Hands-On Design Patterns with Swift

Master Swift best practices to build modular applications for mobile, desktop, and server platforms

Florent Vilmart
Giordano Scalzo
Sergio De Simone

BIRMINGHAM - MUMBAI

Hands-On Design Patterns with Swift

Commissioning Editor: Kunal Chaudhari
Acquisition Editor: Devanshi Doshi
Content Development Editor: Francis Carneiro
Technical Editor: Sachin Sunilkumar
Copy Editor: Safis Editing
Project Coordinator: Kinjal Bari
Proofreader: Safis Editing
Indexer: Mariammal Chettiyar
Graphics: Alishon Mendonsa
Production Coordinator: Priyanka Dhadke

First published: December 2018

Production reference: 1211218

Published by Packt Publishing Ltd.
Livery Place
35 Livery Street
Birmingham
B3 2PB, UK.

ISBN 978-1-78913-556-5

www.packtpub.com

`mapt.io`

Mapt is an online digital library that gives you full access to over 5,000 books and videos, as well as industry leading tools to help you plan your personal development and advance your career. For more information, please visit our website.

Why subscribe?

- Spend less time learning and more time coding with practical eBooks and videos from over 4,000 industry professionals

- Improve your learning with Skill Plans built especially for you

- Get a free eBook or video every month

- Mapt is fully searchable

- Copy and paste, print, and bookmark content

Packt.com

Did you know that Packt offers eBook versions of every book published, with PDF and ePub files available? You can upgrade to the eBook version at `www.packt.com` and as a print book customer, you are entitled to a discount on the eBook copy. Get in touch with us at `customercare@packtpub.com` for more details.

At `www.packt.com`, you can also read a collection of free technical articles, sign up for a range of free newsletters, and receive exclusive discounts and offers on Packt books and eBooks.

Contributors

About the authors

Florent Vilmart, M.Sc., is a full stack engineer in Montreal. Born in France, he moved to Montreal shortly before graduating, seeking exciting opportunities in the francophone metropole of North America. He honed his skills with Objective-C before jumping to Swift when it was released. He is a polyglot, and you can find his open source work on the parse community GitHub project, where he is one of the core maintainers. He has spoken at conferences, including the GitHub CodeConf in 2016 and, most recently, the 2017 Swift Summit in San Francisco. Currently, he is working full-time with BusBud in Montreal, using mainly TypeScript alongside Swift.

Writing a first book is a daunting challenge, even more so when you have three children to take care of at the same time. I want to start by thanking Elodie, my life partner, without whom writing this book would never have been possible. She has provided both support and encouragement during the process. Elodie, thank you many times over.

Many thanks to Francis at Packt Publishing for keeping my spirits up in the darkest days, always encouraging and looking forward.

I also wish to thank all the leaders and makers of the Swift community that I had the chance to meet in person or online, many of whom are a source of inspiration through their open source work, blogs, and conferences. Without such a vibrant community, this book would not have been possible.

Many thanks are due to my mom and dad. They both taught me that anything and everything is possible in this world, and my brothers, with whom I had the best time and who helped me to disconnect and take a step back when I needed it the most.

Giordano Scalzo is a developer with 20 years of programming experience, since the days of the ZX-Spectrum. He has worked in C++, Java, .NET, Ruby, Python, and in a multitude of other languages. After years of backend development, Giordano has developed extensively for iOS, releasing more than 20 apps which he wrote for clients, enterprise applications, or for his own benefit. Currently, he is a contractor in London where, through his company, Effective Code Ltd., he delivers code for iOS. For Packt, he has written two books on Swift, *Swift by Example* and *Swift 2 by Example*, and has reviewed a number of Swift books and videos, including *Learn Swift by Building Applications, Introduction to Server-Side Swift,* and *Swift Functional Programming.*

> *I'd like to thank my better half, Valentina, who lovingly supports me in everything I do: without you, none of this would have been possible. Thanks to my bright future, Mattia and Luca, for giving me lots of smiles and hugs when I needed them. Thanks to Francis, for making this book better. Finally, my gratitude goes to my mom and my dad, who piqued my curiosity and supported me in the pursuit of my passions, which begun one day when they bought me a ZX-Spectrum.*

Sergio De Simone has been working as a software engineer for over twenty years across a range of different projects and companies, including work environments such as Siemens, HP, and small start-ups. For the last few years, his focus has been on developing mobile platforms and related technologies. He is currently working for BigML, Inc., where he leads iOS and OS X development. Additionally, he likes writing about technology, as well as programming tools, techniques, and languages, with a special focus on Swift evolution, for InfoQ.

About the reviewers

Tibor Bödecs is an enthusiastic software developer with more than a decade of experience in the IT industry. Previously, Tibor was the technology leader at one of the biggest mobile development-focused companies in Hungary. He is a self-taught programmer with a true passion for Swift. He has the ability to work with different languages and technologies, and has extensive experience in product management. Nowadays, he is a freelance developer focusing predominantly on web, mobile, and server-side Swift projects. Tibor has a personal blog where he regularly writes about the Swift programming language.

Nikola Brežnjak is an engineer at heart and a jack of all trades. Currently, he's the director of mobile engineering at Teltech, where he is responsible for the management, mentoring, and coaching of mobile app developers. He loves his job! He has written books on the Ionic Framework and the MEAN stack, and has been a technical reviewer for a number of Packt books. He likes to help out on Stack Overflow, where he's a top contributor. He records a podcast called DevThink with his friend, Shawn Milochik, and runs a local meetup called MeCoDe.

I wish to thank my wife for supporting me in all my geeky endeavors and my parents for teaching me the power of hard and consistent work.

Packt is searching for authors like you

If you're interested in becoming an author for Packt, please visit `authors.packtpub.com` and apply today. We have worked with thousands of developers and tech professionals, just like you, to help them share their insight with the global tech community. You can make a general application, apply for a specific hot topic that we are recruiting an author for, or submit your own idea.

Table of Contents

Preface

Hands-on Design Patterns in Swift provides a complete overview of how to implement classic design patterns in Swift. Swift is a modern language, and for users coming from a purely object-oriented language background, it may feel overwhelming. It has peculiar characteristics that create new programming paradigms, such as protocol programming, and appropriate solutions to problems such as type erasure. Both of these are covered in this book.

Design patterns do not live in isolation, however, but they help to solve real-world problems. Particular attention is given to presenting them in a number of realistic scenarios.

The goal of Swift is to create robust and maintainable apps, be they mobile or server. However, well-known techniques such as dependency injection and automatic testing are taken from other programming languages.

Finally, since most of the modern software relies upon open source, the final chapter shows how to release and maintain a Swift open source package.

Who this book is for

This book is designed for intermediate and advanced developers who already have experience of another programming language and some experience of Swift.

Those readers with no previous experience in Swift may find an examination of the basics in the first part of the book beneficial.

The second part demonstrates how to implement the classic creational, behavioral, and structural design patterns, as well as those peculiar to Swift patterns. In this section, experienced developers will find both similarities and differences with their favorite programming language.

This isn't an academic book, but it aspires to show readers how to implement an app in a pragmatic and practical way. Consequently, the third part is devoted to how to implement an application architecture, presenting patterns such as MVC and MVVM, as well as how to create a couple of modules loosely with dependency injection, and how to handle asynchronous code with futures, promises and reactive programming.

The final part shows how to make apps robust and maintainable. After providing advanced readers with an overview of the Swift testing ecosystem, particular attention is given to the open source maintainers between the readers, showing how to release and maintain a Swift open source package or app.

What this book covers

Chapter 1, *Refreshing the Basics*, introduces the building blocks that facilitate the writing of Swift code: classes, structs, enums, functions, and closures. Those basics are essential to the Swift language and for successfully applying efficient design patterns and best practices.

Chapter 2, *Understanding ARC and Memory Management*, describes the particular memory management strategy Swift uses. From its origins in Objective-C, during the pre-ARC era, to today, we'll discover how to properly manage our memory and object life cycles.

Chapter 3, *Diving into Foundation and the Swift Standard Library*, discusses the powerful framework that comes with Swift. Alongside basic data structures such as arrays and dictionaries, it also comes with a fully featured concurrency management abstraction library (GCD), a full modern networking API (URLSession), and many more features besides.

Chapter 4, *Working with Objective-C in a Mixed Code Base*, covers the basics of interoperability, nullability, naming conventions, and lightweight generics, as well as the common pitfalls to avoid when bringing Objective-C code to Swift.

Chapter 5, *Creational Patterns*, dives into the traditional creational design patterns. Examples of Singleton, Abstract Factories, Prototype, Factory, and Builder are shown by means of detailed use cases.

Chapter 6, *Structural Patterns*, explores the most popular structural patterns, starting with the adapter pattern. We'll follow that up with implementing decorators, facades, and proxies, and finish with exploring composite, bridge, and flyweight patterns.

Chapter 7, *Behavioral Patterns*, shows patterns that identify common communication strategies between different entities. We'll see examples of the state pattern, observer/observable, memento, visitor, and the strategy pattern.

Chapter 8, *Swift-Oriented Patterns*, presents patterns peculiar to Swift. After introducing protocol programming, it shows how to implement the classic template pattern using protocol programming. Finally, it shows the type erasure pattern, a powerful tool for mastering generics.

Chapter 9, *Using the Model-View-Controller Pattern*, explores some best practices and decoupling strategies to keep the view controllers as lean as they should be. The classic Model View Controller pattern is discussed, as are other popular controllers available in UIKit and AppKit.

Chapter 10, *Model-View-ViewModel in Swift*, explores an extension of MVC, the Model-View-ViewModel pattern. MVVM is a very popular and flexible pattern that avoids the "bloated view controller" effect.

Chapter 11, *Implementing Dependency Injection*, covers the different flavors of dependency injection and examines how each can solve a particular set of problems in real-world scenarios.

Chapter 12, *Futures, Promises, and Reactive Programming*, discusses how to solve the most common asynchronous code problems. It explores futures and promises as an encapsulation of work being done. Finally, it provides an overview of signals and reactive programming.

Chapter 13, *Modularize Your Apps with Swift Package Manager*, shows how Swift Package Manager can power your workflow and keep your project in check, all while increasing the modularity and maintainability of your code base.

Chapter 14, *Testing Your Code with Unit and UI Tests*, shows how to write unit tests, what they are, what you should look for, and how to get started with testability. The chapter on dependency injection concludes with a presentation of the different types of test doubles to test in isolation, along with an introduction to UI testing.

Chapter 15, *Going Out in the Open (Source)*, discusses the steps required before you can put your project in the open, documenting the source code with Jazzy, using continuous integration with Travis, and automating release with Fastlane.

To get the most out of this book

This book uses Xcode version 10 and Swift 4.2. If you use a different version of Xcode, you will likely encounter syntax difference. To upgrade the Swift syntax and update the code examples of this book to a newer version of Xcode, you can use Xcode's **Edit** | **Convert** | **To Current Swift Syntax** option.

Visit `https://developer.apple.com/xcode/` to download Xcode.

Download the example code files

You can download the example code files for this book from your account at www.packt.com. If you purchased this book elsewhere, you can visit www.packt.com/support and register to have the files emailed directly to you.

You can download the code files by following these steps:

1. Log in or register at www.packt.com.
2. Select the **SUPPORT** tab.
3. Click on **Code Downloads & Errata**.
4. Enter the name of the book in the **Search** box and follow the onscreen instructions.

Once the file is downloaded, please make sure that you unzip or extract the folder using the latest version of:

- WinRAR/7-Zip for Windows
- Zipeg/iZip/UnRarX for Mac
- 7-Zip/PeaZip for Linux

The code bundle for the book is also hosted on GitHub at https://github.com/PacktPublishing/Hands-On-Design-Patterns-with-Swift. In case there's an update to the code, it will be updated on the existing GitHub repository.

We also have other code bundles from our rich catalog of books and videos available at https://github.com/PacktPublishing/. Check them out!

Download the color images

We also provide a PDF file that has color images of the screenshots/diagrams used in this book. You can download it here: https://www.packtpub.com/sites/default/files/downloads/9781789135565_ColorImages.pdf.

Conventions used

There are a number of text conventions used throughout this book.

CodeInText: Indicates code words in text, database table names, folder names, filenames, file extensions, pathnames, dummy URLs, user input, and Twitter handles. Here is an example: "Mount the downloaded WebStorm-10*.dmg disk image file as another disk in your system."

A block of code is set as follows:

```
func translate(point : Point, dx : Double, dy : Double) {
    point.x += dx
    point.y += dy
}
```

When we wish to draw your attention to a particular part of a code block, the relevant lines or items are set in bold:

```
func translate(point : Point, dx : Double, dy : Double) {
    point.x += dx
    point.y += dy
}
```

Any command-line input or output is written as follows:

```
$ gem install jazzy
$ jazzy
```

Bold: Indicates a new term, an important word, or words that you see on screen. For example, words in menus or dialog boxes appear in the text like this. Here is an example: "Navigate to the **Diagnostics** tab."

Warnings or important notes appear like this.

Tips and tricks appear like this.

Get in touch

Feedback from our readers is always welcome.

General feedback: If you have questions about any aspect of this book, mention the book title in the subject of your message and email us at customercare@packtpub.com.

Errata: Although we have taken every care to ensure the accuracy of our content, mistakes do happen. If you have found a mistake in this book, we would be grateful if you would report this to us. Please visit www.packt.com/submit-errata, selecting your book, clicking on the Errata Submission Form link, and entering the details.

Piracy: If you come across any illegal copies of our works in any form on the internet, we would be grateful if you would provide us with the location address or website name. Please contact us at copyright@packt.com with a link to the material.

If you are interested in becoming an author: If there is a topic that you have expertise in, and you are interested in either writing or contributing to a book, please visit authors.packtpub.com.

Reviews

Please leave a review. Once you have read and used this book, why not leave a review on the site that you purchased it from? Potential readers can then see and use your unbiased opinion to make purchase decisions, we at Packt can understand what you think about our products, and our authors can see your feedback on their book. Thank you!

For more information about Packt, please visit packt.com.

Refreshing the Basics

1

In order to properly kick-start our journey through Swift's best practices and design patterns, I believe it's important that we take some time to go back to the basics. It's important to always keep your foundation strong; the more we advance through this book, the more we'll rely on those concepts.

I'll assume that you have a proper understanding of **object-oriented programming (OPP)** fundamentals, classes, inheritance, composition, and other techniques, as well as a fundamental understanding of the differences between value and reference types. If you're rusty on these concepts, you shouldn't worry too much, as we'll cover them shortly.

This chapter will dive deeply into the Swift language. What is a `struct`, and what is a `class`? What are their differences? Should you use an `enum` or an `OptionSet`? All of these questions will be answered in this chapter. We'll go back to the basics of classes and inheritance, and we'll discover the power of value types and immutability. We'll look it functions, closures, and currying. If you're unfamiliar with these constructs, or if you just want to get a refresher, you should tag along as we go back to the basics. These basics are essential to the Swift language, and are required to successfully apply efficient design patterns and best practices.

In this first chapter, we'll take the time to go back to the basics by covering the following topics:

- Classes and structs: what they are, and how they behave
- Exploring enums and their capabilities and extensibility
- Getting functional with closures and functions
- Introducing protocols and scratching the surface of extending protocols
- Concluding with other useful language constructs, such as type aliases, tuples, and generics

Classes and structs

Let's start with a quick refresher on classes and structures. Both of them help to encapsulate functionality by defining methods and properties. While they share the same semantics, they differ in many ways. In this section, we'll quickly refresh you on the differences between classes and structs, and we will show you a simple refactoring from classes to structs.

Classes

Let's start with an example of a simple class that represents a Point in an x, y coordinate system (Cartesian). Consider the following:

```
class Point {
    var x: Double
    var y: Double

    init(x: Double, y: Double) {
        self.x = x
        self.y = y
    }
}
```

Now, let's define a simple translate function that will mutate the x and y properties of the point objects by adding dx and dy to x and y, respectively:

```
func translate(point : Point, dx : Double, dy : Double) {
 point.x += dx
 point.y += dy
}
```

Now, we can create a point instance with, for example, an initial value of 0.0, and translate it to the position 1.0:

```
let point = Point(x: 0.0, y: 0.0)
translate(point: point, dx: 1.0, dy: 1.0)
point.x == 1.0
point.y == 1.0
```

Because classes follow reference semantics, only a reference to the point object is passed to the translate function; x and y are defined as var, and all of this code is valid.

Struct

Now, let's try to port our `Point` class into a `struct`. Consider the following:

```
struct Point {
    var x: Double
    var y: Double
}
```

We have defined a simple `struct`; as you should notice, there's no need to add a constructor, as the compiler will synthesize it for us:

```
let point = Point(x: 0.0, y: 0.0)
translate(point: point, dx: 1.0, dy: 1.0)
```

If we keep the original implementation, our program won't compile. `Point` is a value type now, and it's forbidden to mutate a value inside of a function! We need to add the `inout` keyword to indicate that this function will mutate the contents of the value that is passed. When the function returns, the value will be assigned back to the original variable.

With those changes complete, we also need to change our call to indicate that our `point` variable can be modified by our `translate` function with the & (ampersand) character. We also need to mark our point as `var`; otherwise, the `inout` function cannot modify its contents:

```
func translate(point: inout Point, dx : Double, dy : Double) {
    point.x += dx
    point.y += dy
}

var point = Point(x: 0.0, y: 0.0)
translate(&point, dx: 1.0, dy: 1.0)
point.x == 1.0 // true
point.y == 1.0 // true
```

We've successfully ported this function, but we can do better.

With structs, you will often see that this pattern is cumbersome. We may want the `translate` function to return a mutated copy of the value we passed in, as follows:

```
func translate(point: Point, dx : Double, dy : Double) -> Point {
    var point = point
    translate(point: &point, dx : dx, dy : dy)
    return point
}
```

We'll be able to use the previously defined function with the following code:

```
let point = Point(x: 0.0, y: 0.0)
let translatedPoint = translate(point, dx: 1.0, dy: 1.0)
point.x == 0.0
point.y == 0.0
translatedPoint.x == 1.0
translatedPoint.y == 1.0
```

With this new implementation, we're not mutating the value anymore, but the `translate` function is always returning a new `Point` value. This has many benefits, including the ability to chain such calls together. Let's add a method to our `Point` struct:

```
extension Point {
    func translating(dx: Double, dy: Double) -> Point {
        return translate(point: self, dx: dx, dy: dy)
    }
}
```

 You don't need to declare this new method in your `struct`, but you can declare it anywhere in your program.

Using our newly crafted extension, we can easily create new `Point` values and translate them:

```
let point = Point(x: 0.0, y: 0.0)
    .translating(dx : 5.0, dy : 2.0)
    .translating(dx : 2.0, dy : 3.0)
point.x == 7.0
point.y == 5.0
```

Enums

Enums are one of the basic constructs that the Swift language offers. At the same level as classes, structs, and functions, they are used to represent values that can only have a finite amount of states.

Take the `Optional` enum, for example; it is represented by an enum perfectly. It represents a value that can have two, and only two, states, represented by the two members of the `Optional` enum. It can either be initialized to `.none` or filled with a value, `.wrapped(value)`.

Enums are incredibly powerful in Swift. From very simple cases to generics, they are among the most powerful tools that we have for writing our programs.

Simple enums

Let's say you're building a smart light remote control; you can easily represent the state of this light with the following enum:

```
enum State {
    case on
    case off
}

let anOnLight = State.on
```

This is a very simple example, and we could have used a Boolean value, but with the enum, we set ourselves up for expansion.

Adding methods

Now, we may want to add a method to this State enumeration. After all, it's very common to just toggle the switch on and off without thinking:

```
extension State {
    mutating func toggle() {
        self = self == .off ? .on : .off
    }
}

var state: State = .on
state.toggle()
state == .off // true
```

As in the previous section, we can just extend the State enum to add the toggle functionality. Enums follow value semantics; therefore, we have to mark the toggle method as mutating.

Associating values

Enums can also contain associated values. In our scenario, we can leverage this to represent a dimmer. A dimmer changes the intensity of the light, so we can represent it with a third member-the dimmed member:

```
enum State: Equatable {
    case on
    case off
    case dimmed(value: Double)
}
```

You may have noticed that we needed to add the `Equatable` conformance. This is required, as otherwise, the compiler can't synthesize equality anymore without our hint. This implementation works, but we lack a few things. First, not all `Double` values are valid; we'd probably like to keep these in a reasonable span (between 0 and 1, for example). But perhaps not all of our lights support such values between 0 and 1. Others may want to support between 0 and a 100 or integers between 0 and 255.

Generic enums

In the following example, we will build a fully generic light:

```
enum State<T>: Equatable where T: Equatable {
    case on
    case off
    case dimmed(T)
}

struct Bits8Dimming: Equatable {
    let value: Int
    init(_ value: Int) {
        assert(value > 0 && value < 256)
        self.value = value
    }
}

struct ZeroOneDimming: Equatable {
    let value: Double
    init(_ value: Double) {
        assert(value > 0 && value < 1)
        self.value = value
    }
}
```

```
let nostalgiaState: State<Bits8Dimming> = .dimmed(.init(10))
let otherState: State<ZeroOneDimming> = .dimmed(.init(0.4))
```

The dim type is now specified as a part of the `State` type. This gives us a lot of flexibility, as well as validation. Wrapping the value into a small `struct` adds very little overhead in terms of performance, and allows us to ensure that the values are sane before being set into our `enum`.

Raw type enums

A raw type is a base type for all enumeration members; in our example, we can hardcode presets for our dimming, as follows:

```
enum LightLevel: String {
    case quarter
    case half
    case threequarters
}

let state: State<LightLevel> = .dimmed(.half)
```

Thanks to the generic implementation and the fact that `String` is equatable, we can use this raw value in our `dimmed` state.

With the `LightLevel` enum, which has a raw type of `String`, the compiler will use the member name as the underlying raw value:

```
LightLevel.half.rawValue == "half" // == true
```

You can override these by specifying them, as follows:

```
enum LightLevel: String {
    case quarter = "1/4"
    case half = "1/2"
    case threequarters = "3/4"
}
```

When using `Int` as a raw type, the underlying raw values will follow the order of the cases:

```
enum Level: Int {
    case base // == 0
    case more // == 1
    case high = 100
    case higher // == 101
}
```

Switching the state of light

With our final case, let's look at how to interpret the current state of the light:

```
switch state {
case .on:
    doSomething()
case .off:
    doSomething()
case .dimmed(let value):
    switch value {
    case .quarter:
        doSomething()
    case .half:
        doSomething()
    case .threeQuarters:
        doSomething()
    }
}
```

The `switch` statement in Swift is very different from the one in Objective-C. First, the cases do not fall through each other, so there's no need to add the `break` statement after each case.

If you want multiple cases to be handled with the same code, you can use the following strategy:

```
switch state {
case .on, .off:
    doSomething()
default:
    break
}
```

Falling through is somehow not encouraged in Swift, so always try to adapt your code in order not to leverage this. If you can't avoid it, the following code shows how it should be implemented:

```
switch state {
case .off:
    doSomethingOff()
    fallthrough
case .on:
    doSomething()
default:
    break
}
```

If state is off, both doSomethingOff and doSomething will be called. If state is on, only doSomething will be called.

Closures, functions, and currying

Closures are blocks of code that can be executed later, and functions are a special case of closures. Functions and closures can be passed around in your code, returned by other functions or closures. You can store a closure or a function in a variable, and execute them later:

```
let runMe = { () -> Int in
    print("run")
    return 0
}
runMe()
```

The preceding code is equivalent to the following:

```
func runMe() -> Int {
    print("run")
    return 0
}
runMe()
```

Closures and functions are almost always interchangeable, except when it comes to class or struct members:

```
class MyClass  {
    var running = false
    lazy var runWithClosure: () -> Void = {
        self.running = true
    }

    func runWithFunction() {
        self.running = true
    }
}
```

While both implementations are somewhat equivalent, we rarely want this function to be overridable at runtime. The closure can't reference self inside of it, unless marked lazy. Marking it lazy forces the implementation to be var, which, in turn, doesn't reflect what we want to express. In practice, we never declare instance methods as closures.

Currying

Functions and closures don't have to be defined at the top level. This can be unintuitive, when coming from languages such as Objective-C and Java. Swift, like JavaScript, lets you define functions and closures anywhere in your code. Functions can also return functions. This mechanism is known as currying.

Imagine that you want to create a `logger` method that will print a single argument, but it will always pretend to be a string to find it easily in your logs.

Let's start with the following basic implementation:

```
private let PREFIX = 'MyPrefix'

private func log(_ value: String) {
    print(PREFIX + " " + value)
}

class MyClass {
    func doSomething() {
        log("before")
        /* complex code */
        log("after")
    }
}
```

While this works properly in the scope of a simple class, if you need to reuse the `log` method or change the internal implementation, this will lead to a lot of duplication.

You can use currying to overcome that issue, as follows:

```
func logger(prefix: String) -> (String) ->  Void {
    func log(value: String) {
        print(prefix + " " + value)
    }
    return log
}

let log = logger(prefix: "MyClass")
log("before")
// do something
log("after")

// console:
MyClass before
MyClass after
```

Using closures as callbacks

Functions and closures can capture the current scope, which means all of the declared variables outside of the function or closure definition, such as local variables or `self`. In the case of `self`, you can inadvertently extended the lifetime of your objects and leak memory:

```
class MyClass {
    var running = false
    func run() {
        running = true
        DispatchQueue.main.asyncAfter(deadline: .now() + 10) {
            self.running = false
        }
    }
}

var instance: MyClass? = MyClass()
instance?.run()
instance = nil
```

Can you spot the potential issue in this code?

Depending on the use case, you may want `instance` to be destroyed when it is not referenced by any owner. In our case, we'll probably cause a memory leak, as the dispatch block is referencing `self` without any memory management qualifier.

Using weak and unowned

Swift provides us with two keywords that indicate how we want to extend the lifetime of an object in a closure. While both prevent creating retain cycles, they are fundamentally different.

Using `weak` will wrap the captured value inside of an optional, indicating that the instance may have been deallocated before the closure was executed:

```
class MyClass {
    var running = false
    func run() {
        running = true
        DispatchQueue.main.asyncAfter(deadline: .now() + 10) { [weak self]
 in
            self?.running = false
        }
    }
}
```

```
var instance: MyClass? = MyClass()
instance?.run()
instance = nil
```

In this execution, `instance` will immediately be deallocated when set to `nil`.

Using `unowned` indicates that the variable won't be owned by the block. Another mechanism should be responsible for ensuring that the lifetime of the captured object is properly extended until the block is executed:

```
class MyClass {
    var running = false
    func run() {
        running = true
        DispatchQueue.main.asyncAfter(deadline: .now() + 10) { [unowned
self] in
            self.running = false
        }
    }
}

var instance: MyClass? = MyClass()
instance?.run()
instance = nil
```

In this case, your program will crash when the block is executing, because the `self` variable will be deallocated upon the execution of the block:

```
Fatal error: Attempted to read an unowned reference but object
0x7f80bc75a4e0 was already deallocated
```

Protocols

The following is from Apple's *Swift Programming Language* book:

> "*A protocol defines a blueprint of methods, properties, and other requirements that suit a particular task or piece of functionality. The protocol can then be adopted by a class, structure, or enumeration to provide an actual implementation of those requirements. Any type that satisfies the requirements of a protocol is said to conform to that protocol.*"

> *– Apple Inc., The Swift Programming Language (Swift 3.0.1), iBooks*

Protocol-oriented programming is a vast topic that also deserves coverage. It is the subject of many discussions, and I won't dive into it in depth. However, let's go over the basic concepts, as they will be useful for understanding some concepts that will be explained later in this book.

Declaring a protocol

You declare protocols using the `protocol` keyword, as follows:

```
protocol Toggling {
    mutating func toggle()
}
```

Now that this protocol has been declared, any time that you declare a type conforming to `Toggling`, you'll be required to implement a mutating `toggle()` function.

You can use protocols in your type declarations, method declarations, or variable declarations. While it is technically possible to use protocols as interfaces for your objects or structs, that is usually not how they are used in Swift. Often, you will find yourself conforming to protocols when declaring your custom types or later in your code base, part of extending your existing type to bring additional functionality to it.

Conforming to a protocol

We have just declared this new toggling protocol. If we go back to the previous section about enums, you may remember that the `State` enum had a `toggle()` method. We can now declare that our `enum`, `State`, conforms to `Toggling`. As mentioned previously, we have many ways to declare our conformance.

Conformance at declaration

The first method to declare a conformance is to do it at the top level, when you declare your custom type. You'll notice that the raw representation comes first, then the protocol conformance:

```
enum State: Int, Toggling {
    case off = 0
    case on
    mutating func toggle() {
        self = self == .on ? .off : .on
    }
```

```
}

var state: State = .on
state.toggle()
assert(state == .off)
```

Conformance in an extension

The second way to declare a conformance is to add the conformance to an extension. The main benefit is that you can add functionalities, in the form of extensions, to existing types. The other main benefit of declaring a conformance inside of an extension is that you can scope this conformance to a particular file or module, with the `private` modifier.

For example, suppose that we want to add the `toggle` method to the `Bool` type, but only for the current file or your framework. You may not want it to leak outside, as the implementation may conflict with another one:

```
internal extension Bool: Toggling {
    mutating func toggle() {
        self = !self
    }
}

var isReady = false
isReady.toggle()
assert(isReady)
```

Protocol extensions

With protocol extensions, it is possible to provide an implementation for the required methods, without letting the conforming types provide that implementation.

We have updated the `Toggling` protocol with an additional required member: `isActive`. With the protocol extension, we can declare a default implementation for our types, `Bool` and `State`. We can also provide a default implementation for any other type that would choose to conform to the `Toggling` protocol:

```
protocol Toggling {
    mutating func toggle()
    var isActive: Bool { get }
}

extension Toggling where Self == Bool {
```

```
    var isActive: Bool {
        return self
    }
}

extension Toggling where Self == State {
    var isActive: Bool {
        return self == .on
    }
}
```

Default implementations

It is possible to provide default implementations for protocols through extensions. Previously, we provided a partial default implementation for the Toggling protocol on a well-known type. But any other type, that would conform to Toggling needs to provide an implementation on isActive. Using another example, let's look at how we can leverage default implementations in protocol extensions without requiring additional conformance work.

Let's work with a simple protocol, Adder, for the sake of the example:

```
protocol Adder {
    func add(value: Int) -> Int
    func remove(value: Int) -> Int
}
```

The Adder protocol declares two methods: add and remove. And, if we remember our math classes well, we can very well declare remove as a function of add. Removing is just adding a negative value. Protocol extension allows us to do just that:

```
extension Adder {
    func remove(value: Int) -> Int {
        return add(value: -value)
    }
}
```

This may look a bit silly, but in reality, this pattern is really powerful. Remember, we were able to implement remove because we were able to express it as a function of another provided method. Often, in our code, we can implement a method as a function of another. Protocols give us a contract that is fulfilled by either the concrete type or the extension, and we can effectively and expressively compose our programs around those capabilities.

Tuples, type aliases, and generics

This chapter would not be complete if we didn't address some very useful features from Swift. Tuples are very useful types that let you return multiple objects as one, without a strongly typed wrapper. Aliases let you quickly define simple type shortcuts. Finally, we'll cover the basics of generics. While generics could be covered in a whole book, we'll just scratch the surface of their syntax, features, and limits, as we'll make use of them extensively throughout this book.

Tuples

Tuples are used to represent a group of values as a single value. Tuples cannot conform to protocols, nor can they inherit. They cannot declare functions in the same way that we can declare a function on a `struct` or a `class`. They may look limited, but they have their place as first-class types in the language.

Declaring tuples

Tuples can hold any number of values, from any number of types. You can declare a tuple with the same types—let's say a 2D point in `Double`:

```
let origin = (0.0, 0.0)
```

You can also name the parameters, as follows:

```
let point = (x: 10.0, y: 10.0)
```

The two forms are equivalent, but you may want to use the named version, for readability reasons. If you're referencing a size, for example, the tuple would more accordingly be named `(width: Double, height: Double)`. For obvious reasons, this helps to provide a better understanding of your code.

Destructuring tuples

There is a simple method to access tuple values. Take, for example, the `size` pair, as follows:

```
let size = (width: 200, height: 400)
let (w, h) = size
let (width, _) = size
```

In the preceding example, we initialize a tuple on the first line. On the second line, we destructure both parameters as `w` and `h`. On the last line is what we call a partial destructuring: when you're only interested in one part of the tuple, you can extract only a part of it. This is useful when dealing with large tuples.

Using tuples in functions

Tuples are first-class citizens in Swift; you can use them, like any other type, as function parameters. The following code demonstrates how to declare a simple function that computes to the Euclidean distance between two points, a and b, represented by tuples:

```
func distance(_ a: (Double, Double), _ b: (Double, Double)) -> Double {
    return sqrt(pow(b.0 - a.0, 2) + pow(b.1 - a.1, 2))
}
distance(point, origin) == 5.0
```

You may have noticed that the named parameters of the `point` tuple are ignored in this case; any pair of `Double` will be accepted in the method, no matter what they are named.

The opposite is true, as well:

```
func slope(_ a: (x: Double, y: Double),_ b: (x: Double, y: Double)) ->
Double {
    return (b.y - a.y) / (b.x - a.x)
}

slope((10, 10), (x: 1, y: 1)) == 1
```

We've seen examples of using tuples with the same types, but remember that, tuples can contain any type, and as many values as you wish.

Type aliases

Type aliases are a simple addition to the language; they let you reference simple or complex types by an alias. They support all declarations that you can imagine, from the simplest to the most complex.

The following block contains declarations for aliasing the following:

- A string class into a `MyString`
- A function declaration into a `Block`
- A block that takes any argument and returns any value
- A block that takes no argument and returns any value

Let's see the code block; they let you:

```
typealias MyString = String
typealias Block = () -> Void
typealias TypedBlock<T, U> = (T) -> U
typealias ReturningBlock<U> = () -> U
```

We could have also defined `Block` in the function of `ReturningBlock`:

```
typealias Block = ReturningBlock<()>
```

You can also use type aliases for protocol compositions and complex types, as follows:

- You can declare a type that conforms to a protocol and is of a particular class
- You can delete a type that conforms to multiple protocols

Let's see an example, as follows:

```
protocol SomeProtocol {}
protocol OtherProtocol {}

typealias ViewControllerProtocol = NSViewController & SomeProtocol
typealias BothProtocols = SomeProtocol & OtherProtocol
```

You will often find yourself using type aliases, in order to make your code more readable and more expressive. They are a powerful tool for hiding away some of the implementation complexity or verbosity when declaring long conformances. With type aliases, you can be encouraged to craft many protocols, each with a very small requirement list; then, you can compose all of those protocols when you need them, expressed as those types.

Generics

Generics is a complex subject, and would likely require a full book of its own, for extensive coverage extensively. For the purpose of this book, we'll provide a quick refresher on generics, covering the basics that are required to understand the constructions that we'll use in the different design patterns presented in the next chapters.

Generic functions

In Swift, the simplest form of generics would be the generics in functions. You can use generics very simply, with angled brackets, as follows:

```
func concat<T>(a: T, b: T) -> [T] {
    return [a,b]
}
```

The `concat` method knows nothing about the types that you are passing in, but generics gives us many guarantees over using `Any`:

- a and b should be of the same type
- The `return` type is an array of elements that have the same type as a and b
- The type is inferred from the context so you don't have to type it in when you code

You can also leverage protocol conformance in your generic functions, as follows:

```
protocol Runnable {
    func run()
}

func run<T>(runnable: T) where T: Runnable {
    runnable.run()
}
```

In this case, the method that is run can only be called with an object that is `Runnable`.

Generic types

You can also make complex types generic. In our example, we created this wrapper around a list of `Runnable`, called `ManyRunner`. The job of a many runner is to run all of the runnables. The `ManyRunner` is itself `Runnable`, so we have created a kind of type recursion, as follows:

```
struct ManyRunner<T>: Runnable where T: Runnable {
    let runnables: [T]
    func run() {
        runnables.forEach { $0.run() }
    }
}
```

Let's also provide a base object that runs a simple `Incrementer`. Each time the `Incrementer` is run, the static count will increment, to keep track of the number of invocations:

```
struct Incrementer: Runnable {
    private(set) static var count = 0
    func run() {
        Incrementer.count += 1
    }
}
```

When using generics on types, remember that the types have to be the same:

```
// This works
let runner = ManyRunner(runnables: [Incrementer(),Incrementer()])
runner.run()
assert(Incrementer.count == 2)
// runner is of type ManyRunner<Incrementer>


ManyRunner(runnables: [Incrementer(), Runners(runnables: [Incrementer()])]
as [Runnable]).run()
// This produces the following compile error
// In argument type '[Runnable]', 'Runnable' does not conform to expected
type 'Runnable'
```

We'll look at how to overcome these limitations in `Chapter 8`, *Swift-Oriented Patterns*.

Generics, protocols, and associated types

You can also use associated types in your protocols. These associated types let you define protocols that are generics, like this: RunnableWithResult. We can implement a bunch of logic and code around the run() method, without actually knowing anything about the return types. We'll encounter this construction many times in this book, so it's important that you're comfortable with associate types:

```
protocol RunnableWithResult {
    associatedtype ResultType
    func run() -> ResultType
}

struct RunnersWithResult<T>: RunnableWithResult where T: RunnableWithResult
{
    let runnables: [T]
    func run() -> [T.ResultType] {
        return runnables.map { $0.run() }
    }
}
```

Like with generic types, you can't mix and match heterogeneous types. The following example will not compile; later in this book, you'll see strategies for overcoming this common problem when dealing with generics:

```
struct IntRunnable {
    func run() -> Int {
        return 0
    }
}

struct StringRunnable {
    func run() -> String {
        return "OK"
    }
}

let runnables: [RunnableWithResult] = [StringRunnable(), IntRunnable()]
```

This will yield the following dreaded error:

> **Protocol 'RunnableWithResult' can only be used as a generic constraint because it has Self or associated type requirements**

Summary

In this chapter, we covered everything that I consider a prerequisite for the rest of this book. We started with classes, the basic building blocks of OOP. You should now be really familiar with them. Structs are unusual constructions for someone coming from OOP, but they are very useful in Swift, as they behave as values, can be immutable, and have other nice properties. With enums, you'll be able to write even more expressive code.

Functions and closures are first-class citizens in Swift, and should be treated as such. Currying is a powerful pattern that lets you reuse functions; in later chapters, you'll see how to use it to write clean code.

The concept of protocols opens the world of protocol extensions and protocol-oriented programming, which is a complex subject. In the following chapters, we'll look at various use cases for implementing particular patterns through protocol extensions.

In the next chapter, we'll focus on memory management and ARC. While value types are not subject to reference counting, classes, functions, and closures interact with each other, and can lead to memory-related crashes and other issues.

2
Understanding ARC and Memory Management

Swift has a very particular and almost unique memory management strategy: **Automatic Reference Counting (ARC)**. When using ARC, the compiler will inject memory management code for us, but it's very easy to write poor, leaky code, either on purpose or by accident. In this chapter, we'll cover all of the basics for good memory management in Swift. From its origins in Objective-C, to the pre-ARC era, to today, we'll look at how to properly manage our memory and object life cycles. We'll also explore the powerful tools available with Xcode to track memory usage, leaks, cycles, and other defects, through the inspector and the leaks instrument.

In this chapter, we'll cover the following topics:

- A brief history of reference counting
- What is ARC?
- Debugging memory
- Leaks, cycles, and dangling references

A brief history of reference counting

Before we get into the details of ARC, we need to rewind the time machine to a previous epoch. The year is 1988, and Objective-C is licensed by NeXT and starting to make its way into their operating system. In 1996, Apple acquires NeXT, alongside the release of OS X, a new and modern toolchain based on Objective-C. Objective-C is a strict superset of C, which means that any valid C code is valid Objective-C code, but unlike C, Objective-C has a modern and efficient memory management engine, based on reference counting.

Reference counting is a technique that accounts for the exact number of references to a particular object that exist at any given time in the memory. Once there are no references, an object, it is deallocated. This is a very different memory management technique, as compared to garbage collection, which you can find in Java or JavaScript.

Many benefits come with the use of reference counting. As there is no garbage collector, there is no need to freeze the process when the memory is cleaned up. It also provides benefits in performance and power management.

Let's go back to the pre-ARC era and write some Objective-C. Even if you're an avid Swift developer, understanding the origins of reference counting will help you to write more correct and efficient code.

Don't be afraid of Objective-C, even if the language is somehow verbose, with a lot of brackets; this is a very fun and performant language to work with.

The semantics of reference counting

We make a distinction between manual and ARC, as the former requires the developer to write the different calls to the memory management methods alongside the logic of the program, and the latter has that same code injected by the compiler. Let's go over the semantics of manual reference counting in the context of Objective-C.

Retain

Retaining an object increases the number of references to an object. By doing so, we extend the lifetime of the object that received the retained message.

Release

Releasing an object causes the reference count to decrease. When the count of references or `retainCount` becomes 0, the object is deallocated.

Over-releasing is an issue where in an object gets released more than necessary, and could potentially be deallocated before the end of its expected lifespan.

Assign

Any property marked `assign` will not have its retain count increased. It is the equivalent of ARC's `weak`. Marking your property as `assign` in Objective-C without ARC would cause the reference to be nullified when the underlying object was not retained anymore. Delegates are the most notable objects that require this modifier, as we most often do not want to retain the delegate of an object.

Copying

Copying an object doesn't increase its reference count, and ownership can be safely passed from one object to the other. The object's copy will have a reference count of one just after the copying process, no matter what the original object's reference count was.

The `text` property of `UILabel` is marked as `copy`, so any `NSString *` passed as the `text` property can be safely deallocated. If the `text` property of `UILabel` was `assign`, the string would need to be retained by an external object. If it was `retain`, this would probably unnecessarily extend object lifetimes.

In Swift, `String` is a struct that benefits the value type memory behaviors, and it is always copied. It is still possible to disable ARC with Objective-C 2.0, so let's use this modern variant, as it is still very popular in many code bases.

Using and misusing manual reference counting

Now, let's take a look at how we can use and abuse those mechanics, and the kinds of errors that we can litter our code with when using manual reference counting:

```
- (void) doSomething {
    NSString *aString = [[NSString alloc] init];
    // calling alloc returns an object with a retain count of 1

    // do something with the string

    // We're done with the string, call release
    [aString release];
}
```

The preceding is a very simplistic example; many times, you'll pass your objects around, and will need to keep track of when to retain or release your objects. Let's go over some of the issues that you can encounter if you're not careful with your `retain` and `release` calls.

Memory leaks

This issue is probably the most common in Objective-C and Swift. A memory leak occurs when an allocated object is not referenced anymore, but still has a retain count greater than 0. In Objective-C, those are very easy to write, as follows:

```
- (void) doSomething {
    NSString *string = [[NSString alloc] init];
    // do something with the string
    [string retain];

    // Do more things with the string
    [string release];
}
```

Unlike the previous example, there's an additional call to `retain`, and this call will increment the retain count effectively. Every `alloc` and `retain` call should be balanced by `release`, and we failed to do so in the example. You now have a leak in your program. There are many ways to generate leaks in Swift, and in later sections of this book, we'll cover chapter how they can appear, how to debug them, and how to fix them.

Dangling pointers

Dangling pointers are the opposite of over-retained objects. You can encounter dangling pointers when trying to access a deallocated object. This is best illustrated by the following example:

```
- (void) doSomething {
    MyObject *myObject = [[MyObject alloc] init]; // retainCount is +1
    [myObject release]; // retain count is 0; object is deallocated

    // More things happening in this method

    [myObject myMethod];
}
```

This may not cause a crash all of the time, as `myObject` could be properly set to `nil`. When it crashes, you'll face the dreaded `NSInvalidArgumentException`, which, upon first glance, doesn't make much sense:

```
*** Terminating app due to uncaught exception 'NSInvalidArgumentException',
reason: '-[<insert a type here> myMethod]: unrecognized selector sent to
instance 0x12345679
```

We never have a call to `myMethod` on any other type. This crash often means that the contents of the memory at the `myObject` address have been replaced by some other object. Because we called `release` too early, the memory has been reclaimed, and potentially replaced by another object.

In order to overcome the burden of writing the manual reference counting, Apple introduced ARC. In the next section, we'll look at what this compiler feature can do, in order to provide efficient memory management.

ARC – what is that?

Automatic Reference Counting was introduced at the 2011 WWDC, in Session 323. If you want to see the original presentation, feel free to visit `https://developer.apple.com/videos/play/wwdc2011/323/`.

ARC is made possible by Clang and LLVM. LLVM and Clang are two technologies that enable compiling C, C++, and Objective-C code. LLVM is also used alongside the Swift compiler. With ARC, a Clang feature, developers don't have to write the tedious `retain` and `release` calls. There are multiple benefits to letting the compiler handle it, as follows:

- Memory management is difficult
- The compiler is often more correct than you are
- There are fewer lines of code to write
- It has the same performance as manual reference counting

With Swift being a modern language and the successor of Objective-C, you've never had to call `retain`. Swift programs leverage ARC, in order to simplify memory management. In Swift, there are multiple memory management concepts to master, and we'll cover them in this section.

Value types

First, we need to distinguish value types from reference types. Value types aren't reference counted, as they are values. Think of a simple integer; the value in an integer isn't shared across all of its assignments, but copied whenever it's assigned to a new variable:

```
struct Box {
    var intValue: Int
}
```

```
let box = Box(intValue: 0)
var otherBox = box
otherBox.intValue = 10
assert(box.intValue == 0) // box and otherBox don't share the same
reference
assert(otherBox.intValue == 10)
```

When you're passing a struct around, the value is behaving like it's copied. This is the same behavior seen when capturing values inside blocks.

Strong references

Strong references are the default. Any time that you set a property on an object or capture a reference inside a block, the reference count increases on the object, and the lifetime of the object is extended:

```
class Child {

}

class Parent {
    let children: [Parent]
}

let c = MyClass()
let other = MyOtherClass(class: c)
```

Weak references

With weak references, you can safely store a reference to another object without increasing its retain count. This prevents creating cycles with all of the required safety. The weak references are always wrapped into Optionals and, unlike unowned references, when a weak reference gets deallocated, you can safely access it through the Optional interface and check that the object is still set and present at runtime:

```
class Task {
    let description: String
    weak var worker: Worker?
    init(description: String) {
        self.description = description
    }
}
```

```
class Worker {
    var name: String
    var currentTask: Task?
    init(name: String) {
        self.name = name
    }
}

let worker = Worker(name: "John Snow")
let task = Task(description: "Night's Watch Commander")
worker.currentTask = task
task.worker = worker

// John snow is the night watch's commander

worker.currentTask = nil

// the task will be deallocated
```

Unowned references

You can use unowned references when you can guarantee that the owner of another object will never exist when the reference is deallocated. Let's look at the following example:

```
class CreditCard {
    let number: String
    let expiry: String
    unowned let owner: Person
    init(owner: Person) {
        self.owner = owner
        self.number = "XXXXXXXXXXXXXXX"
        self.expiry = "XX/YY"
    }
}

class Person {
    let name: String
    var cards: [CreditCard] = []

    init(name: String) {
        self.name = name
    }
}
```

In this example, one person can have many credit cards. Each card needs to have an owner, which is immutable.

Let's look that how to use such an API:

```
let me = Person(name: "John Smith")
let card = CreditCard(owner: me)
let otherCard = CreditCard(owner: me)
me.cards = [card, otherCard]
```

In this example, me has two credit cards; each card has a back reference to its owner. In this particular case, we can always guarantee that the owner will never be deallocated before the cards. A CreditCard without an owner doesn't make any sense, and if we're trying to access the owner property of such a card, our program is probably not sane anymore. The behavior to notice here is that, compared to the weak modifier, the owner property on the CreditCard is not required to be an optional.

In this particular example, if we omitted the unowned qualifier, when there were no references left to Person, the back references from the cards would keep the object alive, effectively leaking both the credit cards and the owner of the cards.

Now that we've covered the semantics of memory ownership, we can dive deeply into the memory management and debugging tools that come with Xcode.

Memory debugging

Xcode and Swift come with a powerful memory debugging infrastructure, letting you inspect the contents of existing and destroyed objects, inspect the contents and relationships between your objects, and more. In this section, we'll get you started with these powerful tools, so that later on, you'll be able to debug complicated pieces of code with ease.

Configuring your project

In order to see the memory allocation backtraces, we need to enable **Malloc Stack** in our Scheme. You can do so by following these steps:

1. Open your **Scheme** settings with ⌘ | <, or by navigating to **Product** | **Scheme** | **Edit Scheme...**
2. Navigate to the **Diagnostics** tab

3. Ensure that you select the options shown in the following screenshot:

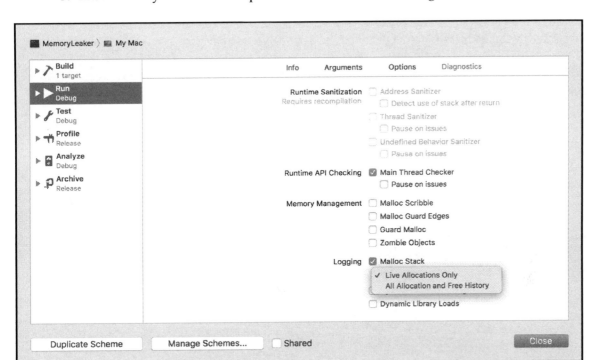

With this configuration on your Scheme, you can run your project again, and we'll be able to debug memory issues in depth, right into Xcode.

Using the memory graph hierarchy tool

Now that we've properly configured our project, let's take a look at the tool itself.

Let's use the following code, for the sake of having a simple, working command-line `Hello World!` application:

```
class Hello {
    func world() {
        print("Hello, World!")
    }
}

let hello = Hello()
hello.world() // set a breakpoint here
```

The preceding code is pretty simple; it just prints `Hello, World!` in the console.

With a breakpoint set on the `hello.world()` line, run your program, and, in the Debug toolbar, hit the icon that looks like a graph. It will open the **Memory Graph Hierarchy** tool:

You can also access it from the debug navigator menu, as follows:

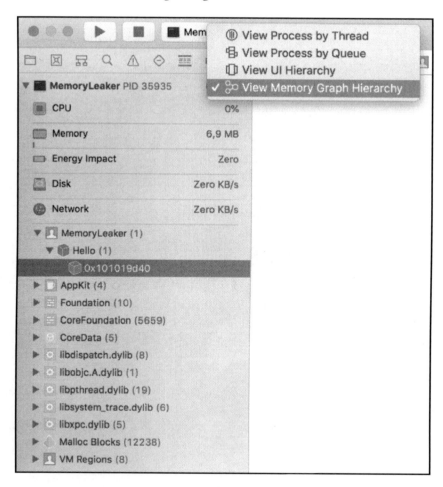

Voilà! We get the result shown in the following screenshot:

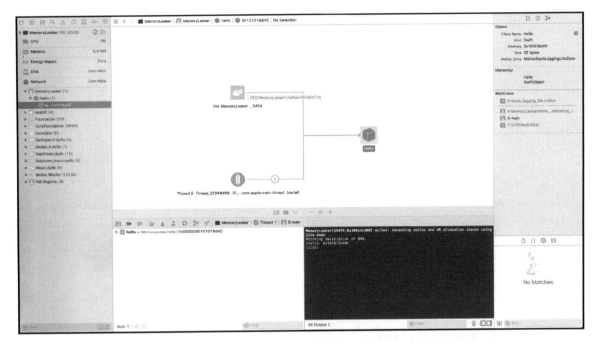

Grandiose memory debug tool

This is the grandiose memory debug tool. As with many tools within Xcode, the screen is split into three main components:

- On the left, you have a list of all of the allocations that are still living in the process, and our single **hello** instance is currently selected
- In the center, there's an interactive view of the memory, with the relations that our object has with other objects
- On the right, there's the information panel for the selected object, with some details, and, most importantly, the stack that led to its allocation

There are two very useful shortcuts that are also presented in this screen, shown as follows:

The shortcuts are as follows:

- The first icon, which looks like a book, jumps to the definition of the object
- The second one prints the description in the debugger

This tool is very powerful, and it's very important to master it. It will ultimately help you to better understand how your applications and projects behave. While for the sake of demonstration we used very simple code examples, and they didn't yield any issues, in the next section, you'll see the most common issues that you may encounter while tracking down memory leaks.

Leaks, cycles, and dangling references

Let's dive into examples of the two most common issues: leaks and crashes related to memory issues. A memory leak occurs when one or many objects become unreachable from the rest of your program but still, in one way or another, form a cycle.

In the first example, we'll look at how to effectively leak memory, using Xcode's powerful memory graph hierarchy tool to track down issues.

In the second example, we'll explore how to debug and investigate crashes related to accessing properties that may have been deallocated.

Leaking with cycles

One common way to leak objects and their memory is to create **strong** references between different instances, and cut off any external references.

Let's consider the following code:

```
class MemoryLeak {
    var ref: MemoryLeak?
    init(ref: MemoryLeak) {
```

```
        self.ref = ref
    }

    init() {
        ref = self
    }
}
```

As you can see, this is some code that you'd be unlikely to write on your own, as it doesn't have a purpose, aside from showcasing a memory leak.

The `MemoryLeak` class has two initializers, as follows:

- One initializer can take a reference, on to which the instance will hold
- The other initializer creates a `self` reference

As you can imagine, this will not bode well if we use that class in code.

A simple leak

Now, let's write a function that creates an instance, and does nothing else:

```
func createLeak() {
    let leak = MemoryLeak()
}

createLeak()
```

When we create the new `MemoryLeak` instance, a `self` reference is set, and the retain count will be two for the duration of the function call. When the function returns, the local `leak` variable is not referenced anymore, so the retain count is still one, and, if there are no references to this instance in the program, we will have a leak.

 In a garbage collected language, this would never happen, as unreachable objects are deallocated automatically.

Now, let's use the memory graph tool to investigate this issue:

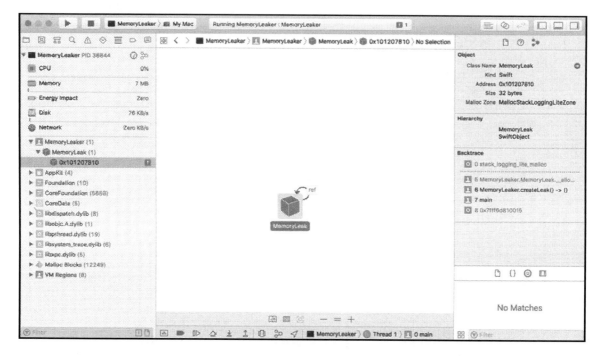

Using this tool, at a glance, we can see the following:

- Leaks are denoted with the purple issue icon
- Upon clicking on the leaking object, we can see the issue
- The dark arrows in the memory graph are for strong references

In one go, it is now really easy for you to identify what might be wrong with your programs.

Fixing the leak

Now that we've seen a simple leak, we have to change our implementation, in order to prevent the leaks from occurring. In our case, this can lead to other unexpected behavior. We have multiple options to resolve this particular `self` reference, as follows:

- Using `weak`
- Using `unowned`
- Ensuring that we never set `ref = self`

Let's investigate the solutions that involve `weak` and `unowned`.

Using weak

Using `weak` will ensure that we never create a strong reference in `ref`, but will not retain the objects, either. If the object passed in `ref` is never retained by any other object, it will automatically be deallocated. This will lead to unexpected behavior, as the chain will be deallocated, and only a returned object will be kept in the memory:

```
class MemoryLeak {
    weak var ref: MemoryLeak?
    init(ref: MemoryLeak) {
        self.ref = ref
    }
    init() {
        ref = self
    }
}

func test() -> MemoryLeak {
    let a = MemoryLeak()
    let b = MemoryLeak(ref: a)
    let c = MemoryLeak(ref: b)
    a.ref = c
    return a
}

let result = test()
assert(result.ref != nil)
```

In the preceding code, we changed the `MemoryLeak` class, in order to keep a `weak` reference in `ref`. Unfortunately, the program will crash at the assertion line, as the `ref` property will be deallocated.

This is often the behavior that you are looking for with delegation. Using weak for the delegate lets you safely avoid thinking about the potential reference cycle; however, the delegates should be retained on their own.

Using unowned

In our particular example, we cannot guarantee the duration of the life cycle of our objects, so unowned is unfit us example. Also, unowned provides fewer guarantees than weak, in terms of safety, can't be applied to Optionals. If you can't use weak for logic reasons, then there's little chance you'll be able to use unowned.

Let's investigate another piece of code involving credit cards, borrowed from Chapter 1, *Refreshing the Basics*.

First, let's see the code without the unowned modifier under the memory debugger:

```
class Card {
    let owner: Person
    init(_ owner: Person) {
        self.owner = owner
    }
}

class Person {
    let name: String
    var cards = [Card]()
    init(name: String) {
        self.name = name
    }
}

func runTests() {
    let batman = Person(name: "Batman")
    batman.cards.append(Card(batman))
    batman.cards.append(Card(batman))
    batman.cards.append(Card(batman))
}

runTests()
```

This simple program should not leave any objects behind after runTests() finishes running; however, because we have a strong reference cycle between Person and Card, that is not the case, and all of the created objects will leak:

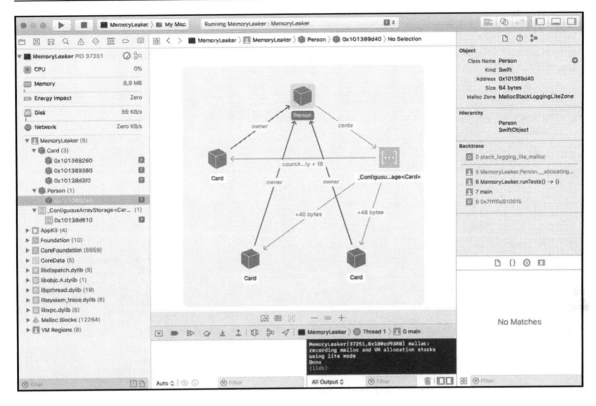

All of our objects have leaked, as shown in the preceding screenshot. This example is perfect for using `unowned`. The `Card` object can't live without an owner. So, whenever the owner is deallocated, all of the cards should be destroyed as well, as we'll never reference a card without its owner. We need to update our `Card` class to reflect that the `Card` objects are not retaining their owner:

```swift
class Card {
    unowned let owner: Person
    init(_ owner: Person) {
        self.owner = owner
    }
}
```

With this addition, the card cannot be allocated without a `Person`, and this person has to exist to be a valid card. In the next section, you'll see the issues that `unowned` can cause, and how we can prevent them.

Dangling references

Now that we've seen the powerful weak and unowned modifiers and have regained control over our memory management, we are thrilled to use it everywhere. That is, until we see a crash in the form of the following:

Fatal error: Attempted to read an unowned reference but object 0x10132c0f0 was already deallocated.

This is the same issue as the, which the dangling pointer one that we saw earlier in this chapter.

Let's reuse the example, as follows:

```
func getCard() -> Card {
    let batman = Person(name: "Batman")
    let card = Card(batman)
    batman.cards.append(card)
    return card
}

let card = getCard()
print("\(card.owner.name)")
```

In this code, we explicitly return a card, but the owner of this card is not in the memory anymore, as it was properly deallocated after we exited the scope. Let's break it down, line by line, and try to get an idea of the counts, as shown in the following table:

Line of code	batman	card	Explanation
let batman = Person(name: "Batman")	1	0	Person is allocated and referenced by the batman variable.
let card = Card(batman)	1	1	Card is allocated and referenced by the card variable. batman is unowned.
batman.cards.append(card)	1	2	card is added to the array, and it retains it.
return card	0	1/0	card is returned. batman is deallocated (no more references). In turn, it removes ref from the cards array. The ownership of card is passed to the caller.

With this in mind, we can now see why the program crashes, as there's nothing left to retain the owner of the card.

This can be seen as unsafe, but it should not be. This example, while valid, is a perfect example where the relationship is unowned because it can't be anything else. weak would have forced us to write the owner as an optional, which is incorrect, and using a strong relationship ultimately leads to cycles and leaks being retained.

To overcome this issue, we have to re-evaluate our code and ensure that we never return a card disassociated from its owner. The unowned references preserve the semantics of your program, while ensuring that the memory management is sane.

Summary

In this chapter, we explored the origins of ARC, the performant memory management paradigm available in Swift. With great power comes great responsibility, so you're still required to design your memory model with ARC in mind; failing to do so will lead to memory leaks or crashes caused by dangling pointers. By now, you should be comfortable with the advantages and drawbacks of both weak and unowned references. You should also understand why weak or unowned don't apply to value types. Last but not least, you should now be comfortable with setting your project up to efficiently debug memory with the tools from Xcode.

ARC sits at the compiler level, injected into your code as it is built. In the next chapter, we'll continue to refresh the basics and stretch our muscles, as we explore Foundation and the standard library.

Diving into Foundation and the Standard Library

3

Now that you have had a good refresher of the core language features and the memory model, we can continue our journey with the Standard Library and the Foundation Framework.

The Standard Library is responsible for bringing high-level features, and it provides powerful implementations for common data types, such as strings and numbers. Along with these basic types, it implements efficient storage and algorithms for common data structures, such as arrays, dictionaries, and sets. Finally, it exposes a trove of protocols that can help to reduce boilerplate in your own implementations, as well as implement common features like `Equatable`, `OptionSet`, or `Collection`.

Foundation is at the core of all Apple SDKs, providing a base layer for your programs in Swift, including (but not limited to) networking, file management, persistence, date arithmetic, and more.

In this chapter, we will cover the following topics:

- Swift's basic types
- Exploring container types and generics
- Mastering concurrency with `Dispatch`
- Communicating via HTTP with `URLSession`

Swift basic types

Swift comes with a number of basic types that are at the root of all of your programs. All of your programs leverage these basic types, one way or another. Let's take some time to revisit these types and their main features, along with some hidden gems.

We can organize all of the Swift's basic types into the following categories:

- Logical types: Bool
- Numeric types: Int, Double, and Float, among others
- Range types: Range and ClosedRange
- Errors: Error protocol
- Optionals: Optional enum

I don't believe it's necessary to introduce the Bool, Int, Double, and Float types, as they are all very common in all languages. Perhaps their most interesting feature is that they are defined as structs, and not primitive types, like in Java.

Working with ranges

Ranges come in two flavors: Range and ClosedRange. The difference between Range and ClosedRange is the inclusion of the upper bound. In a ClosedRange, the upper bound is included; in Range, it isn't.

If you want to include all numbers between 0 and 10, not including 10, you can represent it in two ways, as follows:

```
let range1 = 0..<10
let range2 = 0...9

range1.contains(10) // false
```

The two ranges are equivalent, and they contain the same numbers. They read differently and carry different meanings, however depending on what you want to express, you may want to pick one over the other. Ranges work with the Comparable protocol, which means that any type that conforms to this Comparable protocol is suited for creating ranges.

For example, you could create a Range type of Strings, as follows:

```
let uppercased = "A"..."Z"
uppercased.contains("C") // true
uppercased.contains("c") // false
```

You can also use the ~= operator, which is an alias for the contains method:

```
uppercased ~= "Z" // true
```

Range as Sequence

When using `Range<Int>` or `ClosedRange<Int>`, in addition to others, the Standard
Library provides conditional conformance to the `Sequence` type, as follows:

```
extension Range: Sequence where Bound: Strideable, Bound.Stride :
SignedInteger {
    public typealias Element = Bound
    public typealias Iterator = IndexingIterator<Range<Bound>>
}
```

Extract from Swift Core source code (`https://github.com/apple/swift/blob/master/`
`stdlib/public/core/Range.swift`).

This means that you can use this range as the source for iterating on it, as shown in the
following example:

```
let doubles = (1..<10).map { $0 * 2 } // [2,4,6,8,10,12,14,16,18]

for i in 1..<10 {
    // do something with i
}
```

 Because the `Sequence` conformance is provided as a conditional
conformance, you can also define your own types that will allow for
transforming `Ranges` to `Sequences`.

Throwing and catching errors

Swift has an error handling mechanism that is based on throwing and catching errors, very
similar to JavaScript or Java. In Swift, `Error` is simply a protocol. Any of your custom types
conforming to the `Error` protocol can be used, and can also be thrown. This provides us
with the ability to be as expressive as possible with the underlying types that we'll be using.

Unlike in Java, for example, it is not possible to specialize error catching, but you can
always leverage pattern matching to determine the kind of error that's been thrown. You
may want to define functions that throw, in order to indicate that an abnormal operation
has run, and therefore, the execution of the program should properly handle these
abnormal operations.

Let's look at our credit card example and suppose that we can create charges on a prepaid card:

```
class CreditCard {
    private(set) var balance: Int // balance is in cents

    init(balance: Int) {
        self.balance = balance
    }

    func charge(amount: Int) {
        balance -= amount
    }
}

let card = CreditCard(balance: 10000)
card.charge(amount: 2000)
card.balance == 8000
```

This implementation is now completely unsafe, due to the following:

- A developer can increment the balance by providing a negative amount
- The balance can become negative, and we may want to include restrictions

We could use UInt instead of Int, but, for the sake of the example, we'll write our own error handling logic.

Let's rewrite our example, as follows:

```
class CreditCard {
```

Let's define ChargeError as an enum, which encompasses the two expected errors. Using an enum lets you safely define a finite possibility of values, while ensuring that the consumer will always implement all of the cases, and therefore, handle all of the error types:

```
enum ChargeError: Error {
    case invalidAmount
    case insufficientFunds
}

/* unchanged implementation of init / balance */
```

We can now mark our `charge` method with the `throws` keyword, to indicate to anyone using this method that it can fail:

```
func charge(amount: Int) throws {
    guard amount >= 0 else { throw ChargeError.invalidAmount }
    guard balance >= amount else { throw ChargeError.insufficientFunds
}

    balance -= amount
    }
}
```

Let's take a look at how to use this API now:

The first way is to use the `do...catch` pattern and cast the error as the one thrown, as follows:

```
let card = CreditCard(balance: 10000)
do {
    try card.charge(amount: 2000)
} catch CreditCard.ChargeError.invalidAmount {
    /* handle invalidAmount */
} catch CreditCard.ChargeError.insufficientFunds {
    /* handle insufficientFunds */
} catch {}
```

If you're not interested in catching errors, you can also use `try?`:

```
try? card.charge(amount: -1000) // this will fail safely and nicely
```

Error handling is a fundamental feature in Swift, when you need to interact with failable code. Throughout the course of this book, you'll see other patterns that encapsulate error management differently, and which many Swift users prefer over the default `do...catch...throw` pattern. However, for now let's continue our exploration of the Standard Library with the different container types.

Container types

Container types are data types that are useful for containing other types. We'll spend this section covering the most prominent features of the most widely known and used containers:

- Array
- Dictionary
- Set

Arrays are unordered collections of the same element; dictionaries are keyed collections of elements; sets are unordered collections of unique elements.

Arrays

Unlike in Objective-C, a Swift array can only hold elements of the same type, and it's a value type.

The following code declares an `Array` container of three `Int` types, 1, 2, and 3:

```
let ints = [1,2,3] // Array<Int> or [Int]
```

As an example, if you wanted them to be `Doubles`, you could easily force the type on it:

```
let doubles: [Double] = [1,2,3]
```

Mutability and operations

These arrays are immutable, as they are defined as `let`; it is therefore not possible to add or remove elements from them. Hopefully, we can still make mutable copies of them:

```
var otherDoubles = doubles
otherDoubles.append(4)
let lastDoubles = otherDoubles.dropFirst()

print(doubles)
print(otherDoubles)
print(lastDoubles)
```

Take a minute to think about what will be printed in the console, and why:

```
[1.0, 2.0, 3.0]
[1.0, 2.0, 3.0, 4.0]
[2.0, 3.0, 4.0]
```

The first array, `doubles`, was never mutated, as we called `append(4)` on a copy of it. So the copy, `otherDoubles`, has the value `4.0` appended to the end. Finally, the `dropFirst()` call returns another copy of the array, and doesn't mutate in place. This is crucial to understand these, as this behavior is consistent across all Swift Standard Library value types.

Iterating, mapping, and reducing

Starting with Swift 3, C-style statements that are usually used when iterating through arrays have been removed, so you can no longer write the following:

```
for var i = 0; i < otherDoubles.count; i++  {
    let element = otherDoubles[i]
}
```

Instead, we use more powerful syntax:

A simple iterator is as follows:

```
for value in doubles  {
    print("\(value)") // 1.0, 2.0, 3.0
}
```

You can use an enumerator as follows:

```
for (idx, value) in doubles.enumerated()  {
    print("\(idx) -> \(value)") // 0 -> 1.0, 1 -> 2.0, 2 -> 3.0
}
```

Similarly, you can use the `forEach` method that will invoke a closure for each element, passing it as the first parameter:

```
doubles.forEach { value in
    // do something with the value
}
```

Next, we can transform the current array into another array of the same dimensions, through the `map` method:

```
let twices = doubles.map { value in
    return "\(value * 2.0)"
} // twices is [String] == ["2.0", "4.0", "6.0"]
```

Finally, when you need to change the dimensions of your array, change the type, or any other transformation, you can use the `reduce` method to do the following:

- Calculate a `sum`, as follows:

  ```
  let sum = doubles.reduce(0) { $0 + $1 }
  ```

- Create a new array, larger than the original one, as follows:

  ```
  let doubleDoubles = doubles.reduce([]) { $0 + [$1, $1] }
  doubleDoubles == [1.0, 1.0, 2.0, 2.0, 3.0, 3.0]  // true
  ```

Dictionaries

Let's take a look at the definition of the `Dictionary` type:

```
public struct Dictionary<Key, Value> where Key : Hashable
```

In an array, you can only carry a single type of object, but there is no constraint on this type of object. Dictionaries can hold any `Value`, but the `Key` has to conform to the `Hashable` protocol. The reason is simple: in order to efficiently index a dictionary and compare two dictionary keys, Swift uses the hash value of the key, instead of the key itself. This also helps us to write a variety of dictionary types that can make our programs more expressive.

Many types conform to the `Hashable` protocol, and you can make your own types conform to this protocol if you need to create you own custom dictionary keys.

Initialization and mutability

Dictionaries are value types, and they follow the same mutability and initialization as other value types.

Let's use some important dates—the release dates for Swift—to work with dictionaries:

```
let swiftReleases = [
    "2014-09-09": "Swift 1.0",
    "2014-10-22": "Swift 1.1",
    "2015-04-08": "Swift 1.2",
    "2015-09-21": "Swift 2.0",
    "2016-09-13": "Swift 3.0",
    "2017-09-19": "Swift 4.0",
    "2018-03-29": "Swift 4.1",
    "2018-09-17": "Swift 4.2"
] // Swift release dates, source Wikipedia
```

As you can see, the dictionary type is quite simple; it's `Dictionary<String, String>`, which we can also denote as `[String: String]`.

Similar to the `Array` and other value types, using the `let` keyword makes the dictionary immutable, which means the following:

- You cannot replace the contents of `swiftReleases` with a new dictionary
- You cannot add another key/value pair
- You cannot remove an existing key/value pair

- You cannot replace an existing key/value pair
- You cannot use any function or method that have an effect from above

While having the release date as a string is practical for writing the code, it becomes quite impractical if we want to do any kind of date comparison or computation.

In the next sections, we'll explore what we can do with dictionaries.

Iterating, mapping, and reducing

Dictionaries are collections; literally, `Dictionary` conforms to the `collection` type. Therefore, it gains lots of the features of collections.

The element type of the `[Key: Value]` collection is a `(Key, Value)` tuple.

Let's take a look at the different syntax, as follows:

```
for (key, value) in swiftReleases {
    print("\(key) -> \(value)")
}

// Output:
2016-09-13 -> Swift 3.0
2015-09-21 -> Swift 2.0
2017-09-19 -> Swift 4.0
2015-04-08 -> Swift 1.2
2014-09-09 -> Swift 1.0
2014-10-22 -> Swift 1.1
2018-03-29 -> Swift 4.1
```

As you can see, the order of keys is not preserved; this may affect your programs, if you expect the order to be consistent across runs.

- Using `forEach`: This is very similar to using the `for in` pattern:

```
swiftReleases.forEach { (key, value) in
    print("\(key) -> \(value)")
}
```

Technically, you can pass any function or closure in the execution block, which can make your code clearer, by extracting the implementation of the iterator outside.

- Using `enumerated()`: You can also get an enumerator from your dictionaries, if you need to get the index of the current `key/value` pair:

```
swiftReleases.enumerated().forEach { (offset, keyValue) in
    let (key, value) = keyValue
    print("[\(offset)] \(key) -> \(value)")
}

// Output:
[0] 2016-09-13 -> Swift 3.0
[1] 2015-09-21 -> Swift 2.0
[2] 2017-09-19 -> Swift 4.0
[3] 2015-04-08 -> Swift 1.2
[4] 2014-09-09 -> Swift 1.0
[5] 2014-10-22 -> Swift 1.1
[6] 2018-03-29 -> Swift 4.1
```

- Mapping values: You can easily transform values from a dictionary to the same type, or to another type completely. This is done with the `mapValues` method. Our Swift releases dictionary is raw data, and we'll probably want to parse the version in a proper semantic versioning `major`, `minor`, `patch` tuple. First let's declare `Version` as `typealias`, as it's very simple, and it's unlikely that we'll need it to be `struct` or `class`, at this point:

```
typealias Version = (major: Int, minor: Int, patch: Int)
```

Now, we need a simple method, which will transform a `string` version into a proper `Version`. Because not all strings are valid versions, we mark the method as `throws`, to encompass the cases where the string is invalid:

```
func parse(version value: String) throws -> Version {
    // Parse the string 'Swift 1.0.1' -> (1, 0, 1)
    fatalError("Provide implementation")
}
```

Finally, we'll apply the mapping to our dictionary object:

```
let releases: [String: Version] = try swiftReleases.mapValues {
(value) -> Version in
    try parse(version: value)
}
```

You can also use a shorter syntax, such as the following:

```
let releases = try swiftReleases.mapValues(parse(version:))
```

Or, you could use the following:

```
let releases = try swiftReleases.mapValues(parse)
```

- Mapping keys with a reducer: Transforming values is very easy with the `mapValues` method, but Swift doesn't provide a `mapKeys` method to transform the keys into other types or use other values for them. This is where the `reduce` method comes into play. We can use a reducer to transform our releases into another dictionary of the type, `[Date: Version]`, as follows:

```
let releases: [String: Version] = ... // the mapped values from
previous examples
let versionsByDate = try releases.reduce(into: [Date: Version]()) {
(result, keyValue) in
    let formatter = // NSDateFormatter...
    if let date = formatter.date(from: keyValue.key) {
        result[date] = keyValue.value
    } else  {
        throw InvalidDateError()
    }
}

assert(versionsByDate is [Date: Version])
```

We have now fully, and safely converted our original dictionary of strings into valid Swift objects, upon which we can perform more complex operations; these objects are more suited for handling in your programs. You will often find yourself transforming data from one type to another, so remember the `map`, `reduce`, and `mapValues` methods.

Mastering concurrency with Dispatch

Grand Central Dispatch (GCD) is a technology that provides a high-level API for safely dealing with concurrency and leveraging multicore architectures. With Dispatch, you don't need to deal with threads and thread pools anymore; instead, you'll work with operations and queues.

Using GCD, you'll be able to write efficient, multitasking code that scales from few to many CPU cores. Let's begin with the basic concepts of queues and tasks; then we'll cover the different techniques for synchronizing tasks.

Tasks and queues

Queues are objects that abstract series of operations to execute. The system creates many queues for you, but the most important one is probably the main queue. Queues come in two major flavors, as follows:

- **Serial**: A serial queue guarantees that no two operations will be executed at the same time. This is a particularly interesting feature if you need to write thread-safe code.
- **Concurrent**: A concurrent queue will let different operations run in parallel, which can also be a very interesting feature.

As we mentioned previously, a serial queue is a queue that guarantees that no two operations will be run in parallel. The main queue of our apps, which you can access through `DispatchQueue.main`, is a serial queue. This is helpful to know, as the UI of iOS and macOS apps is run on the main thread. The execution of tasks on the main thread will be in order.

Let's consider the following code:

```
DispatchQueue.main.async {
    print("operation 1")
    DispatchQueue.main.async {
        print("operation 1.1")
    }
}

DispatchQueue.main.async {
    print("operation 2")
}
```

 Take a minute to think about what order you expect the logs to be printed in.

The output is as follows:

```
operation 1
operation 2
operation 1.1
```

The operations are executed in the order that they were enqueued. This is why `operation 2` runs before `operation 1.1`. This is guaranteed, because the main queue is a serial queue. In a concurrent queue, this would not be guaranteed, and operations could be run out of order.

Let's spice things up and run this series multiple times, with different queues, considering the following function run, which takes a queue and a number of executions. This function will run as many times as it is asked, on the provided queue, using the same logic that we ran previously:

```
func run(queue: DispatchQueue, times: Int) {
    (0..<times).forEach { i in
        queue.async {
            print("\(i) operation 1")
            queue.async { print("\(i) operation 1.1") }
        }
        queue.async {
            print("\(i) operation 2")
        }
    }
}
```

When calling with `run(queue: .main, times: 3)`, the results are consistent with a serial queue:

```
0 operation 1
0 operation 2
1 operation 1
1 operation 2
2 operation 1
2 operation 2
0 operation 1.1
1 operation 1.1
2 operation 1.1
```

All operations are executed in the order in which they have been enqueued. However, can you guess what will happen if we plug in a concurrent queue? See the following:

```
let queue = DispatchQueue(label: "com.run.concurrent",
                          attributes: .concurrent)
run(queue: queue, times: 3)
```

 Take a minute to write on a piece of paper what you can suppose about the concurrent queue execution order.

The execution is actually unpredictable. Running the program multiple times will always yield a different output. Let's take a look at the following table:

Run 1	Run 2	Run 3
0 operation 1	0 operation 1	0 operation 1
0 operation 1.1	0 operation 2	0 operation 1.1
0 operation 2	0 operation 1.1	0 operation 2
1 operation 1	1 operation 1	1 operation 1
1 operation 2	1 operation 2	1 operation 2
2 operation 1	1 operation 1.1	2 operation 1
2 operation 2	2 operation 1	1 operation 1.1
1 operation 1.1	2 operation 2	2 operation 2
2 operation 1.1	2 operation 1.1	2 operation 1.1

As we can clearly see in the preceding table, every run has a slightly different execution order. We've repeated these simple tasks just a few times, and we didn't execute large computations or slow operations that would amplify this behavior.

Let's take a look at how we can use the Dispatch library to coordinate multiple operations with precision, and ensure the order of execution.

Synchronization with Dispatch

Dispatch provides powerful tools that help you to write thread-safe code. Let's dive into the different techniques and patterns that are widely used, based upon Dispatch.

Thread safety through serial queues

Sometimes, in your code, you want to guarantee that no two concurrent threads will write to the same memory. You can use the @synchronized(self) section in Objective-C, but in Swift, you can leverage Dispatch and serial queues. As you saw in the previous section, the execution order will be preserved, as well as additional guarantees that the previous task enqueued on a serial queue will be completed before the next one starts.

You can ensure that access to the balance property of CreditCard is thread-safe, which guarantees that no other thread or code is writing while you are reading the value:

```
class CreditCard {
    private let queue = DispatchQueue(label: "synchronization.queue")
    private var _balance: Int = 0
    var balance: Int {
        get {
            return queue.sync { _balance }
```

```
        }
        set {
            queue.sync { _balance = newValue }
        }
    }
}
```

In the preceding example, we use a shadow variable (`balance`) to provide public access to the underlying `_balance`. The shadow variable will guarantee that the `_balance` object/variable will always be accessed in a thread safe manner.

Organizing execution with groups and semaphores

Groups and semaphores help you to organize the execution of your program when you need to do the following:

- Wait for one or more tasks to complete
- Ensure that a resource has proper access control, across multiple contexts

Example of a counting semaphore

In the following example, we'll use a semaphore to suspend the execution of the current thread until a long-running task has completed:

```
let semaphore = DispatchSemaphore(value: 0)
let queue = DispatchQueue(label: "com.run.concurrent",
                          attributes: .concurrent)

// Run a block 1 second of the future
queue.asyncAfter(deadline: DispatchTime.now() + 1) {
    print("Will Signal")
    semaphore.signal()
    print("Did Signal")
}
print("Will Wait")

// wait for the semaphore, this suspends the current thread
semaphore.wait()
print("Done")
```

This will give us the following output:

```
Will Wait
Will Signal
Did Signal
Done
```

As you can see, this code successfully waited till the long-running operation was done, and signal() has been called on the semaphore.

Note that blocking the main thread with a semaphore may result in a deadlock if the semaphore is expected to be signaled on the main thread.

While semaphores are very powerful tools for coordinating the execution of many threads, sometimes, you may not know how many tasks you'll need to synchronize. Also, with semaphores, it is very easy to deadlock a thread as to continue execution; you'll need to balance all wait calls with signal calls. DispatchGroups are suited for this task.

Using groups

Dispatch groups let you organize tasks and execute a block when many tasks have completed. Let's suppose that we need to wait for many long-running tasks to complete, but we don't really know ahead of time how many tasks we need to run, so using a semaphore is not a good solution. For this particular problem, using DispatchGroup is one of the best-suited solutions:

```
/**
Performs some work on any thread
- parameter done: A block that will be called when the work is done
- note: This method may not be thread safe
*/
func doWork(done: @escaping () -> ()) {
    /* complex implementation doing important things */
}
```

Consider the previous function, which could be provided by a third-party SDK or your own API. It performs some work, and, at a later point, the callback, done will be called.

Now, let's suppose that we need to execute it a certain number of times; we could write it as follows:

```
// completion block
let complete = {
```

```
    print("DONE!")
}
// initialize a count for the remaining operations
var count = 0
for i in 0..<4 {
    count += 1 // add one operation
    doWork {
        count -= 1 // one operation is done
        if count == 0 { // yay! we're finished
            complete()
        }
    }
}
```

This is very, very bad code, for many reasons, including the following:

- Poor readability
- Unsafe access to the count variable from many threads
- Not reusable

For all of these issues, use DispatchGroup, as follows:

```
let group = DispatchGroup()

// Iterate through all our tasks
for i in 1..<4 {
    // tell the group we're adding additional work
    group.enter()
    // Do the piece of work
    doWork {
        // tell the group the work is done
        group.leave()
    }
}

// tell the group to call complete when done
group.notify(queue: .main, execute: complete)
```

As you can see, this approach has many benefits:

- The code is more readable and easier to follow
- There is no unsafe incrementation of variables
- You have better control over the execution of your completion block
- It allows for higher order abstractions

Let's take a look at an abstraction over `DispatchGroup` that you can use in your projects to synchronize many executions together:

```swift
// Typealiases so it's easier to reference them all
typealias Block = () -> ()
typealias FunctionWithCallback = (@escaping Block) -> ()

/**
Runs asynchronous functions and calls completion when all is done
- parameter functions: List of functions to run
- parameter completion: A block to call when all functions have completed
*/
func runAll(functions: [FunctionWithCallback], completion: @escaping Block)
{
    // Create a group
    let group = DispatchGroup()
    functions.forEach { (function) in
        group.enter()
        function {
            group.leave()
        }
    }
    group.notify(queue: .main, execute: completion)
}
```

In the preceding example, we created a very high abstraction over simple invocations that complete in the future; thanks to `DispatchGroup`, this implementation is thread safe, easy to understand and maintain, and highly reusable.

HTTP with URLSession

`URLSession` is a class that manages tasks related to network data transfers. You use `URLSession` when you want to download or upload data to an HTTP server.

Combined with `Codable` types, `URLSession` provides a very convenient abstraction over your network requests, if you're using a JSON-based API, for example. In this section, we'll look at how we can use `Encodable` and `Decodable` to represent request and responses bodies in a generic and compile time-safe manner.

Making your first call with URLSession

Let's take a look at the anatomy of a simple URL task:

```
let url = URL(string: "https://api.website.com/")!
let task  = URLSession.shared.dataTask(url: url) { data, response, error in
    if let error = error { return } // handle the error somehow
    guard let response = response as HTTPURLResponse,
        let data = data else { return }
    // data: Data is set, and all good
}
task.resume()
```

If the call has succeeded, the data variable will be set and will contain the data downloaded from the remote server.

Parsing responses with Decodable

A Decodable object is an object that can be transformed from Data to a pure Swift object or struct, through Decoder. This section will not provide a full coverage of codables, but rather, a quick example that shows how you can leverage this when communicating with a server in a generic way.

Let's re-work the previous example a bit and improve the code; instead of returning data, we want to return a pure Swift object:

```
func get<T>(url: URL, callback: @escaping (T?, Error?) -> Void) ->
URLSessionTask where T: Decodable {
    let task = URLSession.shared.dataTask(with: url) { data, response,
error in
        if let error = error {
            callback(nil, error)
            return
        }
        // Very simple handling of errors, you may wanna
        // have a more in depth implementation
        if let data = data {
            do {
                let result = try JSONDecoder().decode(T.self, from: data)
                callback(result, nil)
            } catch let error {
                callback(nil, error)
            }
        } else {
            callback(nil, nil)
```

```
            }
        }
        task.resume()
        return task
    }
```

The preceding `get` method will fetch the contents of a URL, and then try to parse the received data into the expected type. You can use it the following way:

```
struct MyResult: Decodable {
    /*
    you can put anything decodable here
    the compiler will generate the decodable implementation
    */
}

func handle(result: MyResult) {
    print(result)
}

func handle(handle: Error) {
    print(handle)
}

_ = get(url: URL(string: "http://example.com")!) { (result: MyResult?,
error) in
    switch (result, error) {
    case (.some(let result), _):
        handle(result: result)
    case (_, .some(let error)):
        handle(handle: error)
    default: // both are nil :/
        break;
    }
}
```

In the preceding example, we'll get the contents of `http://example.com`, and the `get<T>` function will automatically try to map the contents of the response body into the expected `MyResult`. This gives you a compile time guarantee that only valid response bodies will be processed further down your application, which is very interesting when building robust clients.

Now that we have implemented a simple `get` method and a parser, let's look at how we can tie the loop with another method.

Sending requests with Encodable

The counterpart to Decodable is Encodable; an object that conforms to both Encodable and Decodable is Codable. Now that you have seen how to download data from a server and parse it into a pure Swift object, you'll probably want to send data to the server from pure Swift objects:

```
func post<T, U>(url: URL, body: U, callback: @escaping (T?, Error?) ->
Void) throws
    -> URLSessionTask where T: Decodable, U: Encodable {
    var request = URLRequest(url: url)
    request.httpBody = try JSONEncoder().encode(body)
    request.httpMethod = "POST"
    let task = URLSession.shared.dataTask(with: request) { data, response,
error in
        // Exact same code as in the get<T> callback, extracted
        handleResponse(data: data,
                       response: response,
                       error: error,
                       callback: callback)
    }
    task.resume()
    return task
}
```

As you can see, we have now minimally changed the implementation of the original get<T>. That begs for a higher level of abstraction on both URLSession and URLRequest:

1. We can make the URLRequest class aware of the body parsing logic, as follows:

```
extension URLRequest {
    enum HTTPMethod: String {
        case GET
        case POST
        case PUT
        case DELETE
    }
    init<T>(url: URL, method: HTTPMethod, body: T?) throws where T:
Encodable {
        self.init(url: url)
        httpMethod = method.rawValue
        if let body = body {
            httpBody = try JSONEncoder().encode(body)
        }
    }
}
```

2. Let's update `URLSession` with the response parsing logic, over the `dataTask` call:

```
extension URLSession {
    func dataTask<T>(with request: URLRequest,
                     callback: @escaping (T?, Error?) -> Void)
                     throws -> URLSessionTask where T: Decodable {
        return URLSession.shared.dataTask(with: request) { data,
response, error in
            handleResponse(data: data,
                           response: response,
                           error: error,
                           callback: callback)
        }
    }
}
```

3. With those abstractions done, we can finally use our enhanced `URLSession` all over our program. Let's start with the new `URLRequest`:

```
let request = try! URLRequest(url: URL(string:
"http://example.com")!,
                              method: .POST,
                              body: MyBody())
```

4. We can then get `URLSessionDataTask` from `URLSession`:

```
let task = try? URLSession.shared.dataTask(with: request) {
(result: MyResult?, error) in
    // Handle result / error
}
task?.resume()
```

You now have the basic building blocks required to build a type-safe and powerful network client. You'll be able to reuse these patterns across your programs, as they are very generic.

Summary

In this chapter, we have explored the Swift Standard Library, Dispatch, and a piece of Foundation with URLSession. You should now be comfortable with basic types, containers (such as dictionaries and arrays), modern enumeration, mapping, and reducing techniques. With Dispatch, you now have a good understanding of the differences between threads and queues, how serial and concurrent queues can be used to effectively make your programs more performant (but also unsafe), and ultimately, how to use synchronization techniques to organize the execution of your programs in a safe manner. Finally, we scratched the surface of the Codable protocols and applied them to URLSession in a generic way. This will allow you to write a type-safe client with excellent error handling and resilience against malformed responses.

Not all projects are written solely in Swift; many still share implementations with Objective-C. Now that you have a good grasp of the Standard Library, in the next chapter, we will look at all of the kinks and quirks involved with working in a mixed-code base.

Working with Objective-C in a Mixed Code Base

4

Swift builds upon the strong heritage of Objective-C. When Apple released the first version of Swift, they also reassured all developers that their Objective-C code bases would be able to integrate Swift progressively thanks to a strong interoperability layer. Even today, many applications haven't fully migrated to Swift, and interoperability is key to ensure that the Objective-C code isn't bringing instability and unsafe types into your shiny Swift modules.

In this chapter, we'll have a look at techniques to write safer Objective-C code:

- How to import Swift code in Objective-C and vice versa
- How to add nullability to Objective-C
- How to expose renamed methods to Swift
- How to leverage lightweight generics in Objective-C
- How the Cocoa design patterns translate in Swift

Setting up your project

Setting up for Swift from an existing Objective-C project just takes a minute and Xcode is usually able to do it for you, but in case you're lost, you've faced an issue, or you want to know exactly how everything works, this section is for you.

Importing Objective-C in Swift

This is usually how we discover the interoperability layer. An existing Objective-C code base is getting upgraded to Swift and you need to expose existing Objective-C classes to your new Swift code.

In Swift, all of your classes are available in the current module, depending on their access control scopes. In Objective-C, one developer need is to import a header through the `#import "MyClass.h"` directive or the module through `@import ExternalLibrary`. In order to expose your classes to Swift, you'll need to use a **bridging header**. Its responsibility is to expose only the classes you wish to the Swift compiler.

The bridging header is a header file that contains all of the import statements of the libraries and classes that are available to Swift. Once exposed this way, those classes are automatically available in all of the Swift code.

Let's set up a project for bridging:

1. Add a header file to your project; call it `Bridging-Header.h`, for example
2. In your **Project Build** settings, set `SWIFT_OBJC_BRIDGING_HEADER` to the path relative to your project root to your `Bridging-Header.h` file
3. Add the required imports to your header

 In step 2, you may need to double-check where your header file is located. If it's in a subfolder called `MyClasses`, then the value should be `MyClasses/Bridging-Header.h`.

Exposing Swift to Objective-C

In order to expose Swift to Objective-C, Xcode will generate a header for you, which contains all Swift classes and modules that can be exposed to Objective-C. In Xcode, you can set the value of that header by controlling `SWIFT_OBJC_INTERFACE_HEADER_NAME`.

There are many reasons why a Swift class can't be exposed to Objective-C, including the following:

- Using types that don't directly bridge to Objective-C
- Using generics
- Using pure Swift structs and classes

`SWIFT_OBJC_INTERFACE_HEADER_NAME` is usually set to `$(SWIFT_MODULE_NAME)-Swift.h` at the project level, which is a good default and unlikely to conflict with any other header declaration. Most of the time, `$(SWIFT_MODULE_NAME)` will be the name of your app.

Whenever you need to import Swift code in your Objective-C implementation files use the following:

```
#import "MyProject-Swift.h"
```

This will properly import all of your Objective-C compatible declarations from Swift.

Now that we have properly bridged the two worlds of Swift and Objective-C, let's explore the interoperability layer with one of the most important features of Swift, nullability. In Objective-C, sending a message to `nil` or calling a method on a `nil` object has no effect, but it's unlikely that the developer on purpose left that in the code. Unlike Java, the program will not crash, nor raise an exception. In Swift, calling a method on a `nil` value results in a crash. As Objective-C can produce `nil` values, we need to reconcile these two worlds with nullability annotations.

Nullability and optionals in Objective-C

Objective-C provides a facility to work at compile time with nullability and optionals. While it's not as powerful as Swift optionals, it still provides a decent amount of safety for pure Objective-C programs. Lastly, it can be used to better interoperate with Swift.

Let's first consider this simple Objective-C interface:

```
@interface AnObject: NSObject

@property (nonatomic, copy) NSString* string;

@end
```

This is exposed in Swift as the following:

```
class AnObject: NSObject {
    var string: String!
}
```

As you might notice, the string is a forced unpacked string, but this is unlikely what you would expect. Before Swift 4, the following code was valid but would crash at runtime:

```
// Swift 3
let object = AnObject()
let string = object.string // String!
string.appendContentsOf("SwiftObject")
// fatal error: unexpectedly found nil while unwrapping an Optional value
```

Starting with Swift 4, however, the forced unpack optionals have not been accessible without using the ? operator:

```
// Swift 4
let object = AnObject()
let string = object.string // String!
string?.appending("SwiftObject") // safe to use
```

While this works properly and is now quite safe to use, this is often not what we expect to expose. Most of our objects don't have optional properties.

Using NS_ASSUME_NON_NULL_BEGIN and NS_ASSSUME_NON_NULL_END

We can use NS_ASSUME_NON_NULL_BEGIN and NS_ASSUME_NON_NULL_END in order to express broadly that all properties, method arguments, and return types are non-optional:

```
NS_ASSUME_NONNULL_BEGIN

@interface AnObject: NSObject

- (NSString *)sayHello; // return @"Hello World"
- (NSString *)append:(NSString *)aString with:(NSString *)anotherString;
@end

NS_ASSUME_NONNULL_END
```

The following snippet shows how to use it in Swift:

```
// Swift 5
let object = AnObject()
let string = object.sayHello() // String
let returnValue = object.append("First String", with: "Next String")
let otherString = string.appending(" From Swift") // safe to use
assert(otherString == "Hello World From Swift")
```

As you can see, nothing is an optional anymore and it properly expresses the need for non-optional parameters in Objective-C.

So far, we're able to mark large portions of code as non optional, but often, you'll need to mark just a few arguments or return types as optional.

Using nullable, nonnull, _Nullable, and _Nonnull

With NS_ASSUME_NON_NULL_BEGIN/_END, you may need to mark particular properties as nullable as all of the code enclosed will be translated without optionals.

These four keywords are used to mark individual arguments or properties—their usage is straightforward:

- nullable
- nonnull
- _Nullable
- _Nonnull

Using a nullable property will produce Optional, which you'll safely need to unpack in Swift. Using nonnull will produce non-optional properties or variables. nullable and nonnull keywords are exclusively used in the context of declaring @property on Objective-C interfaces.

_Nullable and _Nonnull keywords are used in all other cases:

- Declaring local variables
- Arguments to methods
- Return types of methods
- Declaring ivars

You can use the following table as a reference if you ever need to quickly look up the different possibilities and how they translate in both languages:

Swift	Objective-C
var myString: String?	@property(nullable) NSString *string;
func run(string: String?)	- (void) run:(NSString * _Nullable) string;
var myString: String	@property(nonnull) NSString *string;
func run(string: String)	- (void) run:(NSString * _Nonnull) string;

Naming, renaming, and refining Objective-C for Swift

You may also find yourself in a situation where the generated names for your classes or methods are suboptimal. Thankfully, Clang provides macros that help us rename classes, methods, and more.

Setting Objective-C names from Swift

When you write Swift class names, we follow the recommendation of not prefixing our class names or extensions with a two or three letter code. However, back in Objective-C, those conventions are quite important for a number of reasons, but principally to avoid naming collisions with other objects from different frameworks.

Let's consider the following code snippet that defines a movie:

```
class Movie {
    let title: String
    let director: String
    let year: Int
    /* Initializers */
}
```

As it is right now, it is not possible to use it in Objective-C as the `Movie` object doesn't inherit `NSObject`. Also, because you're exposing your class to Objective-C and not following the naming conventions of Objective-C with the prefix, we should probably rename the class with the `@objc(...)` declaration:

```
@objc(FVMovie)
class Movie: NSObject {
    /* Original code */
}
```

The previous class will be exposed to Objective-C as `FVMovie` and not `Movie` and can be used properly and naturally in your Objective-C code.

Let's now imagine, you have written an extension for `String` in Swift called `leftPad` and you'll need it in Objective-C now. In Objective-C, we deal with `NSString`, not `String`, so the extensions are not exposed by default:

```
extension String {
    static let padCharacter = " "
    func leftPad(to length: Int, with character: String = .padCharacter) ->
```

```
String {
        /* Your left pad implementation */
    }
}
```

There are multiple steps required to expose it to Objective-C:

- @objc cannot be applied to String as it's a struct, and Swift structs can't be exported to Objective-C
- The leftPad name should be prefixed, as per Objective-C recommendations
- String doesn't exist in Objective-C, but NSString does

Let's create an extension on NSString:

```
extension NSString {
    func leftPad(to length: Int, with character: String = .padCharacter) ->
String {
        return (self as String).leftPad(to: length, with: character)
    }
}
```

You'll realize that the method is still not exposed to Objective-C as the extension is not exposed by default. You can remedy that by marking the full extension @objc:

```
@objc
extension NSString { /* */ }
```

Now you can use the leftPad method in Objective-C:

```
NSString * padded = [@"Hello" leftPadTo:10 with:@" "];
// padded == @"     Hello"
```

There are a few things we should improve before we can move on with that implementation:

- The default character used in padding (String.padCharacter) isn't available
- The method name isn't the best for Objective-C
- This doesn't follow the recommended prefixed naming conventions

In order to expose the default implementation that requires only the target length, we need to add an additional method:

```
extension NSString {
    func leftPad(to length: Int) -> String {
        return (self as String).leftPad(to: length)
    }
}
```

This will leverage the original default implementation in Swift, so it's usable in Objective-C as well:

```
NSString * padded = [@"Hello" leftPadTo:10];
// padded == @"     Hello"
```

Now let's put proper names on the methods:

```
extension NSString {
    @objc(flv_leftPadToLength:)
    func leftPad(to length: Int) -> String

    @objc(flv_leftPadToLength:withCharacter:)
    func leftPad(to length: Int, with character: String) -> String
}
```

Now you'll be able to use those implementations in Objective-C with the following:

```
[@"Hello" flv_leftPadToLength:10]; // @"     Hello"
[@"Hello" flv_leftPadToLength:10 withCharacter:@"*"]; // @"*****Hello"
```

In this section, we've focused on adapting our Swift code to Objective-C so it's easier to use and more natural in the Objective-C style. In the next section, we'll focus on the opposite, making our Objective-C code more natural to Swift.

Setting Swift names from Objective-C

Clang also provides macros that help to rename Objective-C classes and methods for Swift: NS_SWIFT_NAME.

Let's start with an example that could arise if you're writing a cooking application or any other app that requires measuring. When cooking, you'll often be hit with multiple volumes, units, and so on. It is possible to abstract it with a Measure class:

```
// A measuring unit
typedef NS_ENUM(NSInteger, FVMeasureUnit) {
    FVLiters,
```

```
        FVMilliliters,
        FVCups
    };

    //  The Measure class,
    @interface FVMeasure : NSObject

    @property (nonatomic, readonly) double amount;
    @property (nonatomic, readonly) FVMeasureUnit unit;

    + (instancetype) measureWithAmount:(double) amount unit:(FVMeasureUnit)
    unit;
    + (instancetype) withCups:(double) value;

    - (double) valueInUnit:(FVMeasureUnit) unit;
    /* more convenience initializers */
    @end
```

While the previous code is not explicitly bad, it is not very Swift-y:

```
    let measure = FVMeasure(amount: 10, unit: FVMeasureUnit.cups)
    let inMilliliters = measure.value(in: .milliliters)
```

Renaming classes

The first step would be to rename the classes and enums so they don't expose this ugly FV prefix:

```
    typedef NS_ENUM(NSInteger, FVMeasureUnit) {
     /* ... */
    } NS_SWIFT_NAME(MeasureUnit); // notice the attribute is 'after'

    // And for interfaces the attribute is before
    NS_SWIFT_NAME(Measure)
    @interface FVMeasure : NSObject
```

We can now rewrite our Swift to the following:

```
    let measure = Measure(amount: 10, unit: MeasureUnit.cups)
```

The class and enum names are quite better but we can go further.

Renaming methods and enum cases

Is is also possible to apply the NS_SWIFT_NAME macro to enum cases as well as class and instance methods:

```
// A measuring unit
typedef NS_ENUM(NSInteger, FVMeasureUnit) {
    FVLiters NS_SWIFT_NAME(l),
    FVMilliliters NS_SWIFT_NAME(ml),
    FVCups,
} NS_SWIFT_NAME(MeasureUnit);
```

Let's also rename one of the static initializers and the conversion method's name to something shorter:

```
+ (instancetype) withCups:(double) value NS_SWIFT_NAME(init(cups:));
- (double) valueInUnit:(FVMeasureUnit) unit NS_SWIFT_NAME(in(unit:));
```

Notice how you declare an initializer with the init(cups:) syntax; this follows the same conventions as when you specify selectors in Swift.

Now it is possible to use the shorthand enum value when referencing the unit:

```
let tenCups = Measure(cups: 10)
let tenCupsInLiters = tenCups.in(unit: .l)
```

In this section, we've covered how to adapt your legacy Objective-C code naming style to the modern Swift feel. We're almost done with interoperability, and still have to cover a great feature added to the Objective-C language: lightweight generics.

Lightweight generics in Objective-C

Swift has made a big use of generics through the standard library. Arrays, dictionaries, enums, and more leverage generic types in order to ensure contained types are not swallowed by the language. In order to improve compatibility and interoperability, Apple has introduced lightweight generics to Objective-C.

Using typed NSArray* in Objective-C

In Objective-C, for example, arrays can hold any object type:

```
NSArray * array = @[@"Hello", @1, @{@"key": @2} [NSObject new], [NSNull
null]];
```

```
[array enumerateObjectsUsingBlock:^(id _Nonnull obj, NSUInteger idx, BOOL
* _Nonnull stop) {
    // Do something with the object
}];
```

In the previous code, we see `id _Nonnull obj` as being the first parameter of our enumeration block. This is very far from being useful as a consumer of the array has no idea what kind of objects are contained. At compile time, it is impossible to enforce a safe usage of the arrays. This is where lightweight generics come in:

```
NSArray<NSString *> * stringArray = @[@"Hello", @1];
// WARNS: Object of type 'NSNumber *' is not compatible with array element
type 'NSString *'
```

While the compiler doesn't explicitly prevent us from initializing the array, a warning is issued with the correct resolution. In this case, only strings can be added to `stringArray`.

Generic classes in Objective-C

Let's craft a class especially for our demonstration purposes. It has the following features:

- It is a generic class, similar to Swift's generic classes
- It exposes generic types (in the form of arrays)
- It exposes a generic type that is bound to the classes' own generics

Consider the following `MyGeneric` class:

```
NS_ASSUME_NONNULL_BEGIN

@interface MyGeneric<__covariant T> : NSObject

@property (nullable, nonatomic, retain) NSArray<T> *genericArray;

- (NSArray *)untypedArray;
- (NSArray<NSString *> *)stringArray;
- (NSArray<__kindof NSString *> *)kindofStringArray;

@end

NS_ASSUME_NONNULL_END
```

The previous code is a fully generic Objective-C class and introduces two new keywords:

- __covariant is used to make the MyGeneric class generic with a type that will be determined when creating an instance
- __kindof is used to allow not only the provided type (NSString *) but also all subclasses.

In Objective-C, we can now use it this way:

```
MyGeneric * untypedGeneric = [MyGeneric new];
NSArray* objects = [untypedGeneric genericArray];

MyGeneric<NSNumber *> * numberGeneric = [MyGeneric new];
NSArray<NSNumber *> * numbers = [numberGeneric genericArray];
```

As you can see, in Objective-C, you can always use the non-generic type; the compiler doesn't force you to specialize. You can also do unsafe casts from one type to another:

```
MyGeneric<NSNumber *> * casted = (MyGeneric<NSNumber *> *) untypedGeneric;
```

This is valid Objective-C code, but will likely crash at runtime when accessing the objects.

And from Swift's perspective, it is as follows:

```
let generic = MyGeneric<NSNumber>()

assert(generic.untypedArray() is [Any])
assert(generic.stringArray() is [String])
assert(generic.kindofStringArray() is [String])
assert(generic.genericArray is [NSNumber]?)
```

There are multiple things to note from the Swift code:

- You cannot create an instance of MyGeneric **without** the specialization to a particular type
- You cannot create an instance of MyGeneric **with a value type** as a specialization; for example, MyGeneric<String>() won't work
- You cannot create extensions of MyGeneric in Swift, you'll be hit by: **Extension of a generic Objective-C class cannot access the class's generic parameters at runtime**

With that reference in mind, you can come back to it whenever you need to bridge Objective-C code in Swift. The last step in our introduction is to cover the basic Cocoa design patterns, how they translate and apply to Swift, and how to put them in practice safely and efficiently.

Cocoa design patterns in Swift

In this section, we'll recapitulate how the most common Cocoa design patterns translate to Swift. You may already be very familiar with those design patterns as they are found throughout Cocoa.

Originally, Cocoa was designed as the high-level API to interface with macOS in Objective-C. Originally, it comprised three frameworks:

- Foundation
- AppKit
- Core Data

These frameworks are designed with a common rationale and a set of design patterns we encounter and work with constantly through all Apple SDKs.

Delegation

Delegation is one of the most common design patterns when working with Apple SDKs. Delegation is a pattern that facilitates the communication between two objects, the first one, which we'll call the source and the other, the delegate. The source can be anything from a view, such as `UITableView` / `UITableViewDelegate`, or a manager, such as `CLLocationManager` / `CLLocationManagerDelegate`.

In every case, the delegation pattern facilitates a **many-to-one** communication. A single delegate can handle as many sources as needed; however, a source can only have one and only one delegate.

Delegation should not be used if a single source object instance needs to communicate with different delegates. You will encounter race conditions or other issues.

Using delegation

Let's create a simple class that has a location manager, which will receive location updates:

```
class LocationAware: NSObject {
    let manager = CLLocationManager()

    override init() {
        super.init()
```

```
            manager.delegate = self
    }
}
```

Then, we need to mark `LocationAware` as being `CLLocationManagerDelegate`. Delegation uses protocols to ensure the methods that may be called are properly implemented on the delegate:

```
extension LocationAware: CLLocationManagerDelegate {
    func locationManager(_ manager: CLLocationManager, didUpdateLocations
locations: [CLLocation]) {
        // do something with the updated location
    }

    /* more delegation methods */
}
```

Now, with that example in mind, let's create our own delegation pattern that will facilitate communications between two objects.

Implementing delegation

Imagine you're building an interactive cookbook. Cookbooks are often confusing as all of the steps may be on the same page, without images, and you believe that a full page with videos and so on will provide a better experience.

We can break down the cookbook into multiple recipes—each recipe has an ingredient list and multiple steps to accomplish in order, only one step after the other. We don't really need to focus right now on the ingredient list, but more on how we can use delegation in order to easily abstract away the realization of a recipe:

```
class Step: Equatable {
    let instructions: String = ""
    weak var delegate: StepDelegate?
}
```

`Step` is merely a simple abstraction over a recipe step:

```
class Recipe {
    let steps: [Step]
    init(steps: [Step]) {
        self.steps = steps
    }
```

```
    func step(after: Step) -> Step? { /* implement me */ }
    func step(before: Step) -> Step? { /* implement me */ }
}
```

`Recipe` is just defined for now as an ordered collection of steps, as well as a simple helper method for getting the next and previous step. As an exercise, you can implement them, and then generalize to `Array` or `Collection` types through the power of extensions:

```
protocol StepDelegate: NSObjectProtocol {
    func didComplete(step: Step)
}

extension Step {
    func complete() {
        delegate?.didComplete(step: self)
    }
}
```

The `StepDelegate` protocol is defining a single method that will be invoked when the step is marked as completed:

```
class RecipeCookingManager: NSObject {
    weak var delegate: RecipeCookingDelegate?
    private let recipe: Recipe

    init(recipe: Recipe) {
        self.recipe = recipe
    }

    func start() {
        guard let step = recipe.steps.first else { fatalError() }
        run(step: step)
    }

    private func run(step: Step) {
        step.delegate = self
        // Make the step available to the UI layer, present it etc...
        // When the user finishes the step, ensure to call step.complete()
    }
}
```

In the previous code, it is very important to mark the delegate `weak`. Failing to do so would create a strong relationship between the object that originates the events and the delegate, which, in turn, would likely prevent the safe and timely deallocation of both objects.

`RecipeCookingManager` is responsible for coordinating the user experience involved in cooking a recipe. Its most important responsibility is to be able to move forward through the recipe:

```
protocol RecipeCookingManagerDelegate: NSObjectProtocol {
    func manager(_ manager: RecipeCookingManager, didCook recipe: Recipe)
    func manager(_ manager: RecipeCookingManager, didCancel recipe: Recipe)
}
```

`RecipeCookingManagerDelegate` is responsible for communicating back to the creator, application, or manager when the recipe is complete or the cooking is cancelled and the user wants to exit the current step:

```
extension RecipeCookingManager: StepDelegate {
    func didComplete(step: Step) {
        step.delegate = nil // no need for the delegate anymore
        if let nextStep = recipe.step(after: step)  {
            run(step: nextStep)
        } else {
            delegate?.manager(self, didComplete:recipe)
        }
    }
}
```

In the previous extension, we are putting the logic that will move forward to the next step or complete the recipe when there is no more steps to accomplish in the recipe.

Let's now have a look at how we can use this `RecipeCookingManager`. In this case, we can write `AutomaticCooker` that would help us run tests quickly and ensure we can show any kind of recipe on screen properly:

```
class AutomatedCooker: NSObject, RecipeCookingManagerDelegate {
    func cook(recipe: Recipe) {
        let manager = RecipeCookingManager(recipe: recipe)
        manager.delegate = self // self is a RecipeCookingManagerDelegate
        manager.start() // start cooking the first step should be in
progress!
        /* complete all steps */
        recipe.steps.forEach { $0.complete() }
        // the did cook method should have been be called!
    }

    func manager(_ manager: RecipeCookingManager, didCook recipe: Recipe) {
        // We're done!
    }

    func manager(_ manager: RecipeCookingManager, didCancel recipe: Recipe)
```

```
    {
            // The user cancelled
        }
    }
```

Now, you should be more comfortable with the delegation design pattern, how to implement it effectively, and how to use it in your programs.

Lazy initialization

In Objective-C, we may want to initialize some properties lazily as they may only be accessed at a future time, we don't want to block the init() call with a long-running operation, or when a required instance property will only be accessible at a later time.

In Swift, we are blessed by the presence of the lazy keyword.

Let's start with this code and see how we can improve it:

```
class MyView: NSView   {
    let image: NSImage!
    let imageView = NSImageView(frame: .zero)
    init(imageName: NSImage.Name, frame: NSRect) {
        image = NSImage(named: imageName)
        super.init(frame: frame)
    }

    func setup() {
        addSubview(imageView)
        imageView.frame = bounds.insetBy(dx: 5.0, dy: 5.0)
        imageView.image = image
        imageView.imageAlignment = .alignCenter
    }
}
```

The previous code isn't completely bad, but we can refactor it so we have better performance, readability, and maintainability.

The first thing we may want to do is to leverage lazy for the image property. There's probably no need to perform it at initialization:

```
class MyView: NSView   {
    private let imageName: NSImage.Name
    lazy var image = NSImage(named: imageName)
    let imageView = NSImageView(frame: .zero)

    init(imageName: NSImage.Name, frame: NSRect) {
```

```
            self.imageName = imageName
            super.init(frame: frame)
        }
        /* original code */
    }
```

Now, when you create a new instance of `MyView`, the image is not initialized; it will be when `setup()` is called.

We can also fix `imageView`:

```
class MyView: NSView {
    private let imageName: NSImage.Name
    lazy var image = NSImage(named: imageName)
    lazy var imageView = NSImageView(frame: self.bounds.insetBy(dx: 5.0,
dy: 5.0))
    init(imageName: NSImage.Name, frame: NSRect) {
        self.imageName = imageName
        super.init(frame: frame)
    }

    func setup() {
        addSubview(imageView)
        imageView.image = image
        imageView.imageAlignment = .alignCenter
    }
}
```

This is getting better! The last step would be to completely configure `imageView` at initialization time:

```
class MyView: NSView {
    private let imageName: NSImage.Name
    lazy var image = NSImage(named: imageName)
    lazy var imageView: NSImageView = {
        let frame = self.bounds.insetBy(dx: 5.0, dy: 5.0)
        let imageView = NSImageView(frame: frame)
        imageView.image = self.image
        imageView.imageAlignment = .alignCenter
        return imageView
    }()
    init(imageName: NSImage.Name, frame: NSRect) {
        self.imageName = imageName
        super.init(frame: frame)
    }
```

```
func setup() {
    addSubview(imageView)
}
}
```

Now, our `setup()` method is nice and clean and, within the `imageView` property, it becomes fully initialized. This is probably one of my favorite initialization patterns in Swift as it lets you configure a property completely, before it's consumed by the called.

The `imageView` initialization happens within a self-executing closure. You can replace it with a function call. This is very helpful if you have common initializations or variables to set (such as the `bounds` inset we apply):

```
private func getImageView(image: NSImage, bounds: NSRect)
-> NSImageView { /* */ }

let imageView = getImageView(image: self.image, bounds:
self.bounds)
```

Summary

In this chapter, we have extensively covered many different aspects of writing and maintaining code bases that share Objective-C and Swift code. Now you should be able to use Swift classes in Objective-C and import your Objective-C classes to Swift, as well as write safe Objective-C with the help of nullability annotations. Not only can your Objective-C code, and should, be safer, with the help of nullability annotations, but you will also tailor your method names so they feel natural in Swift. Lastly, lightweight generics should hold no secrets for you.

With all of these powerful tools in mind, we can continue our journey to the next step: creational design patterns.

Now the design pattern journey can begin. We have prepared ourselves for this in the first chapters. Next in line is the study and implementation of creational design patterns. They are design patterns that are aimed at solving issues related to the creation of object instances. If you feel it isn't always desirable to expose a constructor, the next chapter is for you. If you feel constructors are just fine, then the next chapter is even more for you.

5

Creational Patterns

Now that we've refreshed ourselves on the basics of Swift programming, we can get started with the first series of design patterns: creational patterns.

We use creational patterns to hide the complexity of creating instances of fully featured objects, decouple different part of your applications, and gear your code toward high maintainability.

In this chapter, we'll dive into those traditional patterns, from theoretical to concrete examples, through detailed use cases. We'll see how they're adapted from traditional languages such as Java, and how we can enhance them with the unique features of Swift.

We'll start with two very common and widespread patterns, the singleton and the lazy initialization. We'll follow up through the chapter with the most powerful and useful creational patterns in Swift.

In this chapter, we'll dive deep into the following topics:

- The singleton pattern
- The factory method pattern
- The abstract factory pattern
- The builder pattern
- The prototype pattern

The singleton pattern

The singleton pattern is one of the most used (and misused) creational patterns. It is seen throughout the Cocoa libraries, UIKit, AppKit, and many other Apple frameworks. Be aware that its use can lead to a central state point that gets mutated across your whole program, which can lead to nasty bugs.

In this section, we'll go back to basics with the singleton and focus on its use cases.

Using singletons

Singletons are fairly easy in Swift. A singleton is an object of which there can never be more than one instance in your program. The first instance of a singleton object will be the last. As a corollary, singletons never die, and their lifespan is always your whole program.

In Swift, we have to be particularly cautious about retain cycles. Any object that will be retained by your singleton will ultimately live till the end of your program. It's not an understatement to say: you have to be very cautious with them.

Here's an example:

```
class Earth {
    static let current = Earth()

    private init() {}

    func spinAroundTheSun() { /* */ }
}


let planetEarth = Earth.instance
planetEarth.spinAroundTheSun()
```

Here, we have an `Earth` class. There is only one Earth (as far as we know), so it's safe to assume that we can use the singleton pattern to represent that, through `static let current = Earth()`.

The initializer is also marked as private—this way we prevent accidental initialization of additional Earths.

 Here we used `current` as the static property on our class to denote the accessible singleton. You can use anything you see fit, such as `shared`, `instance`, or `sharedInstance`—but always try to keep it short. Unlike in Java, we don't recommend using a getter.

You may remember the good old Objective-C singleton syntax, as follows:

```
@implementation Earth

+ (id)currentEarth {
    static Earth *sharedEarth = nil;
    static dispatch_once_t onceToken;
    dispatch_once(&onceToken, ^{
        sharedMyManager = [[self alloc] init];
    });
```

```
    return sharedEarth;
}

@end
```

You may wonder why it is not necessary to write an exact translation of that code block in Swift. The reason is quite simple—the compiler does it for us.

In Objective-C, there were two main features of this static + (id)currentEarth method:

- It is thread-safe, as dispatch_once is thread-safe
- It is lazy, as static Earth *sharedEarth is nil until there's a call to currentEarth

Those two features are handled for us by the compiler! So worry not, using static let shared = Earth() is as safe and as performant as the good old Objective-C code.

Singletons in a nutshell

In Swift, you may want to use a singleton in order to ensure only a single instance of your object is ever created. This is very often seen in the facade pattern.

Let's see how to go about creating a singleton:

1. Identify the class you want to refactor as a singleton, ensuring it doesn't grow in memory too much over time
2. Make the initializer private. A singleton can never be instantiated from outside
3. Add a static immutable member, which will be the single instance of your object
4. Replace all occurrences of the now inaccessible constructor with the shared reference

The factory method pattern

The factory method pattern is designed to solve the following design problems:

- How to create different implementations of your objects, based on the creator class
- How to let subclasses define how to instantiate your objects

The factory method pattern lets you decouple the call site from the instantiation site in your code. This makes it easier to refactor, update, or change the instantiation of the target object without compromising the consuming part of your code.

The factory method will be responsible for instantiating objects, instead of the call site. It usually comes in multiple flavours:

- Letting subclasses define different implementations and classes
- Using parameters to define the kind of object returned by the factory

Using the factory method pattern

Let's see how we can leverage the factory method pattern in order to improve existing code.

Let's say you're building an app that let users poke, message, or call their contacts, as follows:

```
enum ContactAction {
    case call
    case message
    case poke
}

class ContactController: NSViewController {
    let callButton = NSButton(title: "Call", target: self, action:
#selector(processAction(from:)))
    let messageButton = NSButton(title: "Message", target: self, action:
#selector(processAction(from:)))
    let pokeButton = NSButton(title: "Poke", target: self, action:
#selector(processAction(from:)))
    private func action(for button: NSButton) -> ContactAction {
        switch button {
        case callButton:
            return .call
        case messageButton:
            return .message
        case pokeButton:
            return .poke
        default:
            fatalError("Unknown button")
        }
    }

    func processAction(from button: NSButton) {
        let action = self.action(for: button)
```

```
        let controller: NSViewController?
        switch action {
        case .call:
            controller = CallController()
        case .message:
            controller = MessageController()
        case .poke:
            // TODO: confirm the poke is sent
            controller = nil
        }
        guard let viewController = controller else
            return
        }
        presentViewControllerAsModalWindow(viewController)
    }
}
```

Let's start refactoring this code.

There are two points at which we can leverage factory methods. The first is button creation. All buttons are created inline, the titles are set inline, nonlocalized, and so on. Ultimately, that is a lot of specific code, which could be replaced with a factory method.

Let's first extend the ContactAction with the associated button titles, as follows:

```
extension ContactAction {
    private var buttonTitle: String {
        switch self {
        case .call:
            return "Call"
        case .message:
            return "Message"
        case .poke:
            return "Poke"
        }
    }

    var localizedTitle: String {
        return NSLocalizedString(buttonTitle, comment: "\(self) button
title")
    }
}
```

With that extension in place, we can now enhance our ContactController in order to simplify the button instantiation:

```
class ContactController: NSViewController {
    lazy var callButton = makeButton(for: .call)
```

```
        lazy var messageButton = makeButton(for: .message)
        lazy var pokeButton = makeButton(for: .poke)
        func makeButton(for action: ContactAction) -> NSButton {
            let button = NSButton(title: action.localizedButtonTitle,
                                    target: self,
                                    action: #selector(processAction(from:)))
            // Additional common configuration for the button
            return button
        }

        /* original code */
    }
```

This is our first factory method! We've hidden the implementation details for NSButton and its configuration. If we add an additional action case, we'll be easily able to add the new button, without duplicating code.

The second part we can improve with the factory method is the action-processing part. There are two issues in the code:

- As processAction takes a button, which is related to the UI, we can't programmatically process an action
- The presentation logic is tightly coupled to the UI logic

Let's tackle the first issue, by adding an additional method:

```
@objc
private func processAction(from button: NSButton) {
    handle(action: action(for: button))
}

func handle(action: ContactAction) {
    let controller: NSViewController?
    switch action {
    case .call:
        controller = CallController()
    case .message:
        controller = MessageController()
    case .poke:
        // TODO: confirm the poke is sent
        controller = nil
    }
    guard let viewController = controller else {
        return
    }
    presentViewControllerAsModalWindow(viewController)
}
```

That's better now. Next, we'll add another factory method that will help us produce the right `ViewController` to present when handling the chosen action:

```
func controller(for action: ContactAction) -> NSViewController? {
    switch action {
    case .call:
        return CallController()
    case .message:
        return MessageController()
    default:
        return nil
    }
}

func handle(action: ContactAction) {
    guard action != .poke else {
        // handle the poke
        return
    }

    guard let controller = controller(for: action) else {
        return
    }
    presentViewControllerAsModalWindow(controller)
}
```

Et voilà! We now have a very clean way to handle our actions. The factory method helped us abstract away the complexity of instantiating objects, as well as providing a clean way for subclasses to provide a different implementation.

For example, in our button case, if you're visiting your own profile, you may not want to call yourself. It is easily solved in a subclass with the following implementation:

```
class MyContactController: ContactController {
    override func makeButton(for action: ContactAction) -> NSButton {
        let button = super.makeButton(for: action)
        button.isEnabled = false
        return button
    }
}
```

We have successfully leveraged the factory method pattern to:

- Hide implementation details from the call sites
- Improve the testability of the code
- Improve our ability to modify the behavior of our programs using subclasses

Advanced usage of the factory method pattern

The factory method pattern is particularly suited to configuring the objects provided by SDKs in a reliable manner. For example, we may want to have a common way to instantiate alerts for our users when there's an error in the app.

Let's see how we can apply this with the popular iOS view controller `UIAlertController`. This controller is used to display a message to the user, either in the form of an alert or an action sheet.

In object-oriented languages, we'd create a factory object, and issue the objects from a factory, as follows:

```
class UIAlertControllerFactory {
    static let sharedFactory = UIAlertControllerFactory()
    private init() {}

    func alertControllerFor(error: Error,
                            onOK handler: @escaping (UIAlertAction) ->
Void)
                            -> UIAlertController {
        /* implementation goes here */
    }
}


let alertController =
UIAlertControllerFactory.shared.alertControllerFor(error: error) {

}
```

However, this is not very *Swifty*—it's very long, verbose, and impractical. Discovering the method on `UIAlertControllerFactory` is quite painful for developers who have just joined your project, and even yourself—after a while, you may even forget about this factory.

In Swift, we can leverage extensions to provide additional initializers, methods, and static methods. This is the preferred way when you want to implement factory methods that help you define additional configuration for your objects, as follows:

```
extension UIAlertController {
    static func forError(_ error: Error,
                         onOK handler: @escaping (UIAlertAction) -> Void)
-> UIAlertController {
        let title = NSLocalizedString("There was an error", comment: "Error
alert title")
```

```
        let message = error.localizedDescription
        let OK = NSLocalizedString("OK", comment: "Error alert OK button
title")
        let controller = UIAlertController(title: title,
                                           message: message,
                                           preferredStyle: .alert)
        let okAction = UIAlertAction(title: OK, style: .cancel, handler:
handler)

        controller.addAction(okAction)

        return controller
    }
}
```

And we can use it anywhere else in the code, having a standard error AlertController to display our errors, as follows:

```
do {
    // Call something that may fail...
} catch let e {
    present(
        UIAlertController.forError(e) { (action) in
            // user tapped OK
        },
        animated: true,
        completion: nil)
}
```

Alternatively, Swift provides the powerful ability to declare **convenience initializers** in class extensions. Instead of a static method, it is possible to refine the previous implementation with a convenience init:

```
extension UIAlertController {
    convenience init(forError error: Error, onOK handler: @escaping
(UIAlertAction) -> Void) {
        let title = NSLocalizedString("There was an error", comment: "Error
alert title")
        let message = error.localizedDescription
        let OK = NSLocalizedString("OK", comment: "Error alert OK button
title")
        self.init(title: title, message: message, preferredStyle: .alert)
        let okAction = UIAlertAction(title: OK, style: .cancel, handler:
handler)
        ddAction(okAction)
    }
}
```

Using the following implementation is even simpler:

```
do {
    // Call something that may fail...
} catch let e {
    present(
        UIAlertController(forError: e) { (action) in
            // user tapped OK
        },
        animated: true,
        completion: nil)
}
```

While all these implementations are very similar, they all carry a different weight. If you find yourself using the `static` or `class` method to create new instances of a particular object, always ponder whether a convenience initializer would be more fitting.

Wrapping up

In our example, we successfully refactored our `ContactsController` with the help of multiple factory methods. As you will have noticed, we haven't created a factory object—factory methods are simply methods that create new instances of objects each time.

In order to implement the factory method pattern you will need to:

1. Identify in your code the areas that produce similar objects. In our case, these are `String`, `NSButton`, and `NSViewController`.
2. Find the common denominator for the generation of those objects. For `String` this was `ContactAction` and `enum`; it was `ContactController` for `NSButtons` and `NSViewControllers`.
3. Replace all the call sites where you were creating the instances with the factory method calls.

Unlike other patterns, this one is not defensive. Usually, you can keep the old code as it is; you're not forced to use the factory methods in your whole code base.

The next pattern we'll discuss is all about simplifying the management of multiple implementations at runtime. Let's dive into the abstract factory pattern.

The abstract factory pattern

You will probably find yourself needing to implement the abstract factory pattern when your program needs different concrete class implementations behind the same interface. Instead of writing the logic in terms of concrete classes, this will let you write programs based on exposed interfaces.

At runtime, the abstract factory will let you easily swap and choose concrete classes when they are instantiated at a single point, instead of writing lengthy and unmaintainable code.

To illustrate this, we'll use an example that you may relate to: registering push notifications and keeping up with changing APIs in a cross-platform environment.

Using the abstract factory pattern

With every **Worldwide Developers Conference (WWDC)**, a new set of OSs is released. This often means tweaking our current projects to accommodate new APIs, provide backwards compatibility, and explore new and shiny features. All those changes can be tedious; even more so if you're maintaining multiple platforms such as iOS, watchOS, tvOS, Linux, and so on.

Let's focus on a simple case: registering for push notifications. We can abstract the intention of *registering* with the following protocol:

```
typealias ResultBlock = (Bool, Error?) -> Void
protocol PushNotificationService {
    func register(_ done: ResultBlock)
}
```

`PushNotificationService` is an object that has a `register(:)` function, with a `ResultBlock` output that will indicate whether the operation was successful or not.

Now let's say we're supporting macOS and iOS apps in our code base. They both have different push notification APIs, which we need to consume in order to register our application for push.

I will not go into the details of the implementation, but we can abstract this for iOS as follows:

```
struct iOSPushNotificationService: PushNotificationService {
    func register(_ done: ResultBlock) { /* Your implementation here */ }
}
```

This is how we do it for macOS:

```
struct macOSPushNotificationService: PushNotificationService {
    func register(_ done: ResultBlock) { /* Your implementation here */ }
}
```

The `struct` for each one conforms to the same protocol, defined as `PushNotificationService`.

Now that we have those objects, we could use them directly—but for every single place in our app that we require those implementations, we'd need to test whether we're on macOS or iOS. Also, we may have further services based on either the iOS or macOS platform, or even want to add additional platforms in the future.

As such, we'll create a `ServicesFactoryType` protocol that will represent all those services we may need, as follows:

```
protocol ServicesFactoryType {
    func getPushService() -> PushNotificationService
    /* Add more services here as your project grows */
}
```

Now, with that interface defined, we can implement a `ServicesFactoryType` for each platform:

```
struct macOSServicesFactory: ServicesFactoryType {
    func getPushService() -> PushNotificationService {
        if #available(OSX 10.9, *) { // Mavericks and above only
            return macOSPushNotificationService()
        }
        /* add additional platform support here */
        fatalError("Push notificaitons are not supported on macOS < 10.9")
    }
}

struct iOSServicesFactory: ServicesFactoryType {
    func getPushService() -> PushNotificationService {
        if #available(iOS 10.0, *) { // New API based on UNNotification
            return iOSPushNotificationService()
        }
        /* additional platform support here */
        fatalError("Push notificaitons are not supported on iOS < 10.0")
    }
}
```

Our two structs will properly create instances of `PushNotificationService`, based on availability, and we can use `macOSServicesFactory` and `iOSServicesFactory`.

Before we do that, let's abstract one further layer, so our application has no knowledge of which kind of factory there is for which kind of platform support.

```
struct ServicesFactory {
    static let shared: ServicesFactoryType = {
        if #available(OSX 10.0, *) {
            return macOSServicesFactory()
        } else if #available(iOS 1.0, *) {
            return iOSServicesFactory()
        }
    }()

    private init() {}
}
```

Now, throughout our applications and projects, we'll have a single simple interface that will let us register our users for push notifications (or throw a `fatalError` when the platform is unsupported):

```
let pushService = ServicesFactory.shared.getPushService()
pushService.register { (success, error) in
    // handle success
}
```

We successfully leveraged the abstract factory pattern in order to hide complex implementation details from the eyes of the developer.

Let's dive a bit further in and see how to expand upon it with common use cases.

Going further with factory methods

Now we've seen the basic implementation, let's have a look at how we could perform common tasks based on the pattern to extend it without breaking either the pattern or the paradigm.

Default implementations

It is very common to share default implementations between your objects, and only implement the difference when needed.

Let's first start by adding a new service to our factory for registering for localization services. Luckily for us, `CoreLocation` is the same SDK for both iOS and macOS, so we're able to share our implementation between the two platforms, as follows:

```
protocol UserLocationService {
    func getUserLocation(done: (CLLocation) -> Void)
}

struct CommonUserLocationService: UserLocationService {
    func getUserLocation(done: (CLLocation) -> Void) {
        // TODO: Implement me
    }
}
```

Let's now add it to our `ServicesFactoryType`:

```
protocol ServicesFactoryType {
    func getPushService() -> PushNotificationService
    func getUserLocationService() -> UserLocationService
    /* Add more services here as your project grows */
}
```

Now, we have our `UserLocationService` interface, with a default implementation, and we've added the requirement to our protocol. However, our current code will break, as neither `iOSServicesFactory` nor `macOSServicesFactory` implement `func getUserLocationService() -> UserLocationService`.

There are multiple ways to move forward, knowing that this implementation is shared by all platforms.

Inheritance

Through inheritance, we can make our `ServicesFactory` into a `ServicesFactoryType` and then ensure that, instead of conforming to `ServicesFactoryType`, both `iOSServicesFactory` and `macOSServicesFactory` inherit from `ServicesFactory`.

All common services can then be implemented on `ServicesFactory`, instead of repeatedly on each `ServicesFactoryType` implementation, as follows:

```
class ServicesFactory: ServicesFactoryType {
    static let shared: ServicesFactoryType = {
        /* same implementation */
    }()
    internal init() {}
    func getPushService() -> PushNotificationService {
        fatalError("abstract method, implement in subclasses")
    }
    func getUserLocationService() -> UserLocationService {
        return CommonUserLocationService()
    }
}
```

Now, `ServicesFactory` is a properly abstract class, as it implements all methods from `ServicesFactoryType` and provides a default implementation for `getUserLocationServices()`.

We also need to update our specific implementations in order to inherit from `ServicesFactory`, and change from `struct` to `class`, as structs don't let you inherit, but only conform to protocols:

```
class macOSServicesFactory: ServicesFactory {
    override func getPushService() -> PushNotificationService { /* */ }
}

class iOSServicesFactory: ServicesFactory {
    override func getPushService() -> PushNotificationService { /* */ }
}
```

And we're done!

You'll notice that this solution is very object-oriented, and leveraging inheritance is not very Swifty. Let's see how we can use protocols to achieve a similar result.

Protocol extensions

We can leverage protocol extensions to provide default implementations for our protocols.

Let's go back to where we were before implementing this whole inheritance chain:

```
protocol ServicesFactoryType {
    func getPushService() -> PushNotificationService
    func getUserLocationService() -> UserLocationService
```

```
        /* Add more services here as your project grows */
    }
```

We can just extend that protocol, as follows:

```
extension ServicesFactoryType {
    func getUserLocationService() -> UserLocationService {
        return CommonUserLocationService()
    }
}
```

We're done—no additional changes, no `override` keyword to add to the implementations. This strategy has one major drawback, however, compared to the inheritance strategy. In the specific iOS and macOS implementations of our `ServicesFactoryType`, it is impossible to access the default one, unlike with inheritance, where it's easy to call `super`.

You can still work around this issue by adding an extra method on the extension, for example, as follows:

```
extension ServicesFactoryType {
    func getUserLocationService() -> UserLocationService {
        return self.defaultUserLocationService()
    }
    func defaultUserLocationService() -> UserLocationService {
        return CommonUserLocationService()
    }
}
```

And then in your platform-specific implementation, you can leverage the default `UserLocationService`:

```
struct iOSServicesFactory: ServicesFactory {
    func getPushService() -> PushNotificationService {
        /* original impl. */
    }
    func getUserLocationService() -> UserLocationService {
        if /* a particular test */ {
            return defaultUserLocationService()
        }
        fatalError("Not supported")
    }
}
```

The later method using protocol extensions would be the preferred Swift way to write default implementations on your abstract factories. It is more powerful, safer, and lets us use `struct` instead of `class`.

While in this particular case we could use either classes or structs, in your projects, choosing the right abstraction is up to you.

Checklist for using the factory method pattern

Before you start adding this pattern everywhere in your code, you need to understand that it solves certain issues, so it's helpful to encounter (and suffer from) those first.

The main use of this pattern is to ensure you do not need to write platform-specific code in your application, and that you keep those pesky `#available` and `os()` checks (or other compile time or runtime checks) hidden from the consumer.

1. First, ensure you have platform-specific code you need to abstract away (iOS vs tvOS, or iOS 9.0 vs iOS 12.0).
2. Define a common interface for the platform-specific objects, as we did with `PushNotificationService` and `UserLocationService`.
3. Implement platform-specific classes for each interface, such as `iOSPushNotificationService`.
4. Define and implement a common service factory interface, such as `ServiceFactoryType`, and implement platform-specific service factories.
5. Define a common and simple way to get the proper `serviceFactory` for the current context. In our scenario, it was the `ServicesFactory.shared` singleton, which was instantiated based on `#availability` APIs; in other contexts, this may be a method.
6. Protect the visibility of your services or factories with proper accessors (private, internal, and so on), in order to prevent accidental instantiation. For example, we don't want the `iOSPushNotificationService` constructor to be used or available outside `iOSServiceFactory`.
7. Replace all occurrences of creating those objects through their (now-unavailable) constructor by creating them through your new abstract factory.

Now that you know everything about the factory method pattern, we can move on to the builder pattern.

The builder pattern

The builder pattern lets you abstract away the construction of objects or values that require a large number of parameters by using an intermediate representation—the builder. While very popular in Java, for example, I haven't seen it in action in recent pure Swift code bases, most likely as it is cumbersome to implement by hand.

We'll see in this section how to put the builder pattern into action, which problems it solves, and how you can leverage metaprogramming in order to deploy it efficiently through your code base.

Model building

In Swift, we have the nice benefit of having structs automatically generate their constructor. This saves a lot of boilerplate code when creating new instances of structs.

Let's consider this `Article` struct. You could use this to represent an article for a blog, for example:

```
struct Article {
    let id: String
    let title: String
    let contents: String
    let author: String
    let date: Date
    var views: Int
}
```

Creating new `Article` instances is quite labor-intensive, as you need to gather all the parameters and use them at once in the same code place. However, using the builder pattern, you could pass the builder around your code and, when the whole content is ready, create the article structure.

In editors such as IntelliJ for Java, you could automatically generate the builder for this struct. In Swift, Xcode doesn't provide such capacities, but a tool such as Sourcery or SourceKit could help you generate the builder:

1. We can place the builder in an extension, so as not to pollute the original struct with the builder code, as follows:

   ```
   extension Article {
   ```

2. Create a nested `Builder` class. We do not use a struct here, so we can do the chaining:

```
class Builder {
```

3. Next we can declare all the temporary properties, all optional, and with default values for some that we may want default values for, as follows:

```
private var id: String = randomIdGenerator()
private var title: String?
private var contents: String?
private var author: String?
private var date: Date = Date()
private var views: Int = 0
```

4. After this, we can declare all the setter methods. Note that each setter will let you chain the calls for easily setting multiple values:

```
func set(id: String) -> Builder {
    self.id = id
    return self
}
func set(title: String) -> Builder {
    self.title = title
    return self
}

func set(contents: String) -> Builder {
    self.contents = contents
    return self
}

func set(author: String) -> Builder {
    self.author = author
    return self
}

func set(date: Date) -> Builder {
    self.date = date
    return self
}

func set(views: Int) -> Builder {
    self.views = views
    return self
}
```

5. Finally, we create the most important method, the `build()` method, which returns the new instance of the original type:

```
func build() -> Article {
    return Article(
        id: id,
        title: title!,
        contents: contents!,
        author: author!,
        date: date,
        views: views)
    }
}
}
```

Now, you can use this builder across all your applications.

Imagine you have a series of forms that will let you fill in an article, one step after another. For example, you can imagine this form builder is available as a command line tool, each prompt executing after each other, gathering data from the user input:

```
let builder = Article.Builder()

builder.set(author: prompt("What's your name?"))
// ask the user for the title
builder.set(title: prompt("What's the title for your article"))

// later in the code, get the message
builder.set(contents: prompt("What do you want to say?"))

let article = builder.build()
show(article)
```

While the builder pattern is very powerful for passing data around, it is very cumbersome to write the code manually. However, great tools such as Sourcery can help us generate the code.

Going further: metaprogramming with Sourcery

The builder pattern is one of the best examples for getting started with metaprogramming. Sourcery can help us generate the code, and we'll quickly see how it is possible to add a simple builder stencil.

Sourcery is a command-line tool, quite popular in the Swift community, that can help you generate code. I recommend you take some time to read the documentation as well as digging into the tutorials.

First, you will need to install Sourcery on your machine. There are multiple methods, but the best way is to follow the instructions at `https://github.com/krzysztofzablocki/Sourcery#installation`.

My preferred method would be to install it with Homebrew.

Once you have Sourcery, you can familiarize yourself with it. I'll focus on the particular stencil we'll use to generate our builders. First, we need to add a conformance to our article class. Sourcery works by looking up the types exposed, and it's easier to find the type when you mark it with a particular protocol, in our case `Buildable`, as follows:

```
protocol Buildable {}

struct Article: Buildable {
/* ... */
}
```

Once this is done, you can create your `.stencil` file, which will hold the template for our builder classes.

Sourcery looks for files with a `.stencil` extension, and, by default, will create a Swift file with the same name, but a `.generated.swift` extension. For example, if your file is named `Buildable.stencil`, the generated source code will be `Buildable.generated.swift`.

Create your `Buildable.stencil` file as follows:

1. First, loop all the `Buildable` types. In our case, this only applies to `Article` now:

   ```
   {% for type in types.implementing.Buildable %}
   ```

2. Declare an extension for the current `Buildable` type, and a nested `Builder` class:

   ```
   extension {{ type.name }} {
       class Builder {
   ```

3. Declare all the variables as optionals, based on the parent's variable names and types:

```
// MARK: private members
{% for member in type.variables %}
private var {{ member.name }}: {{member.typeName}}?
{% endfor %}
```

4. Declare all the setters:

```
// MARK: - Setters
{% for member in type.variables %}
func set({{ member.name }}: {{member.typeName}}) -> Builder {
    self.{{ member.name }} = {{ member.name }}
    return self
}
{% endfor %}
```

5. Add the build method that will return a new instance:

```
// MARK: Builder method
func build() -> {{type.name}} {
    return {{type.name}}(
        {% for member in type.variables %}
        {{ member.name }}: {{ member.name }}!{% if not
forloop.last %},{% else %}){% endif %}
        {% endfor %}
      }
    }
}
{% endfor %}
```

Et voilà—running Sourcery against our article type will generate a valid `Builder.generated.swift` that we can use in our code.

The generated code doesn't have the default values, but is generic enough to help you implement the builder pattern in a much quicker way than by hand. Once you have the stencil for builders, you can copy/paste the generated code in your programs. This is still much faster than writing it out by hand!

The builder pattern in a nutshell

In conclusion, the builder pattern can be very powerful for a very particular use case in Swift. You should use it when you have an object construction that can span over time, and where it's cleaner to pass your builder around instead of aggregating all partial values.

It makes a lot of sense in Swift to leverage this pattern, instead of polluting your structs or classes with optionals.

To find out whether the builder is the right solution for you, follow these steps:

1. Identify whether there are partial objects created in your app, or large structs.
2. Implement your builder object as a nested class, or (better) use Sourcery and generate the code automatically.
3. Replace the occurrences of your partial object with the builder in your code, and pass the builder around in your code.

The prototype pattern

The prototype pattern defines a `copy()` or `clone()` method on all classes that follow the prototype pattern. Instead of creating new instances of those objects with the constructor, new instances are obtained by calling the `copy()` method. The cloned object will be an exact copy of the original object.

Often, the prototype pattern will be implemented with a shared registry in the form of a factory method that would return the original source object to be cloned. In Swift, this pattern is usually implemented with the help of the `NSCopying` protocol.

Leveraging the prototype pattern

If you're using value types, you will not find yourself needing to implement the prototype pattern, as value types implement copy-on-write.

Let's use our `Article` object from the previous example again, but this time as a class, so we don't benefit from the copy-on-write given by the value types:

```swift
class Article {
    private(set) var id: String
    let title: String
    let message: String
    let author: String
```

```
        let date: Date
        var views: Int

        init(id: String,
             title: String,
             message: String,
             author: String,
             date: Date,
             views: Int) {
            self.id = id
            self.title = title
            self.message = message
            self.author = author
            self.date = date
            self.views = views
        }
    }
```

Now we have `Article` following reference-type semantics, and we needed to add a constructor. Once again, Sourcery can be very helpful for generating this code instead of writing it by hand.

Let's have a look at the copy feature for this object:

```
extension Article: NSCopying {
    func copy(with zone: NSZone? = nil) -> Any {
        return Article(id: id,
                       title: title,
                       message: message,
                       author: author,
                       date: date,
                       views: views)
    }
}
```

Our article doesn't have any mutable fields other than the `views` count. So, if we want this article to be editable, we should probably implement a mutable copy of it:

```
extension Article: NSMutableCopying {
    func mutableCopy(with zone: NSZone? = nil) -> Any {
        return MutableArticle(id: id,
                              title: title,
                              message: message,
                              author: author,
                              date: date,
                              views: views)
    }
}
```

The `MutableArticle` class is pretty much the `Article` class with all members marked as mutable using `var`.

Now, when needing to edit an article, it is possible to use `mutableCopy()` to acquire a copy on which the properties can be edited. `MutableArticle` should also implement `NSCopying` so it is possible to return a copy of the object that will be the `Article` itself:

```
func editContents(article: Article, contents: String) -> Article {
    let mutableArticle: MutableArticle = article.mutableCopy()
    mutableArticle.contents = contents
    return mutableArticle.copy()
}
```

As we have seen, the amount of boilerplate can be high when implementing this pattern as well. Let's have a look how Sourcery can help.

Going further – NSCopying with Sourcery

It is possible to use Sourcery to generate the `NSCopying` and `NSMutableCopying` implementations for simple cases, or even more advanced cases.

In this section, we'll cover different stencils for Sourcery that may help when implementing `NSCopying` and `NSMutableCopying` protocols in the prototype pattern.

Implementing NSCopying automatically

Let's create an `AutoCopy.stencil` protocol, so that `Article` copy implementation can be generated using Sourcery:

```
{% for type in types.implementing.AutoCopy %}
extension {{ type.name }}: NSCopying {
    func copy(with zone: NSZone? = nil) -> Any {
        return {{type.name}}(
        {% map type.variables into vars using var %}
            {{ var.name }}: {{ var.name }}{% endmap %}
        {{ vars|join:"," }})
    }
}
{% endfor %}
```

It will generate the following `AutoCopy.generated.swift`:

```
extension Article: NSCopying {
    func copy(with zone: NSZone? = nil) -> Any {
```

```
        return Article(
            id: id,
            title: title,
            contents: contents,
            author: author,
            date: date,
            views: views)
    }
}
```

 As you may have noticed, this is a simple implementation where the array's contents are not copied through the NSCopying protocol. Recursively, all objects that are copied should be copied by calling the .copy() method, if available.

Implementing mutable objects

Sourcery can also help generate a fully mutable class for your object using AutoMutable.stencil, as follows:

```
{% for type in types.implementing.AutoMutable %}
class Mutable{{ type.name }} {
    {% for member in type.variables %}
    var {{ member.name }}: {{member.typeName}}
    {% endfor %}

    init(
        {% map type.variables into vars using var %}
        {{ var.name }}: {{ var.typeName }}{% endmap %}
        {{ vars|join:"," }}) {
        {% for member in type.variables %}
        self.{{ member.name }} = {{member.name}}
        {% endfor %}
    }
}
{% endfor %}
```

 This stencil will not replicate all instances and class methods—it will only generate a Mutable copy of a plain object.

Implementing NSMutableCopying automatically

With our ability to generate both NSCopying conformance and the Mutable counterpart of objects, it is possible to generate an NSMutableCopying counterpart automatically. NSMutableCopying is a convenience method that returns an instance of an object known to have mutable members.

Create your stencil as follows:

```
{% for type in types.implementing.AutoMutableCopy %}
extension {{ type.name }}: NSMutableCopying {
    func mutableCopy(with zone: NSZone? = nil) -> Any {
        return Mutable{{type.name}}(
        {% map type.variables into vars using var %}
            {{ var.name }}: {{ var.name }}{% endmap %}
        {{ vars|join:"," }})
    }
}
{% endfor %}
```

This stencil is very similar to the one used to generate the NSCopying protocol conformance.

The prototype pattern in a nutshell

When needing to implement the prototype pattern with classes, remember that the NSCopying protocol is part of Foundation.

1. Identify the need for large classes that are already initialized to be copied.
2. If possible, use structs and value type semantics—this saves a lot of boilerplate code.
3. Using classes, implement NSCopying and NSMutableCopying if necessary.
4. Leverage code generation tools such as Sourcery to help reduce implementation time.
5. Where needed, replace the new instances of the objects with calls to copy() on the prototype object.

To sum up, the prototype pattern is widely used in Foundation through NSArray and NSDictionary. In Swift, you can always leverage value types to benefit transparently from copying your objects. Value types benefit from copy-on-write, which ultimately prevents the mutation of prototype objects.

Summary

In this chapter, we covered four of the most common creational design patterns. We described how to adapt them to the Swift language, and how to best leverage language features and capabilities to implement them effectively.

You should now be able to identify which patterns are used in a code base, and which ones to use to refactor your code efficiently.

Creational patterns often involve a lot of boilerplate, and we discussed why tools such as Sourcery are your greatest ally in implementing them.

As we've covered the creation of entities through creational patterns, it is now time to cover how to link those entities together. The structural patterns discussed in the next chapter will specifically address this topic.

6
Structural Patterns

Structural design patterns help represent and abstract relations between different entities. They facilitate abstraction of those entities and communication between them, to ensure greater maintainability and separation of concerns.

These patterns are found in many code bases, and are often recognized by their keywords. Adapters, proxies, and bridges may sound scary at first, but mastering them is critical for writing clean and maintainable code.

In this chapter, we'll explore the most popular ones:

- The adapter pattern
- Implementing decorators
- Facades and proxies
- Composite patterns
- The bridge pattern
- The flyweight pattern

The adapter pattern

The adapter design pattern is employed when a component in your system doesn't provide an appropriate interface, API, or surface to make it compatible with the rest of the system. Adapters can be thought of as real-world adapters, or dongles.

There are a number of ways to implement the adapter pattern in Swift by leveraging inheritance, aggregation, or extensions.

Using the adapter pattern

When building an app, a program, or a web server, it is good practice to configure logging or analytics so it is easy to inspect program behavior at runtime. When running on a debugger or deployed on a user's device, or on a server, requirements for logging or recording analytics may change. During development, for example, it is not recommended to send analytics to the production server.

The adapter pattern is a great way to abstract and connect different logging or analytics infrastructures or classes, depending on runtime. It is based on the idea that classes will wrap your specialized code, in order to provide a common interface. This is very useful when dealing with third-party libraries, on which the code isn't easily changeable.

For this example, we'll use two very popular tracking libraries as examples: **Mixpanel** and **Google Analytics for Firebase**. We'll demonstrate how it is possible to unify the analytics into a single interface, and how to use one or the other at runtime.

The basics

First, you'll need to define a common protocol or interface that all your objects share. This will ensure all of our adapters share the same interface.

In this particular scenario, we simply want to track events with additional and optional custom properties. It can be defined as follows:

```
public protocol Tracking {
    func record(event: String)
    func record(event: String, properties: [String: String]?)
}
```

Thanks to protocol extensions, it is also possible to define the default implementation of tracking with empty properties:

```
extension Tracking {
    func record(event: String) {
        record(event: event, properties: nil)
    }
}
```

Now that the base tracking protocol is defined, it is possible to expose the shared tracker:

```
public class Tracker: Tracking {
```

Set up a singleton that can be accessed across the program, as follows:

```
public static let shared = Tracker()
```

Keep a reference to the tracking adapter:

```
private var trackingAdapter: Tracking!
```

Next, declare a set method, to register the tracking adapter:

```
public func set(trackingAdapter: Tracking) {
    self.trackingAdapter = trackingAdapter
}
```

Declare the conformance to tracking, so it is possible to forward the calls to the private adapter:

```
public func record(event: String, properties: [String : String]?) {
    trackingAdapter.record(event: event, properties: properties)
  }
}
```

This is optional, and not part of the adapter design pattern. It will help when referencing the specialized analytics tracker across the program. It also forwards calls to the `Tracking` class.

The classes to adapt

In this example, we'll adapt both Mixpanel and Google Analytics for Firebase. Let's have a look at how both look, and how to use them:

```
open class MixpanelInstance: CustomDebugStringConvertible, FlushDelegate,
AEDelegate {
    /* ... */
    open func track(event: String?, properties: Properties? = nil) {
        /* ... */
    }
}
```

It is possible to use Mixpanel to track an event with additional properties:

```
Mixpanel.mainInstance()
    .track(event: "Read Book",
           properties: ["name": "Design Patterns with Swift",
                        "format": "paperback"])
```

Google Analytics for Firebase, however, exposes the tracking method through a static method from Objective-C:

```
NS_SWIFT_NAME(Analytics)
@interface FIRAnalytics : NSObject

/* ... */

+ (void)logEventWithName:(NSString *)name
        parameters:(nullable NSDictionary<NSString *, id> *)parameters
        NS_SWIFT_NAME(logEvent(_:parameters:));

/* ... */

@end
```

To use this library, you will have to use the following code:

```
Analytics.logEvent("Read Book",
                parameters: ["name": "Design Patterns with Swift",
                             "format": "paperback"])
```

Using classes as adapters

The adapter pattern makes use of classes to wrap the functionality of immutable interfaces, such as the two libraries we are using:

```
public class MixPanelTrackingAdapter: Tracking {
```

Wrap the Mixpanel `mainInstance`, as follows:

```
    private let mixpanel = Mixpanel.mainInstance()
```

Next, expose the required methods from the `Tracking` protocol:

```
    public func record(event: String, properties: [String : String]?) {
        mixpanel.track(event: event, properties: properties)
    }
}
```

For Google Analytics for Firebase, it's even more trivial, as there is no singleton to wrap:

```
public class FirebaseTrackingAdapter: Tracking {
    public func record(event: String, properties: [String : String]?) {
        Analytics.logEvent(event, parameters: properties)
    }
}
```

With those two adapters, the implementation of the adapter pattern is complete.

Two classes, `MixpanelInstance` and `Analytics`, now share the same interface through their respective adapters. It is possible now to exchange them at runtime or at startup, which helps you with vendor independence.

Through the program, only the shared tracker should be used, abstracting away the complexity and implementation details for the analytics tracking.

For example, in your AppDelegate's `applicationDidFinishLaunching`, you can set up your tracking library as follows:

```
let tracker: Tracking

if USE_FIREBASE {
    tracker = FirebaseTrackingAdapter()
} else    {
    tracker = MixPanelTrackingAdapter()
}

Tracker.shared.set(trackingAdapter: tracker)
```

This pattern can be used for many use cases throughout your programs, and is particularly powerful for problems such as this one.

Leveraging extensions

In Swift, any class, struct, or protocol can be extended. In this case, we can improve implementation of the adapter pattern for `MixpanelInstance` by using an extension, as follows:

```
extension MixpanelInstance: Tracking {
    func record(event: String, properties: [String : String]?) {
        track(event: event, properties: properties)
    }
}
```

With this pattern, there is no need to create a wrapper instance and forward implementation calls in the wrapper. Depending on your code base, use case, and particularities, you may find it easier to use extensions over wrapping as a method:

```
let tracker: Tracking

if USE_FIREBASE {
    tracker = FirebaseTrackingAdapter()
```

```
} else {
    tracker = Mixpanel.mainInstance()
}

Tracker.shared.set(trackingAdapter: tracker)
```

In this particular use case, it is to be noted that leveraging extensions does not work for the static implementation of the Firebase `Analytics` class. It is a limitation to consider when deciding how to implement the adapter pattern.

The adapter pattern in a nutshell

The adapter pattern is perfectly suited for abstraction of third-party libraries, wrapping legacy code to fit newer interfaces or hiding implementation details or complexity away.

1. Identify the class or classes that need to be adapted.
2. Identify and implement a protocol that represent the common tasks for the objects to accomplish.
3. Implement either wrapper classes or extensions to the existing classes.
4. Remove direct access to the nonadapted classes.

Implementation of the adapter pattern is completely up to you and your requirements. It is good practice to abstract away moving pieces in your programs to avoid vendor lock-in, without needing a full refactor of your code bases.

The decorator pattern

The decorator pattern allows us to add behaviors to objects without changing their structure or inheritance chain. Instead of subclassing, decorators enhance an object's behavior by adding functionalities to it.

Unlike with inheritance, where the chain is directional, the decorator pattern allows for composing behaviors without regard to a particular execution order.

In this section, we'll explain the implementation details of the decorator pattern through the example of assembling a burger to your taste.

Using a decorator

The decorator pattern is extremely powerful when assembling a series of objects together. We'll use a burger as an example, from the point of view of the cashier who processes and bills it.

First, let's define a basic protocol, which will encapsulate the price and the different ingredients in the current burger. In the decorator pattern, this protocol will represent the object that will be decorated over and over:

```
public protocol Burger {
    var price: Double { get }
    var ingredients: [String] { get }
}
```

Then we define a decorator: `BurgerDecorator`. In other languages, it may be implemented as an abstract class.

The decorator is implemented with the following protocol. It also conforms to the type that defines the base object being decorated, in the same way as a proxy:

```
public protocol BurgerDecorator: Burger {
    var burger: Burger { get }
}
```

Here is the corresponding extension, which forwards the calls to the burger object if nothing is implemented in `BurgerDecorator`:

```
extension BurgerDecorator {
    public var price: Double {
        return burger.price
    }
    public var ingredients: [String] {
        return burger.ingredients
    }
}
```

Now, everything is ready for the final implementation. A burger is composed of many things: a bun, patties, cheese, salad, sauces, and more. Customers may be eligible for discounts. Finally, we'll need to apply tax to the bill.

`BaseBurger` will be the basic element—the bun, on which we'll build the rest of our burger:

```
public struct BaseBurger: Burger {
    public var price = 1.0
```

```
        public var ingredients = ["buns"]
    }
```

Now, here is the first decorator, `WithCheese`. Note that adding cheese increases the price by `0.5`:

```
public struct WithCheese: BurgerDecorator {
    public let burger: Burger
    public var price: Double { return burger.price + 0.5 }

    public var ingredients: [String] {
        return burger.ingredients + ["cheese"]
    }
}
```

Next, we can add the Incredible Burger Patty, which will give a great taste (not to mention increase the price by `2.0`):

```
public struct WithIncredibleBurgerPatty: BurgerDecorator {
    public let burger: Burger
    public var price: Double { return burger.price + 2.0 }

    public var ingredients: [String] {
        return burger.ingredients + ["incredible patty"]
    }
}
```

Now, we have a `burger` with the `bun`, `cheese`, and a `patty`. We now need to add the toppings, which are free. Let's do that through an `enum`, as follows:

```
enum Topping: String {
    case ketchup
    case mayonnaise
    case salad
    case tomato
}

struct WithTopping: BurgerDecorator {
    let burger: Burger
    let topping: Topping
    var ingredients: [String] {
        return burger.ingredients + [topping.rawValue]
    }
}
```

We're done with the implementation now. I'll leave it for you as an exercise to implement decorators for both the taxes and the discounts.

The cashier can now implement any kind of burger requested, using the following:

```
var burger: Burger = BaseBurger() // it's just a simple burger
burger = WithTopping(burger: burger, topping: .ketchup) // put the mayo
first
burger = WithCheese(burger: burger) // Add some cheese
burger = WithIncredibleBurgerPatty(burger: burger) // Add the patty
burger = WithTopping(burger: burger, topping: .salad)

assert(burger.ingredients == ["buns", "ketchup", "cheese", "incredible
patty", "salad"])
assert(burger.price == 3.5)
```

We successfully leveraged the decorator pattern in order to build an object over time. With this pattern, it is possible to add new decorators in the future, without changing the original implementation, and therefore propose more options to the consumers of your program very easily.

Let's now see how it is possible to go further with this design pattern.

Going further with decorator

As you may have noticed, most of the decorator interfaces are the same and can be abstracted as (Burger) -> Burger functions. All the constructors take Burger as the first parameter and return a new instance of their class, which is BurgerDecorator, which in turn is a Burger.

It is possible to add a method to the toppings enum so that it can decorate a Burger:

```
extension Topping {
    func decorate(burger: Burger) -> WithTopping {
        return WithTopping(burger: burger, topping: self)
    }
}

// Topping.ketchup.decorate(burger: burger)
```

It would technically be possible to gather all the functions that decorate a burger, and finally apply them to a burger:

```
var decorators = [(Burger) -> Burger]
decorators.append(Topping.ketchup.decorate)
decorators.append(WithCheese.init)
decorators.append(WithIncredibleBurgerPatty.init)
decorators.append(Topping.salad.decorate)
```

In order to build the burger, it is now possible to use a reducer on the array of decorators:

```
let reducedBurger = decorators.reduce(into: BaseBurger()) { burger,
decorate in
    burger = decorate(burger)
}
assert(burger.ingredients == reducedBurger.ingredients)
assert(burger.price == reducedBurger.price)
```

As we appended the decorators in the same order, the ingredients list is the same for both burgers, as is the price.

While this technique works well with the current code, it is separate to the decorator pattern. It is an extension that is possible because all the decorators we defined follow the same interface. Depending on your use case, you may want either to decorate the original objects as you go, or accumulate the function references in an array and resolve the final object by applying a reducer.

Decoration in a nutshell

The decorator pattern is a powerful design pattern that can be leveraged when building objects at runtime, where the final object has features that are defined over time, and where only the final outcome matters:

1. Identify in your program an object that can or should be abstracted with this pattern
2. Define the base protocol for your object (in our case, that was `Burger`)
3. Define the decorator interface, in our case the `BurgerDecorator`, and ensure it conforms to the decorator's interface (`Burger`)
4. Leverage protocol extensions to provide the default values for the decorator
5. Provide at least one constructor or method to decorate the base object (`.init(Burger)` or `.decorate(Burger)`)
6. Build your decorating features out of the decorator's interface
7. Use your decorator objects to build (over time and in multiple steps) your decorated objects out of base implementations

The facade pattern and proxy pattern

Facades and proxies are design patterns that are similar. They both help to reduce the apparent complexity of a subsystem, by exposing a simpler interface.

The main goal of the facade pattern is to simplify the interface of a complete subsystem, while the proxy helps you enhance the capabilities of a particular interface. The client will only interact with the simple, exposed interface.

This yields multiple benefits, from separation of concerns to ease of use for clients. SDKs and third-party libraries often use facades and proxies in order to leverage their powerful capabilities, abstracting away the internal complexity.

In this section, we will show how to implement facades and proxies effectively, and demonstrate their capabilities and limits.

The facade pattern

The facade pattern is particularly suited if you wish to hide multiple tightly coupled subcomponents behind a single object or method. This object will expose a separate set of methods and properties, independent from the ones exposed by objects managed by the facade object.

Building a network cache with the facade pattern

Let's take the example of a resource-caching library. When building our applications or servers, we often need to leverage caching to avoid repeatedly making the same network calls, impacting on the performance of our programs. Server-side, it's particularly important to reduce the number of database or external calls, making our servers faster by saving network round-trips.

Let's call this system `CachedNetworking`, and we'll implement it with the facade pattern.

Such a system may be composed of:

- `URLSession`: A system that fetches a resource based on its `URLRequest`
- `Cache`: The subsystem responsible for storing the results of the resource fetcher

- `CacheCleaner`: The subsystem responsible for periodically running over the cache and actively removing stale data

A `cache` will have a simple interface that abstracts away the storage of the data. With simple setters, removers, and getters, this cache can be used in multiple scenarios, and could potentially be refactored in a generic way:

```
class Cache {
    func set(response: URLResponse, data: Data, for request: URLRequest) {
        // TODO: Implement me
    }

    func get(for request: URLRequest) -> (URLResponse, Data)? {
        // TODO: Implement me
    }
    func remove(for request: URLRequest) {
        // TODO: Implement me
    }

    func allData() -> [URLRequest: (URLResponse, Data)] {
        return [:]
    }
}
```

`CacheCleaner` is a simple object that periodically visits the cache and removes stale data:

```
class CacheCleaner {
    let cache: Cache
    var isRunning: Bool {
        return timer != nil
    }

    private var timer: Timer?
    init(cache: Cache) {
        self.cache = cache
    }

    func startIfNeeded() {
        if isRunning { return }
        timer = Timer.scheduledTimer(withTimeInterval: 10.0, repeats:
        true) { [unowned self] (timer) in
            let cacheData = self.cache.allData()
            // TODO: inspect cache data, and remove cached elemtns
            //that are too old
        }
    }
```

```
    func stop() {
        timer?.invalidate()
        timer = nil
    }
}
```

Now that we have the base objects that have the complex logic, let's implement our facade on a CachedNetworking class. The facade should have a very simple interface, in order to yield the most benefit:

```
class CachedNetworking {
    let session: URLSession
    private let cache = Cache()
    private lazy var cleaner = CacheCleaner(cache: cache)
```

In our case, it's reasonable to let the user of the facade configure the URLSession to be used, or at least the configuration for the URLSession:

```
    init(configuration: URLSessionConfiguration) {
        session = URLSession(configuration: configuration)
    }

    init(session: URLSession) {
        self.session = session
    }

    init() {
        self.session = URLSession.shared
    }
```

With the initializers implemented, we can now get to the run(...) method. Note that we didn't keep the same naming and signature as the URLSession, as the dataTask will be run automatically. There's is no similar method in URLSession.

Other implementations would perhaps use a subclass of URLSession, and the implementations may be different in this case:

```
    func run(with request: URLRequest, completionHandler: @escaping (Data?,
URLResponse?, Error?, Bool) -> Void) {
```

First, when a request comes in, let's poke the cache and check if there is a valid (response, data) pair, and, if there is, call back immediately with the last argument set to true to indicate it came from the cache:

```
        if let (response, data) = cache.get(for: request) {
            completionHandler(data, response, nil, true)
```

```
                    return
        }
```

Otherwise, perform the original request:

```
cleaner.startIfNeeded()
session.dataTask(with: request) { [weak self] (data, response, error) in
        if let data = data,
            let response = response {
```

If we're successful, we have data and a response to cache, so let's save it:

```
self?.cache.set(response: response, data: data, for: request)
        }
```

Finally, call `completionHandler` to notify the caller that the response is available to consume:

```
completionHandler(data, response, error, false)
        }.resume()
    }
```

We finish with a `deinit` call to stop the cleaner and ensure there is nothing leaking:

```
deinit {
    cleaner.stop()
    }
}
```

Now you can use `URLSessionFacade`, and benefit from the caching capabilities. The facade pattern abstracted away three complex components in a simple interface:

- `URLSession`
- `Cache`
- `CacheCleaner`

Those three components are testable on their own, and can evolve independently, reducing the overall maintenance cost.

Let's now have a look at how we could leverage the proxy pattern in order to add logging capabilities to the `CachedNetworking` class.

Using the proxy pattern to implement request/response logging

The proxy pattern is very useful when you need to forward all calls from one object to another. In our case, we could have implemented `CachedNetworking` as a proxy on `URLSession`, effectively giving additional caching capabilities to `URLSession`.

When debugging your applications, it may be useful to log information about networking calls, such as duration, whether they come from the cache, and so on.

The proxy pattern and the decorator pattern are actually quite similar at first glance. They both attempt to solve similar problems in a similar way. However, the proxy pattern is applied at compile time, while the decorator pattern is only applied at runtime, as discussed earlier.

The proxy should have the exact same signature as the object being proxied. We can either subclass or use a common interface in order to achieve this:

```
class LoggingCachedNetworking: CachedNetworking {
    private func log(request: URLRequest) {
        // TODO: implement proper logging
    }
    private func log(response: URLResponse?,
                     data: Data?,
                     error: Error?,
                     fromCache: Bool,
                     forRequest: URLRequest) {
        // TODO: implement proper logging
    }

    override func run(with request: URLRequest, completionHandler:
@escaping (Data?, URLResponse?, Error?, Bool) -> Void) {
        self.log(request: request)
        super.run(with: request) { (data, response, error, fromCache) in
            self.log(response: response,
                     data: data,
                     error: error,
                     fromCache: fromCache,
                     forRequest: request)
            completionHandler(data, response, error, fromCache)
        }
    }
}
```

And now, for example, at application initialization, we may want to leverage compilation directives like this:

```
#if DEBUG
let networking = LoggingCachedNetworking()
#else
let networking = CachedNetworking()
#endif
```

Depending on whether your program is built with the DEBUG flag set, this will use (or not) the proxied CachedNetworking.

Coupled with techniques such as dependency injection, the proxy pattern let you design your programs by enhancing an existing object's features without changing code that is known to be working. This unobtrusive pattern is very interesting if you cannot or do not want to change the implementation of the underlying features.

The composite pattern

The composite pattern helps in writing proper abstractions when dealing with objects that appear in hierarchies; being containers and containees. For example, on a filesystem, a directory can contain files and other directories. In this case, the composite pattern would be a suitable abstraction. Each element of the filesystem can be either a container for other elements (a directory), or a terminal node (file).

In this section, we will see how to set up and implement the composite pattern to represent a series of unit tests organized in test suites.

Using the composite pattern to represent tests and suites

When writing unit tests, it's recommended to group together tests that are closely related to one other. We call a series of tests a *suite*, which can contain subsuites. Whole suites, subsuites, and individual tests can be run. These features makes the composite pattern very suitable for organizing the tests in suites, the suite itself being the composite.

First, we start with the base protocol, `Testable`. The only method it needs is the `run` method, to execute the contents of the test, and we'll use the errors thrown to indicate failure:

```
protocol Testable {
    func run() throws
}
```

The following is the `UnitTest` class, which provides a simple wrapper around a name and a block that can be executed:

```
class UnitTest: Testable {
    let name: String
    private let block: TestImplementation
    init(name: String, block: @escaping TestImplementation) {
        self.name = name
        self.block = block
    }

    func run() throws {
        try self.block()
        print("UnitTest \(name) ran successfully")
    }
}
```

Now, we can implement the composite, `TestSuite`. In the composite pattern, the composite wraps many components, and behaves as a single one. `TestSuite` wraps many `Testable` objects, and also behaves like a single `Testable` object through the implementation of the `Testable` protocol:

```
class TestSuite: Testable {

    let name: String
    private(set) var testables: [Testable]

    init(name: String, _ testables: [Testable] = []) {
        self.name = name
        self.testables = testables
    }

    func add(_ testable: Testable) {
        testables.append(testable)
    }

    func run() throws {
        print("Suite \(name) started")
        let errors = testables.compactMap { (testable) -> Error? in
```

```
            do {
                try testable.run()
            } catch let e {
                return e
            }
            return nil
        }
        if errors.count > 0 {
            throw Errors(errors: errors)
        }
        print("Suite \(name) ran successfully")
    }
    struct Errors: Error {
        let errors: [Error]
    }
}
```

The code here should be pretty straightforward. TestSuite, the **composite**, allows you to add Testable objects onto it. When calling the run method on the TestSuite, this will execute all Testable objects, and if the Testable itself is a TestSuite, the composite will in turn recursively run more tests.

It's time to put this testing framework to good use:

```
let testSuite = TestSuite(name: "Top Level Suite")
testSuite.add(UnitTest(name: "First Test") {})
testSuite.add(UnitTest(name: "Second Test") {})
testSuite.add(
    TestSuite(name: "ChildSuite", [
        UnitTest(name: "Child 1") {},
        UnitTest(name: "Child 2") {}
    ])
)

try? testSuite.run()
```

This code will produce the following output:

```
Suite Top Level Suite started
UnitTest First Test ran successfully
UnitTest Second Test ran successfully
Suite ChildSuite started
UnitTest Child 1 ran successfully
UnitTest Child 2 ran successfully
Suite ChildSuite ran successfully
Suite Top Level Suite ran successfully
```

The composite pattern is particularly suitable for representing systems where complex components behave the same as simple ones, such as filesystems, testing hierarchies, and other tree-like problems.

The bridge pattern

When writing testable code, it is often necessary to decouple implementation from abstractions. For example, when writing a network-based or database-driven application, you may not have access to a database during testing, and you'll probably want to test without the possibility of networking failure.

Using the bridge pattern can help you achieve your goals in terms of architecture and testability. By decoupling interfaces from implementations, the bridge pattern lets you swap at runtime which object performs the work, while retaining the same abstractions.

Anatomy of the bridge pattern

The bridge pattern is oriented around two interfaces:

- Abstraction
- Implementor

Instead of implementing the Abstraction interface directly, the bridge pattern encourages the introduction of the Implementor interface, which in turn will be the top-level interface for feature implementation.

Let's consider the following code. It shows a class that performs some work:

```
class Abstraction {
    func start()
    func stop()
}
```

If we want to be able to swap the implementation of start() or stop() with other implementations, it's quite complicated. We could leverage subclassing, but it may be inconvenient, as it forces us to refactor our entire program.

The bridge pattern can help us with this problem. First, let's extract the interface for Abstraction:

```
protocol AbstractionType {
    init(implementor: ImplementorType)
```

```
        func start()
        func stop()
    }

    extension AbstractionType {
        func restart() {
            stop()
            start()
        }
    }
```

It's important to note that each `AbstractionType` needs to be initialized with an `Implementor`, which will actually perform the work:

```
    protocol ImplementorType {
        func start()
        func stop()
    }
```

It is now possible to implement a concrete `Abstraction`:

```
    class Abstraction: AbstractionType {
        private let implementor: ImplementorType

        required init(implementor: ImplementorType) {
            self.implementor = implementor
        }
        func start() {
            print("Starting")
            implementor.start()
        }

        func stop() {
            print("Stopping")
            implementor.stop()
        }
    }
```

We also need to add more than one `Implementor`:

```
    class Implementor1: ImplementorType {
        func start() {
            print("Implementor1.start()")
        }

        func stop() {
            print("Implementor1.stop()")
        }
```

```
    }

class Implementor2: ImplementorType {
    func start() {
        print("Implementor2.start()")
    }
    func stop() {
        print("Implementor2.stop()")
    }
}
```

We can now benefit from those Abstraction objects that provide different implementations:

```
var abstraction = Abstraction(implementor: Implementor1())
abstraction.restart()

abstraction = Abstraction(implementor: Implementor2())
abstraction.restart()
```

The previous code will output the following:

```
Implementor1.stop()
Implementor1.start()
Implementor2.stop()
Implementor2.start()
```

With this pattern, we have successfully swapped at runtime the implementation of Abstraction without replacing its code.

Now, let's imagine we want to test that the Abstraction object is performing the restart properly; that is, calling stop() and then start() in order.

Let's write TestImplementor, feed it to the Abstraction object, and see how it goes:

```
class TestImplementor: ImplementorType {
    var stopCalled = false
    var startCalled = false
    var inProperOrder = false
    func start() {
        inProperOrder = stopCalled == true && startCalled == false
        startCalled = true
        print("TestImplementor.start() \(startCalled) \(stopCalled)
\(inProperOrder)")
    }
    func stop() {
        inProperOrder = startCalled == false && stopCalled == false
        stopCalled = true
```

```
        print("TestImplementor.stop() \(startCalled) \(stopCalled)
    \(inProperOrder)")
    }
}
```

With `TestImplementor`, we can ensure that the logic of our `Abstraction` object stays sound over time—at least, that the right methods are called in the right order—without worrying about the side-effects of the implementation:

```
let testImplementor = TestImplementor()
abstraction = Abstraction(implementor: testImplementor)
abstraction.restart()

// Check the status of the implementor
assert(testImplementor.inProperOrder)
assert(testImplementor.startCalled)
assert(testImplementor.stopCalled)
```

The following will also have been logged:

```
TestImplementor.stop() false true true
TestImplementor.start() true true true
```

These logs are expected, and the `assert()` should all pass, as `Abstraction` is properly implemented.

We've now successfully leveraged the bridge pattern to decouple abstractions and implementation details, as well as providing three different implementations for the same abstraction, one of which was testing.

Using the bridge pattern

The bridge pattern is a powerful pattern that helps you isolate the objects that actually perform some work from their abstractions. This may help you achieve better testability of the abstractions by letting your tests provide a different implementation, so you can focus on testing the abstractions separately from their implementations.

In order to implement the bridge pattern successfully, you'll need to:

1. Identify which abstractions need to be isolated from their implementations
2. Refactor the `Abstraction` class in order to let the implementation be passed at runtime
3. Ideally, add tests to ensure `Abstraction` is behaving as it should, without interference from the implementation

The flyweight pattern

To conclude this chapter on structural design patterns, we'll dive into the flyweight pattern. You may want to use the flyweight pattern when:

- You create many instances of the same object
- You can afford to use memory to cache instances
- You do not mutate those instances, and can afford to share them across your program

Let's say you want to build an application to help with groceries and recipes. As input, we may have lists of ingredients and their amounts, based on their names, as strings. We want to be able to make lists, organize them, and more.

While we technically could store the strings as our base items, we'll use the flyweight pattern to encapsulate those item names. This will help us be more accurate in the rest of our program. Instead of using strings around, we'll use proper instances.

A shopping list using the flyweight pattern

First, we'll need to identify the object that will be reused over and over in our flyweight pattern—Ingredient:

```
struct Ingredient: CustomDebugStringConvertible {
    let name: String
    var debugDescription: String {
        return name
    }
}
```

The Ingredient object is a simple wrapper around our name, but it could be more complex as our program grows.

Next, we need an object that will manage the creation of those Ingredient objects. As we're leveraging the flyweight pattern, we want to reduce the number of instances of the Ingredient object:

```
struct IngredientManager {
```

The `knownIngredients` dictionary will act as our object cache:

```
private var knownIngredients = [String: Ingredient]()
mutating func get(withName name: String) -> Ingredient {
    // Check if we have already an instance
    guard
        let ingredient = knownIngredients[name] else {
        // Register an instance
        knownIngredients[name] = Ingredient(name: name)
        // Attempt to get again
        return get(withName: name)
    }
    return ingredient
}
var count: Int {
    return knownIngredients.count
}
}
```

The `Ingredients` manager will act as our central store; it will contain all the instances of `Ingredients` we'll possibly ever need, and we'll be able to use it in our `ShoppingList`, as follows:

```
struct ShoppingList: CustomDebugStringConvertible {
    private var list = [(Ingredient, Int)]()
    private var manager = IngredientManager()
    mutating func add(item: String, amount: Int = 1) {
        let ingredient = manager.get(withName: item)
        list.append((ingredient, amount))
    }
    var debugDescription: String {
        return "\(manager.count) Items:\n\n"
            + list.map { (ingredient, value) in
                return "\(ingredient) (x\(value))"
            }.joined(separator: "\n")
    }
}
```

Now, we'll be able to use this shopping list. Let's say your program takes a list of strings as input:

```
let items = ["kale", "carrots", "salad", "carrots", "cucumber", "celery",
"pepper", "bell peppers", "carrots", "salad"]
items.count // 10
```

The user added 10 items, so without the flyweight pattern we'd create 10 different instances of `Ingredients`. Let's add them all to the shopping list, and print the results:

```
var shopping = ShoppingList()
items.forEach {
    shopping.add(item: $0)
}
print(list)
```

Here is the output:

```
7 Ingredients:

kale x 1
carrots x 1
salad x 1
carrots x 1
cucumber x 1
celery x 1
pepper x 1
bell peppers x 1
carrots x 1
salad x 1
```

As there are duplicate ingredients in the list, we successfully reused the same instances of the `Ingredient` objects, reducing the memory footprint by 30%.

In larger applications, the flyweight pattern can yield important improvements; even more so when the program creates a lot of temporary objects for a smaller set of values.

Summary

In this chapter, we covered seven of the most popular structural patterns. These help you design abstractions, objects, and their relationships in a maintainable and efficient way.

Integrating foreign components with **adapters**, as well as using **decorators** to enhance object features and behaviors without cluttering their interfaces, will help when cleaning up existing code bases. When building APIs and public-facing systems, **facades** and **proxy** patterns can help couple complex subsystems and hide their complexity. You can easily introduce external implementations using the **bridge** pattern.

That concludes this chapter on building sound program structures. Next, we'll look at behavioral patterns—or, as it may be put, the art of communicating between different components.

7
Behavioral Patterns

Behavioral patterns are those patterns that identify common communication strategies between different entities. By realizing these patterns, you'll increase flexibility when communicating between different parts of your programs.

We'll start by looking at the state pattern, which helps decouple the behavior of a program from its internal state. We'll follow up with the observer pattern, which encompasses the implementation of event-based data flows.

Next, we'll discuss the memento pattern, a very useful pattern that manages to elegantly abstract the ability to roll back between states. Finally, we'll cover the visitor and strategy patterns, which both help to abstract complexity when implementing algorithms that evolve at runtime.

In this chapter, we will cover the following topics:

- The state pattern
- The observer pattern
- The memento pattern
- The visitor pattern
- The strategy pattern

The state pattern

The state design pattern helps you decouple the behavior of an object, often called the *context*, from its internal state. For each state, the state object will implement the specific behaviors, keeping the context clean and concise.

This design pattern can help transform large switch statements into smaller objects that can perform the underlying specific task.

Let's get started with a simple example of a state machine—a card reader that you can find at a metro station, bus stop, or other public transportation system. From a high-level perspective, these card readers are simple state machines. They follow a simple run loop—wait, detect, read, success or failure—and each state transition is linear. This makes them particularly suitable for demonstrating this pattern.

The card reader

When we think about a finite amount of states, we usually consider using an enum. While this is not wrong, it forces you to pack all the logic either in your context or your enum itself. Let's explore this with an example.

Using enums

First, let's see how this reader could look if we implement its state with an enum:

```
class CardReader {
```

Implement the state with the enum, with all the possible state values, as follows:

```
enum State {
    case unknown
    case waiting
    case reading
    case read(CardInfo)
    case failed(Error)
}
```

Use the `private var state` property so that no one can mutate the state from outside:

```
private var state: State = .unknown
```

The main routine is implemented as follows. For each loop, it will print the current state:

```
func start() {
    while true {
        print("\(state)")
        switch state {
        case .unknown:
            state = .waiting
        case .waiting:
```

When we're `waiting`, we wait for a card to be detected by the radio. When the card is detected, we change the state to `reading`:

```
if seenCard() {
    state = .reading
}
case .reading:
```

When `reading`, we'll wait for this to complete. If it succeeds, we will change the state to `read`, or otherwise indicate the failure as follows:

```
if readCard() {
    state = .read(CardInfo())
} else {
    state = .failed(ReadError())
}
case .read(_):
```

Now that the card is `read`, we can apply the logic. For example, that may involve using an external object to open doors, display a success message on a screen, decrement the number of journeys left on the card, or something more complex.

In any case, whether this logic is implemented in the `enum` or the context, you can clearly see that the state transitions are polluted by each state's logic. The same is true for the failure scenario, as follows:

```
            // Card is read
            // Now we can open the gate
            state = .waiting
        case .failed(_):
            // Display an error message on the screen
            // Prompt to restart after a few seconds
            state = .waiting
        }
        sleep(1)
    }
  }
}
```

We'll start the reader as follows:

```
let reader = CardReader()
reader.start()
```

This program should print, depending on the output of `readCard()` and `seenCard()`, something along the following lines:

```
unknown
waiting
reading
failed(ReadError())
waiting
reading
failed(ReadError())
waiting
reading
read(CardInfo(id: 415))
waiting
waiting
reading
failed(ReadError())
...
```

As we've seen, all the logic is packed into the context, making it very inefficient and hard to maintain. The state design pattern provides a solution for this problem. Let's refactor the code to improve maintainability.

Refactoring for maintainability

A few steps are needed in order to refactor `CardReader`:

1. Define a single protocol for all the states
2. Extract all states as structs or classes
3. Implement the logic and transition inside each state object, instead of the context
4. Refactor the context, in our case `CardReader`, to leverage those states

First, we need to define a single protocol. This protocol abstracts all the different states, and exposes at least one method that lets an external object perform the work in the said state. This method takes the context (`CardReader`) as a parameter, in order to perform the transitions.

Extracting a single protocol

Let's take a look at how to extract a single protocol:

```
protocol CardReaderState {
    func perform(context: CardReader)
}
```

Next, we need to implement all our states as structs or classes, preferring singletons if possible. Let's use structs for this example.

Implementing all states through structs, and moving the logic

Each state will be responsible for its own logic and transitions, so we can start moving the logic into each state:

```
struct UnknownState: CardReaderState {
    static let shared = UnknownState()
    func perform(context: CardReader) {
        // Perform local initialization, When everything is ready
        // Toggle the state to Waiting
        context.state = WaitingState.shared
    }
}
```

As you can see, this is cleaner, as our initialization states are encapsulated. In the example code following, the rest of the logic is even more encapsulated:

```
struct WaitingState: CardReaderState {
    static let shared = WaitingState()
    func perform(context: CardReader) {
        guard seenCard() else { return }
        // we have seen a card!
        context.state = ReadingState.shared
    }
}

struct ReadingState: CardReaderState {
    func perform(context: CardReader) {
        // Read the contents of the card over the radio
        // This is quite complext and can take a while
        if readCard() {
            // Card was read
            context.state = ReadState(card: CardInfo())
        } else {
            context.state = ErrorState(error: ReadError())
        }
    }
}

struct ReadState: CardReaderState {
    let card: CardInfo
    func perform(context: CardReader) {
        // Open the gates to the metro doors
        // And reset back to waiting
```

```
            context.state = WaitingState.shared
        }
    }

    struct ErrorState: CardReaderState {
        let error: Error
        func perform(context: CardReader) {
            // display an error, and go back to waiting
            context.state = WaitingState.shared
        }
    }
```

Refactoring the context object

The `CardReader` object can now be refactored into a much simpler object, which is only responsible for the run loop:

```
class CardReader {
    internal var state: CardReaderState = UnknownState()

    func start() {
        while true {
            print("\(state)")
            perform()
            sleep(1)
        }
    }

    func perform() {
        state.perform(context: self)
    }
}
```

Running `CardReader` is the same as previously.

Note that we also implemented the `perform()` method. As `CardReader` is the context, we can advance each step manually by calling `perform()`.

As you can see, our context object is much simpler. As each state has access to the context, it is also possible to extend capabilities directly within the context, if those capabilities need to be available for every state.

Another interesting feature to note is that with Swift, state objects and their conformance to `CardReaderState` can be decoupled through protocol extensions. You can imagine complex objects being given their state machine capabilities through extensions.

Using state machines

State machines are a powerful pattern that help you decouple states from their transitions and logic. In this section, we have demonstrated the usage of this pattern, replacing `enums` with structs to encompass state and its transitions.

In order to implement your state machine successfully, you will need to do the following:

1. Ensure your program logic can be abstracted as a series of states with clear transitions
2. Identify your context object, which will be passed around each state
3. Define a proper protocol that will be implemented on each state
4. Refactor the context object in order to leverage those state objects and the common protocol

The observer pattern

The observer pattern is used when many objects need to listen to changes in one or many other objects.

`NotificationCenter` is one of the oldest APIs in Foundation, available since macOS 10+ and iOS 2.0, and is used to implement the observer pattern quickly and safely. Using `NSObject`, it is also possible to use **Key-Value Observing (KVO)** to observe changes in objects.

In pure Swift, however, you will need to use a third-party object as the `NotificationCenter` in order to listen to change events. Swift also provides a simple observation mechanism that notifies you when local values are updated.

Event-based programming

Observation is a popular programming strategy that lets you derive the current state of your application from the events you're listening to. Instead of polling for new information, your program will listen to events or notifications in order to update its state.

This strategy is particularly suitable for decoupling event sources from their consumption part. However, always keep in mind that your program can suffer from significant performance hits if you're processing all events without throttling, debouncing, or similar.

Let's get started with `NotificationCenter`, provided by the Foundation framework.

Behavioral Patterns

Using NotificationCenter

`NotificationCenter` is an object that lets you register observers, so that those objects are notified when particular events (notifications) are emitted. When posting a notification to a notification center, only observers registered with that particular notification center will be notified.

For example, on the iOS platform, if you want to be notified when your application will go in the background, you can do it as follows:

```
self.resignObserver = NotificationCenter.default.addObserver(
    forName: NSApplication.willResignActiveNotification,
    object: nil,
    queue: nil) { (notification) in
    print("Application will resign active")
}
```

Don't forget to retain the observer, as you will need to remove it from the notification center once you're done listening for notifications:

```
NotificationCenter.default.removeObserver(self.resignObserver)
```

Now that we're somewhat familiar with the `NotificationCenter` API, let's dig deeper and implement a notification-based application that decouples the model layer from the UI layer through notifications.

First, let's define our custom centers:

```
extension NotificationCenter {
    static let ui = NotificationCenter()
    static let model = NotificationCenter()
}
```

As recommended by Apple documentation, we'll make extensive use of notifications, so let's instantiate custom notification centers to improve performance right away. In the code, we will be able to access those centers with `NotificationCenter.ui` and `NotificationCenter.model`.

The UI center will be responsible for sending view-related notifications, such as a button pressed, or text typed.

The model center will be responsible for sending all model updates. Whether the model is loaded from the database, or was updated after the network call, the model notification center will send notifications of those events.

We'll use two straightforward notification names—one for notifying model changes, and the other for notifying that the user wants to save the object:

```
let modelChangedNotification = Notification.Name(rawValue:
"ModelChangedNotification")
let saveTappedNotification = Notification.Name(rawValue:
"SaveTappedNotification")
```

We'll use three objects:

1. Model, **which contains a few properties as a** struct
2. ModelController, **responsible for loading, and saving the object**
3. ViewController, **responsible for interacting with the user**

```
struct Model {
    var title: String = ""
    var description: String = ""
}

class ModelController {
    private var uiObserver: NSObjectProtocol!
    init() {
        // Setup the observation
        uiObserver = NotificationCenter.ui.addObserver(
            forName: saveTappedNotification,
            object: nil,
            queue: nil) { [unowned self] (notification) in
                guard let model = notification.object as? Model else
{ return }
                self.save(model: model)
        }
    }

    func loadModel() {
        // Load the model from somewhere and emit it
        let model = Model()
        NotificationCenter.model.post(name:
modelChangedNotification, object: model)
    }

    func save(model: Model) {
        var model = model
        // Ensure the title length is never > 20 chars
        model.title = String(model.title.prefix(20))
        // Save the model...
        // Then emit back so we can update the UI
        NotificationCenter.model.post(name:
```

```
        modelChangedNotification, object: model)
            }
        deinit {
            // Do not forget to remove the observer
            NotificationCenter.ui.removeObserver(uiObserver)
        }
    }

    class ViewController {
        private var modelObserver: NSObjectProtocol!
        var model: Model? = nil
        init() {
            modelObserver = NotificationCenter.model.addObserver(
                forName: modelChangedNotification,
                object: nil,
                queue: nil) { [unowned self] (notification) in
                    guard let model = notification.object as? Model
    else { return }
                    self.handle(model: model)
            }
        }

        private func handle(model: Model) {
            self.model = model
            // Print it, our display is the console
            print("\(model)")
        }

        func saveButtonTapped() {
            NotificationCenter.ui.post(
                name: saveTappedNotification,
                object: self.model)
        }
        deinit {
            NotificationCenter.model.removeObserver(modelObserver)
        }
    }
```

As you can see in the preceding code, `ViewController` and `ModelController` are not in direct connection. The display layer is driven by events sent by the model layer, and this helps when decoupling them.

You can test the UI code without connecting the model layer, and vice versa:

```
let modelControler = ModelController()
let viewController = ViewController()

// We have our two instances
```

```
// Load the model, this will emit the event to the UI Layer
modelController.loadModel()

// In the UI, update the title
uiController.model?.title = "Hi! There"
// Tap the saveButton
uiController.saveButtonTapped()

// Attempt to update the title again
uiController.model?.title = "When gone am I, the last of the Jedi will you
be. The Force runs strong in your family. Pass on what you have learned."
uiController.saveButtonTapped()
```

This program will print the following in the console:

```
Model(title: "", description: "")
Model(title: "Hi! There", description: "")
Model(title: "When gone am I, the ", description: "")
```

The first line is logged when calling `modelController.loadModel()`, the second and the third when pressing the **Save** button. In any case, all the calls to `print()` were indirect and the result of mutations or events from the model layer.

`NotificationCenter` is quite powerful, but can be heavy and also lead to complex debugging scenarios. It is well-suited, however, to separating layers from your programs and yet allowing them to communicate loosely.

Keep an eye out for the following issues:

- Always remember to remove observers properly, as otherwise this can lead to crashes.
- Calling `addObserver` with the same objects will register multiple observers.
- Race conditions and thread safety—in our example, all calls are synchronous, but notifications can be dispatched on particular queues asynchronously.

Using Key-Value Observing

KVO is a feature that Swift inherits from Objective-C. It requires that your objects are properly exposed to Objective-C, as it leverages its dynamism.

Not all properties in Objective-C objects support KVO—for example, it's not possible to observe the count in `NSArray` objects in order to be notified when new elements are added.

Using KVO with existing Objective-C APIs

It's often useful to listen for frame or bounds changes, in order to resize other aspects.

Listening to frame changes can be done as follows:

```
let view = NSView(frame: .zero)

let observer = view.observe(\NSView.frame) { (view, change) in
    print("\(view.frame), \(change.oldValue) \(change.newValue)")
}

view.frame = NSRect(x: 0, y: 0, width: 100, height: 100)
// Later in code, in order to stop the observation
observer.invalidate()
```

The preceding code snippet will print the following:

```
(0.0, 0.0, 100.0, 100.0), nil nil
```

As you will note, both `oldValue` and `newValue` are `nil`. It is possible to use a different API if you are interested in the changes.

This is especially powerful when needing to recompute some available space, without the context. This helps isolate further, in line with all the patterns we are seeing in this section:

```
let view = NSView(frame: .zero)
view.observe(\NSView.frame, options: [.new, .old]) { (view, change) in
    print("\(view.frame), \(change.oldValue!) -> \(change.newValue!)")
}
view.frame = NSRect(x: 0, y: 0, width: 100, height: 100)
```

Passing the options to the observer pattern lets you have old and new values passed to the changes. The preceding snippet will print as follows:

```
(0.0, 0.0, 100.0, 100.0), (0.0, 0.0, 0.0, 0.0) -> (0.0, 0.0, 100.0, 100.0)
```

Using KVO with Swift

As mentioned before, KVO leverages Objective-C's dynamism, which means it doesn't work on structs.

In order to use KVO with your own Swift objects, you have to make them dynamic and compatible with Objective-C using the `@objc` annotation:

```
class MyObject: NSObject {
    @objc dynamic
```

```
    var string: String = ""
}
```

Now, the `string` member is observable, and you can use the following code:

```
let object = MyObject()
var changed = false

let observer = object.observe(\MyObject.string) { (obj, change) in
    // Do Something with the new value
    changed = true
}

object.string = "This will emit an event"
assert(changed) // ensure changed was called

observer.invalidate() // Always invalidate!
```

With this technique, it is possible to listen to multiple changes from different call sites and multiple objects. This method is not the most practical in Swift, but still lets you interface properly with Objective-C code and APIs such as Foundation, UIKit, AppKit, and more.

Also, some objects such as AVPlayerItem in AVFoundation are designed to leverage KVO. To keep track of changes in status, or to know when duration has been computed, you'll need to observe for the appropriate properties.

Observation using pure Swift

The last observation technique that we can use is baked right into the Swift language. Unlike the previous techniques, this doesn't let you register multiple observers, only one—the current object. While this is a bit of an aside to the observer pattern, this technique still falls into this category.

Swift exposes `willSet` and `didSet`, which you can use on the properties themselves:

```
struct Article {
    var title: String = "" {
        willSet {
            // here the title is the value before setting
            if title != newValue {
                print("The title will change to \(newValue)")
            }
        }

        didSet {
            // here the title is the value after it's been set
```

```
            if title != oldValue {
                print("The title has changed from \(oldValue)")
            }
        }
    }
}
```

In the preceding code, we print a line each time the title changes from the previous value. It prints the new value as well as the old value, after the new title is set:

```
var article = Article()
article.title = "A Good Title"
article.title = "A Good Title"
article.title = "A Better Title"
```

The output is as follows:

```
The title will change to A Good Title
The title has changed from
The title will change to A Better Title
The title has changed from A Good Title
```

Notice that the second setter doesn't print the following, as we are checking if the values are changing:

```
The title will change to A Good Title
The title has changed from A Good Title
```

This technique is useful if the scope of the observation is constrained to the object itself, for example, if you want to know if your local model has changed. This is particularly useful if, for example, your view has its model set from the outside, and you want to know when the model property is updated in order to render and update the different components that comprise your view.

Using observation

We have covered three different techniques to implement the observer pattern in this section. Each technique comes with its set of constraints and advantages.

1. `NotificationCenter`, which can become resource-intensive
2. KVO observation, which requires deep integration with Objective-C
3. Pure Swift setters, which restrict the number of observers to one

In practice, you'll find yourself using all three techniques over time, as they are core to Swift and Foundation-based programming in general.

The memento pattern

The memento pattern is useful if you need to preserve multiple states of your program or models, which you want to be able to go back or forward to, such as a browsing history or an undo manager.

In this section, we'll implement the memento pattern with a simple example that showcases the different objects required for this pattern.

Components of the memento pattern

The memento pattern requires the implementation of three distinct entities:

- `Memento`: a representation of the internal **state** of `Originator`, which should be immutable
- `Originator`: the original object that can **produce** and **consume** the `Memento`, in order to save and restore its own state
- `CareTaker`: an external object that stores and restores a `Memento` to an `Originator`

 Memento, in other languages, may be implemented as an opaque box so the state can't be mutated. In Swift, we can leverage structs, their immutability, and the fact they are passed by value and not reference. It is critical that different Memento objects do not share memory.

Let's start by implementing a generic memento pattern. Thanks to Swift and its powerful protocols, we can leverage associated types in order to implement the memento pattern.

Let's start with the first important type, `Originator`:

```
protocol Originator {
    associatedtype MementoType
    func createMemento() -> MementoType
    mutating func setMemento(_ memento: MementoType)
}
```

`Originator` has just two responsibilities, to create mementos for `CareTaker` and restore its state using the `setMemento` method. Note that the state of `Originator` should be fully restorable through the `Memento`.

Now, let's have a look at `CareTaker`:

```
protocol CareTaker {
    associatedtype OriginatorType: Originator
    var originator: OriginatorType { get set }

    var mementos: [OriginatorType.MementoType] { get set }
    mutating func save()
    mutating func restore()
}
```

`CareTaker` has a reference to the `Originator` as it should be able to get and restore `Memento` objects from it.

We'll use the associated type again to store the `Memento` objects into an array. This will let us push and pop states easily. With the help of extensions, it is even possible to implement the `save()` and `restore()` methods:

```
extension CareTaker {
    mutating func save() {
        mementos.append(originator.createMemento())
    }

    mutating func restore() {
        guard let memento = mementos.popLast() else { return }
        originator.setMemento(memento)
    }
}
```

With those two protocols in place, we can get started with a more complex example that involves saving the state of a large object.

Implementing the memento pattern

Let's imagine you are building an app that manages a shopping list. On the fly, users can add new items, edit items, and also mark them as done (picked up in-store).

Each element of the shopping list can be represented as an `Item` object:

```
struct Item {
var name: String
    var done: Bool = false
}
```

Again, we'll use a struct, as for the memento pattern we want all the features of value types such as immutability and copy-on-write.

Then we need to represent the `Originator`, `Memento`, and `CareTaker` objects.

A shopping list is just a list. For the sake of our example, we can implement it in many ways, wrapping the list into a `ShoppingList` as the `OriginatorType`, using `[Item]` as the `MementoType`, or introducing a third object as the `CareTaker` for managing undos and redos. As we're in Swift, we can also leverage extensions in order to make the whole program more flexible.

The base type of our shopping list, the `Array` type, is a good candidate for being an `Originator`. As `Array` is a value type, we can guarantee that we can store a copy of it. It is also possible to replace all the contents through `mutating func`, as follows:

```
extension Array: Originator {
    func createMemento() -> [Element] {
return self
    }

mutating func setMemento(_ memento: [Element]) {
self = memento
}
}
```

Now all `Array` types are `Originator` objects, and the `MementoType` is `[Element]`.

The shopping list now can be implemented, but because we don't need another element type, we can call our `CareTaker` the `ShoppingList`:

```
class ShoppingList: CareTaker {

    var list = [Item]()
```

The `Memento` and `Originator` objects are part of the `CareTaker` protocol. `Memento` will store the different states of the list when calling `save()` or `restore()`; the `Originator` is the list of items itself, as explained:

```
var mementos: [[Item]] = []
var originator: [Item] {
    get { return list }
    set { list = newValue }
}
```

Let's also add two convenient methods to add items to the list and toggle them:

```
func add(_ name: String) {
    list.append(Item(name: name, done: false))
}

func toggle(itemAt index: Int) {
    list[index].done.toggle()
}
```

Let's add a few extras for printing our shopping list nicely:

1. First, an extension on `String` to strike through the characters, as follows:

```
extension String {
    var strikeThrough: String {
        return self.reduce("") { (res, char) -> String in
            return res + "\(char)" + "\u{0336}"
        }
    }
}
```

2. Next, a nice description for the shopping list items:

```
extension Item: CustomStringConvertible {
    var description: String {
        return done ? name.strikeThrough : name
    }
}
```

3. Next, let's enhance the description of the shopping list:

```
extension ShoppingList: CustomStringConvertible {
    var description: String {
        return list.map {
            $0.description
        }.joined(separator: "\n")
    }
}
```

Finally, let's consider the following program:

```
// Create a shopping list
var shoppingList = ShoppingList()
// Add some fish
shoppingList.add("Fish")
// Save to the memento
```

```
shoppingList.save()
// Add the Karrots with a typo
shoppingList.add("Karrots")

// Restore to the previous state
shoppingList.restore()

// Check the contents
print("1--\n\(shoppingList)\n\n")

// Add the proper carrots
shoppingList.add("Carrots")
print("2--\n\(shoppingList)\n\n")
shoppingList.save()

// Mark them picked up
shoppingList.toggle(itemAt: 1)
print("3--\n\(shoppingList)\n\n")

// And Restore (didn't pick the right ones)
shoppingList.restore()
print("4--\n\(shoppingList)\n\n")
```

This will output as follows:

```
1--
Fish

2--
Fish
Carrots

3--
Fish
~~Carrots~~

4--
Fish
Carrots
```

As a possible improvement, we could periodically save the contents of the list. Each time there is a mutation, an addition, or an item is toggled, the ShoppingList could call save.

We'd still be following the memento pattern, as the responsibility of the CareTaker to know why and how to save the Originator object's state would not be violated.

Using the memento pattern

Every time you need to store the existing state of an object in order to be able to restore it later, you can probably leverage the memento pattern. The main advantage of this pattern is the opacity of the state. The `CareTaker` isn't really dependent on the `Memento` type, as we've seen.

The protocols we showed can serve as a basis for your custom implementations. Following this pattern lets you implement multiple `CareTaker` objects with different features.

Just to note, in our example, the restoration process means that any redo information is lost. It would be possible to keep this information until the next `save` call by not popping last, but simply moving the current restoration point. Once again, it depends on your needs and the implementation of the `CareTaker` you're looking for.

The visitor pattern

When building complex algorithms, it is practical to separate the algorithm from the objects it operates on. The visitor pattern helps achieve such separation. One of the direct effects of using the visitor pattern is the ability to implement multiple distinct operations, without changing the underlying object structure.

The visitor pattern can be described through the series of protocols that each object has to implement:

1. Define a `Visitable` protocol. Elements that can be visited implement this protocol.
2. Define a `Visitor` protocol. `Visitor` objects implement this protocol, which helps them traverse `Visitable` objects.
3. Extend existing objects to be `Visitable`.
4. Implement one or many `Visitor` objects and their logic.

Visitable and visitor protocols

Thanks to Swift and its expressive generics, it is possible to abstract the visitor pattern through a series of protocols:

```
protocol Visitor {
    func visit<T>(element: T) where T:Visitable
}
```

A `Visitor` is an object that can traverse `Visitable` elements. It implements a single method, which is generic:

```
protocol Visitable {
    func accept(visitor: Visitor)
}
```

`Visitable` objects can be traversed by a `Visitor`. Here we don't use the generics, as they're not needed:

```
// Default implementation for our visitable nodes
extension Visitable {
    func accept(visitor: Visitor) {
        visitor.visit(element: self)
    }
}
```

For the sake of simplicity, and because this is the general use case, we'll want the `Visitable` objects simply to call `visit` on the `Visitor` when they're being visited:

```
// Convenience on Array for visitables
extension Array: Visitable where Element: Visitable {
    func accept(visitor: Visitor) {
        visitor.visit(element: self)
        forEach {
            visitor.visit(element: $0)
        }
    }
}
```

It is possible to extend arrays of `Visitable` objects to be `Visitable` themselves. This may also help with default implementations.

With this base layer of protocols defined, it is possible to retrofit our examples for visitation.

Contributors, thank you notes, and the visitor pattern

We'll now put those protocols to work. Let's imagine you're building an app that helps open source maintainers. New contributors are rare, and it's important to thank them in a timely manner.

Let's implement a simple program that will determine who to send a thank you note to, 3 days after their contribution, out of all the contributions to the repository:

```
struct Contribution {
    let date: Date
    let author: String
    let email: String
    let details: String
}
```

`Contribution` is a simple object of itself, which holds information about the contributor and their contribution.

Now we need to make those `Contribution` objects `Visitable` so we can use `Visitors` on them:

```
extension Contribution: Visitable {}
```

As `Contribution` is `Visitable`, `[Contribution]` will also be so, thanks to the protocol extension on `Array`.

Let's make a logger `Visitor`. This demonstrates the power of the visitor pattern—being able to swap the algorithm without touching the underlying objects. From a single dataset (the list of contributions), it is possible to design multiple algorithms, as follows:

```
class LoggerVisitor: Visitor {
    func visit<T>(element: T) where T : Visitable {
        guard let contribution = element as? Contribution else { return }
        print("\(contribution.author) / \(contribution.email)")
    }
}

let visitor = LoggerVisitor()
[
    Contribution(author: "Contributor", email: "my@email.com", date:
Date(), details: ""),
    Contribution(author: "Contributor 2", email: "my-other@email.com",
date: Date(), details: "")
].accept(visitor: visitor)

// output
Contributor / my@email.com
Contributor 2 / my-other@email.com
```

Now that we know the protocol-based logic works properly, we can implement a proper `Visitor` that will collect the contributor's contact details in order to send them a nice thank-you note:

```
let threeDaysAgo = Calendar.current.date(byAdding: .day, value: -3, to:
Date())!
let fourDaysAgo = Calendar.current.date(byAdding: .day, value: -4, to:
Date())!

class ThankYouVisitor: Visitor {
    var contributions = [Contribution]()

    func visit<T>(element: T) where T : Visitable {
        guard let contribution = element as? Contribution else { return }
        // Check that the contribution was done between 3 and 4 days ago
        if contribution.date <= threeDaysAgo && contribution.date >
fourDaysAgo {
            contributions.append(contribution)
        }
    }
}

// Create an instance of the visitor
let thanksVisitor = ThankYouVisitor()

// Visit this contribution
Contribution(author: "John Duff",
            email: "john@cosmic.tortillas",
            date: threeDaysAgo,
            details: "...")
        .accept(visitor: thanksVisitor)

// We have one as the date is within range
assert(thanksVisitor.contributions.length === 1)

// Visit another contribution
Contribution(author: "Harry Cover",
            email: "harry@cosmic.tortillas",
            date: fourDaysAgo,
            details: "...")
        .accept(visitor: thanksVisitor)

// We have one as the second one is out of range
assert(thanksVisitor.contributions.length === 1)

let allContributions: [Contribution] = ... // get all contributions

allContributions.accept(visitor: thanksVisitor) // visit all contributions
```

```
// Send thanks!
thanksVisitor.contributions.forEach {
    sendThanks($0)
}
```

In the preceding examples, we successfully implemented the visitor pattern in order to extract meaningful information from an existing data structure. You'll have noted that you can use and implement many `Visitor` objects for a particular dataset, as long as the data set is `Visitable`.

Using visitors

As we've seen, the visitor pattern is a powerful design pattern that helps you write algorithms that are independent from the data they consume. The object structure stays untouched, whether arrays, dictionaries, trees, or even more complex structures, and each node or aggregate is enhanced with the `Visitor` object's capabilities.

Swift is particularly suitable for this design pattern, as we can leverage protocols and extensions, allowing the `Visitor` to be defined in completely different call sites.

The strategy pattern

To conclude this chapter, we'll cover the strategy pattern. This design pattern lets you write programs that are able to select different algorithms or strategies at runtime. For example, using the strategy pattern may help in sorting objects in different ways, by letting you specify the comparison function at runtime.

You will find yourself wanting to implement the strategy pattern when faced with:

- Complex classes with multiple algorithms changing at runtime
- Algorithms that may improve performance and need to be swapped at runtime
- Multiple implementations of similar algorithms in different classes, making them difficult to extract
- Complex algorithms that are strongly tied to data structures

The goal of the strategy pattern is to let you isolate those algorithms from the context they operate in.

Components of the strategy pattern

The strategy pattern involves only a few components:

- Context objects, which will have a Strategy member
- Strategy implementations that can be swapped at runtime

Let's attempt to generalize this implementation via protocols.

Strategy is the algorithm that runs the code, and that will be swapped at runtime. At a high level, a strategy is only dependent on its algorithm ReturnType:

```
protocol Strategy {
    associatedtype ReturnType
    func run() -> ReturnType
}
```

In practice, this abstraction lacks some definition, as we're missing some information about what we should pass to the algorithm. For the sake of our demonstration, let's rewrite the run() function with a single argument. As we're using generics, this argument can be anything we want:

```
protocol Strategy {
    associatedtype ReturnType
    associatedtype ArgumentType
    func run(argument: ArgumentType) -> ReturnType
}
```

Now, for all the objects that need a different strategy, we can define a new Context type. This type will need to have an associated StrategyType, and keep a reference to the Strategy:

```
protocol Context {
    associatedtype StrategyType: Strategy
    var strategy: StrategyType { get set }
}
```

With the Context and Strategy protocols defined, we can jump into an example that showcases this design pattern.

The ice-cream shop example

Ice creams are yummy, and you can almost always customize them to your taste—from the number of scoops, to choosing whether you want a wafer cone or a cup, and even whether or not to dip in chocolate for extra crunch.

We're in charge of designing the billing part, but there's a twist. We'll need to be able to run promotions, offer family discounts, and implement a loyal customer program.

This kind of problem is easily solved using the strategy pattern, as it allows us to reconfigure an algorithm (the billing algorithm) at runtime.

First, let's work out the model. For the sake of simplicity, we put all the items into an enum, `IceCreamPart`, and attach their prices right into it. We'll also track the number of scoops into it, instead of externally:

```swift
enum IceCreamPart {
    case waffer
    case cup
    case scoop(Int)
    case chocolateDip
    case candyTopping

    var price: Double {
        switch self {
        case .scoop:
            return 2.0
        default:
            return 0.25
        }
    }
}
```

Adding a debugging string is always welcome, as this will help ensure our program runs smoothly:

```swift
extension IceCreamPart: CustomStringConvertible {
    var description: String {
        switch self {
        case .scoop(let count):
            return "\(count)x scoops"
        case .waffer:
            return "1x waffer"
        case .cup:
            return "1x cup"
        case .chocolateDip:
            return "1x chocolate dipping"
```

```
            case .candyTopping:
                return "1x candy topping"
            }
        }
    }
```

Let's jump into our billing strategies now. `BillingStrategy` is a simple protocol with a single method:

```
protocol BillingStrategy {
    func add(item: IceCreamPart) -> Double
}
```

Each time we call the strategy, we want to know the price at which the item will be billed. This will involve calculating the price for each topping and extra scoop added.

Note that we use the unit prices from each item, as they are part of the menu. What we do here is decouple the pricing of the full ice cream from its parts. This lets us run promotions easily, such as halving the price of each scoop after the first one if we need to:

```
class FullPriceStrategy: BillingStrategy {
    func add(item: IceCreamPart) -> Double {
        switch item {
        case .scoop(let count):
            return Double(count) * item.price
        default:
            return item.price
        }
    }
}
```

Let's say the manager wants to offer a promotion. If a customer buys more than two scoops of ice cream, toppings will be offered at half price. Let's add this strategy as well:

```
class HalfPriceToppings: FullPriceStrategy {
    override func add(item: IceCreamPart) -> Double {
        if case .candyTopping = item {
            return item.price / 2.0
        }
        return super.add(item: item)
    }
}
```

We use inheritance here, as all prices are related to each other, and we don't want to duplicate the code. In other scenarios, you may not need to use inheritance, as the strategies may not be related to each other.

Now that we have our strategies properly defined, we can get into the Context object. In this scenario, this object will be best represented by the customer Bill. This Bill will have a strategy that we can mutate externally, as well as the ability to add ice-cream items, compute the total, and print the receipt:

```
struct Bill {
    var strategy: BillingStrategy
    var items = [(IceCreamPart, Double)]()

    init(strategy: BillingStrategy) {
        self.strategy = strategy
    }

    mutating func add(item: IceCreamPart) {
        let price = strategy.add(item: item)
        items.append((item, price))
    }

    func total() -> Double {
        return items.reduce(0) { (total, item) -> Double in
            return total + item.1
        }
    }
}

extension Bill: CustomStringConvertible {
    var description: String {
        return items.map { (item) -> String in
            return item.0.description + " $\(item.1)"
        }.joined(separator: "\n")
            + "\n----------"
            + "\nTotal $\(total())\n"
    }
}
```

The implementation part is complete, and we now can start serving our first customers:

```
var bill = Bill(strategy: FullPriceStrategy())
// The first customer wants a waffer
bill.add(item: .waffer)
// Then he'll add a single scoop
bill.add(item: .scoop(1))
// Then he'll add the candy toppings
bill.add(item: .candyTopping)
print(bill.description)

// 1x waffer $0.25
// 1x scoops $2.0
```

```
// 1x candy topping $0.25
// ----------
// Total $2.5
```

Let's now welcome the second customer, and start a new bill:

```
bill = Bill(strategy: FullPriceStrategy())
// This one will be in a cup
bill.add(item: .cup)
// 3 scoops!
bill.add(item: .scoop(3))
// Hooray! Toppings are half price
bill.strategy = HalfPriceToppings()
bill.add(item: .candyTopping)
print(bill)

// 1x cup $0.25
// 3x scoops $6.0
// 1x candy topping $0.125
// ----------
// Total $6.375
```

Now, the store manager has introduced a loyalty program. When a customer buys five ice creams, they'll get a sixth one for half price. Thanks to the strategy pattern, it's very simple to implement this new pricing strategy, as follows:

```
class HalfPriceStrategy: FullPriceStrategy {
    override func add(item: IceCreamPart) -> Double {
        return super.add(item: item) / 2.0
    }
}
```

Now, `HalfPriceStrategy` can be applied for loyal customers:

```
bill = Bill(strategy: HalfPriceStrategy())
bill.add(item: .waffer)
bill.add(item: .scoop(1))
bill.add(item: .candyTopping)
print(bill)

// 1x waffer $0.125
// 1x scoops $1.0
// 1x candy topping $0.125
// ----------
// Total $1.25
```

As we can see, we've been able to add new strategies on the fly to perform the calculations, without cluttering `Bill` or `IceCreamPart`.

Using the strategy pattern

We have seen that the strategy pattern is a powerful design pattern that lets you dissociate algorithms from the objects they operate on. In our example, we could have implemented printing and description with the strategy pattern as well. Instead of implementing `CustomStringConvertible` with the strings directly, we could have also used a strategy that generates a string that describes the current bill.

With your implementations, you have to keep an eye on:

- Defining the strategy interface carefully. Different strategies may beg for more complex interfaces; once the strategy interface is defined, refactoring may be very costly.
- Minimizing the logic inside the `Context` object. In our case, the `Bill` was very simple.
- Mutations - strategies can mutate the context, changing the current strategy in turn. In this example, we manipulated the bill strategy from the outside, but equally we could have mutated the strategy inside the strategy itself. This implementation is also interesting, as it keeps the logic outside the core objects.

Summary

In this chapter, we've covered five of the most popular behavioral patterns and how to implement them effectively in Swift. These behavioral patterns will help you to decouple your programs in an effective and maintainable way.

When needing to isolate algorithms from the data they consume, you can use **strategies** and **visitors.** As object behaviors grow, you can refactor using the **state** pattern. Persistence can be represented through the **memento** pattern, and, finally, the **observer** pattern helps when passing information around the program.

We've made great use of some advanced and unique features of Swift: protocols, extensions, generics, and immutable value types, which we will dig deeper into in the next chapter.

8
Swift-Oriented Patterns

Swift is a modern language and, coming from a purely object-oriented language background, can feel overwhelming. With its strong functional capabilities as well as extensive generics support, Swift is an expressive language that generalizes an interesting programming paradigm: protocol-oriented programming.

Protocol-oriented programming doesn't replace object-oriented programming or functional programming—it's another tool that helps you elevate your code bases to new heights. It doesn't magically transform poorly written code into unicorns and rainbows.

Alongside powerful protocols come generics-oriented programming. Generics let you write functions with protocols instead of concrete types. When programming with concrete types, only children of this type, through inheritance, can be used in place of the parent type. With protocols and generics, any type that conforms to, or adopts, the protocol can be used. This leads to a slew of unprecedented capabilities, such as building algorithms that are independent of the data they work with.

In this chapter, we will do the following:

- Define what protocol-oriented programming is, where it comes from, and in which cases you should use it
- Explore how to apply the template pattern through protocol-oriented programming
- Generalize what we've uncovered on generics and protocols
- Learn how to implement effective type erasure and when those techniques may help you in your own code base

Getting started with protocol-oriented programming

Protocols are widespread and available in many languages, such as Swift, Objective-C, and Clojure. In order to have a common definition, let's go back to the source, the Swift language guide (`https://docs.swift.org/swift-book/LanguageGuide/Protocols.html`):

> *"A protocol defines a **blueprint of methods, properties, and other requirements** that suit a particular task or piece of functionality. The protocol can then be **adopted** by a **class, structure**, or **enumeration** to provide an **actual implementation** of those requirements. Any type that satisfies the requirements of a protocol is said to conform to that protocol."*

This first part of the definition is telling us that, contrary to classes or structures, protocols do not provide implementation details, but only the shape. You can think of the protocols as the star, square, and round shaped holes in the popular game for kids. These holes can fit the pieces (instances), as long as the instances have the same shape, but they don't discriminate about the color (different instances).

Let's look at the second part of the definition from the Swift language guide:

> *"In addition to specifying requirements that conforming types must implement, you can extend a protocol to implement some of these requirements or to implement additional functionality that conforming types can take advantage of."*

This tells us that we can extend protocols. Extending protocols is the action of doing the following:

- Adding new features based on the existing functionalities provided by the protocol
- Implementing requirements so the classes adopting it can share the same implementation

With this second feature, we can implement simple (or complex) algorithms on protocols. These algorithms can then be consumed by any concrete type that conforms to the protocol. Unlike inheritance, where the lineage is vertical—a child only inherits from its parent—protocols provide us with a powerful way to share logic and behaviors horizontally.

A refresher on protocols

You define protocols with the `protocol` keyword:

```
protocol BasicProtocol {}
```

The same way classes can inherit from each other, a protocol can inherit from another as well. The syntax is the same as the one for classes:

```
protocol ComplexProtocol: BasicProtocol {}
```

Classes and structures can adopt protocols and a single type can conform to multiple protocols, as in the example:

```
class MyClass: MySuperClass, BasicProtocol, AnotherProtocol {}

struct MyStruct: AnotherProtocol {}
```

Adding requirements to protocols

Empty protocols can be useful as we've seen previously, but protocols are meant to provide requirements.

Protocols can require different aspects of objects:

- Properties, their type, and accessibility
- Methods
- Initializers

```
protocol DemoProtocol {
    var aRequiredProperty: String { get set }
    var aReadonlyProperty: Double { get }
    static var aStaticProperty: Int { get set }

    init(requiredProperty: String)

    func doSomething() -> Bool
}
```

The previous `DemoProtocol` protocol exposes all of the requirements a conforming class should provide:

- `aRequiredProperty` should be `String` that can be read and written.
- `aReadonlyProperty` should be `Double`, but should only be at least readable. Conforming classes can implement it as `let` or as a computed property.
- `aStaticProperty` is a static `Int` member; conforming classes expose them as `vars`.
- Conforming classes should provide an initializer that takes `String` as an argument.
- Conforming classes should expose a `non mutating` function `doSomething()` that returns `Bool`.

You can implement this protocol with a class or a structure or even an enumeration.

Mutation and value types

Some protocols may have methods that mutate the object members or properties. Consider the following protocol:

```
protocol Incrementing {
    func increment() -> Int
}
```

The `Incrementing` protocol requires the implementation of a single method, `increment() -> Int`, which returns the current value after the increment. This protocol may be used whenever we need to count linearly. It also suggests that it increments a local counter:

```
struct Counter: Incrementing {
    private var value: Int = 0
    func increment() -> Int {
        value += 1
        return value
    }
}
```

This implementation will not compile and will emit the following error:

```
Left side of mutating operator isn't mutable: 'self' is immutable
```

This error is emitted because the `increment()` function is not marked `mutable` on the structure. However, we have also to add the `mutating` keyword to the protocol; otherwise, the protocol would still be immutable by default and the structure is not conforming.

```
protocol Incrementing {
    mutating func increment() -> Int
}

struct Counter: Incrementing {
    private var value: Int = 0
    mutating func increment() -> Int {
        value += 1
        return value
    }
}

var counter = Counter()
assert(counter.increment() == 1)
assert(counter.increment() == 2)
```

Protocols are full-fledged types

Protocols don't provide any implementation, but that doesn't mean the only use they have is for conformance on concrete types. You can (and should) use protocols as types. Protocols are first class citizens, as are functions, classes, structures, and enums, which means you can use them anywhere you'd be able to use any other type:

- As a return type—parameter of a function
- As a member—variable or constant
- Within arrays, dictionaries, or other container types

You should already be very comfortable with using protocols as types. Delegation leverages this widely:

```
protocol RunnerDelegate: class {
    func didStart(runner: Runner)
    func didStop(runner: Runner)
}

class Runner {
    weak var delegate: RunnerDelegate?

    func start() {
        // Start the runner
        delegate?.didStart(runner: self)
```

```
    }

    func stop() {
        delegate?.didStop(runner: self)
    }
}
```

In the previous example, we define a delegation protocol, `RunnerDelegate`, which helps convey to another object, `delegate`, actions that were taken on `Runner`.

One interesting feature of protocols as types is the ability to compose these protocols. Instead of creating protocol hierarchies, Swift makes it easy to introduce compounded protocols:

```
typealias HashAndEquatable = Hashable & Equatable
```

As `typealias` is a proper type as well, you can use these composed protocols in your objects.

> Composition is not reserved to protocols—you can also use it with concrete types:
> ```
> typealias RunnerDelegateView = NSView & RunnerDelegate
> ```
> The previous code is a valid `typealias` that would require the variable to be both `NSView` and `RunnerDelegate`. You may use this pattern if you need a specific conformance from a concrete class.

Generics, conditional conformance, and associated types

Programming with generics is a distinct type of programming that implies writing and designing your algorithms in terms of types that will later be fully realized and specified. In Swift, many algorithms in the standard library are implemented with generics, which promotes code reuse but may also impede readability, as it may render the programs harder to reason about.

Generics-based programming

Programming with generics lets you write flexible code that works with any type and that follows the requirements you settle at compile time. Let's first see how generics can be applied to functions and then to classes and structures.

Generic functions

Let's consider the following code, which isn't implemented with generics:

```
func compareInts(_ a: Int, _ b: Int) -> Int {
    if a > b { return 1 }
    if a < b { return -1 }
    return 0
}
```

This works with integers, but how would it work with `Double`? We'd need to implement another method:

```
func compareDoubles(_ a: Double, _ b: Double) -> Int {
    if a > b { return 1 }
    if a < b { return -1 }
    return 0
}
```

Generics-based programming aims to resolve this issue. In Swift, we have the `Comparable` protocol, which we can use in order to implement a generic `compare` function:

```
func compare<T>(_ a: T, _ b: T) -> Int where T: Comparable {
    if a > b { return 1 }
    if a < b { return -1 }
    return 0
}
```

Let's break it down:

- `<T>` indicates that this function is generic, and one type, `T`, will be used in it
- `a: T, b: T` indicates that this method takes two parameters of the `T` type
- `where T: Comparable` indicates that `T` is required to conform to the `Comparable` protocol

With this method, we can use it with any type that is `Comparable`.

Generic everything

Now that we have seen how to implement generic functions, let's have a look at how to implement it with other data structures such as enums.

One of the popular addition swift programmers often like to have in their tool chain is the `Result` or `Either` types. These two types are best represented with `enum` as they can only hold a finite number of different values (two).

`Result` is used when a function can resolve with either a success value or an error (`Error`). `Either` is used when a function can resolve with two different values (a `left` value or a `right` value):

```
enum Result<T> {
    case success(T), error(Error)
}

enum Either<T, U> {
    case left(T), right(U)
}
```

Both of these implementations are **unconstrained generics**, unlike the previous example:

- `Result` is an `enum` with a single generic parameter, `T`.
- `Either` is an `enum` with two generic parameters, `T` and `U`.

Now that we've seen implementations of generics classes and functions, we can go take a look at an example of conditional conformance.

Conditional conformance

Conditional conformance is a feature that lets you provide conformance or extensions to existing types on the condition that a set of requirements is fulfilled.

Let's define a simple protocol:

```
protocol Summable {
    var sum: Int { get }
}
```

The previous protocol defines that any type that is `Summable` should expose a `sum` property of the `Int` type.

We can retrofit this type on `Arrays` of `Int` types as we know how to add integers together to produce a sum:

```
extension Array: Summable where Element == Int {
    var sum: Int {
        return self.reduce(0) { $0 + $1 }
    }
}

[1,2,3,4].sum == 10
```

It's all good, but now we also want to make sums of all number types. In Swift, there is a base protocol, called `Numeric`, that is shared by all number types.

Let's express `Summable` in terms of `Numeric`:

```
protocol Summable {
    associatedtype SumType
    var sum: SumType { get }
}
```

Now we define that the sum type will be defined *a posteriori* at the time a concrete object will declare its conformance to the protocol. We'll dive into more details in the associated types later on:

```
extension Array: Summable where Element: Numeric {
    typealias SumType = Element
    var sum: Element {
        return self.reduce(0) { $0 + $1 }
    }
}
```

Let's break it down:

- `extension Array: Summable` declares that we're extending `Array` to be `Summable`
- `where Element: Numeric` is only for arrays that have their elements of the `Numeric` type.
- `typealias SumType = Element` declares that the sum will be the type of the array `Element` type, not `Numeric`.

Now we can use the following:

```
let intSum = [1,2,3,4,5].sum
let doubleSum = [1.0, 2.0, 3.0, 4.0].sum
let floatSum: Float = [1.0, 2.0, 3.0, 4.0].sum

assert(intSum is Int)
assert(doubleSum is Double)
assert(floatSum is Float)
```

The previous code compiles and is valid; we've successfully extended arrays of the `Numeric` types in order to implement the `Summable` protocol.

Now, let's say you want to use the same `Summable` protocol in order to implement it on `String` arrays:

```
extension Array: Summable where Element == String {
    var sum: String {
        return self.reduce("") { $0 + $1 }
    }
}
```

While the previous code seems reasonable, it doesn't compile and fails with the following error:

```
conflicting conformance of 'Array<Element>' to protocol 'Summable'; there
cannot be more than one conformance, even with different conditional bounds
```

As you may have guessed, we cannot declare multiple conformances with different restrictions; if we want to use the sum computed property to concatenate strings, we need to drop the `Summable` conformance:

```
extension Array where Element == String {
    var sum: String {
        return self.reduce("") { $0 + $1 }
    }
}

["Hello", " ", "World", "!"].sum  == "Hello World!"
```

We just had a peek at protocols with associated types with the `Summable` protocol and we'll go deeper into this feature in the next section.

Associated types

Protocol with Associated Types or **PATs** is a powerful but largely misunderstood feature of Swift; it feels buggy but works as intended. The first encounter with PAT often terminates with the following dreaded error:

```
// Protocol 'MyProtocol' can only be used as a generic constraint because
it has Self or associated type requirements
```

This error is by design and you're not doing anything wrong; it's just a small misunderstanding of how to use associated types or self requirement with protocols, which we'll hopefully explain and fix for now and the future.

Let's consider this popular example:

```
protocol Food {}

protocol Animal {
    func eat(food: Food)
}

struct Cow: Animal {
    func eat(food: Food) {}
}
```

We defined two protocols, `Food` and `Animal`, and added a requirement that `Animal` should eat `food`.

We also defined `Cow` as being `Animal`, which eats `food`—lots of food. While correct, the previous code doesn't convey that cows don't eat *any kind of food*. They prefer `Grass`.

Let's define `Grass` as a structure that conforms to `Food`:

```
struct Grass: Food {}
struct Cow: Animal {
    func eat(food: Grass) {} // Type 'Cow' does not conform to protocol
'Animal'
}
```

Oops. Now that we've refined the `Cow` type to only eat `Grass`, we're not able to feed it anything else, which doesn't match with the requirement on `Animal`, that every animal should eat `Food`.

Associated types are there to solve this problem. We need to refactor the `Animal` type in order to let it work with an associated type, `FoodType`:

```
protocol Animal {
    associatedtype FoodType: Food
    func eat(food: FoodType)
}
```

An associated type can be thought about a generic type added on protocols. `FoodType` is a placeholder that will be determined by the class or structure implementing the protocol. We also conveyed that `FoodType` should conform to the `Food` protocol. Let's be realistic: animals don't eat `String`, `Ints`, or `NotificationCenters`.

With this, the `Cow` struct is now valid and properly compiles, and we can expressively convey that `Lions` eat `Meat`, and not any kind of food:

```
struct Meat: Food {}
struct Lion: Animal {
    func eat(food: Meat) {}
}
```

This is great; now we can feed each animal, but can we feed them all? Let's see:

```
func feed(animal: Animal) { } // Protocol 'Animal' can only be used as a
generic constraint because it has Self or associated type requirements
```

So we previously saw that protocols were types and could be used as types, unless they have `Self` or associated type requirements.

How can we solve this? The answer is, by using `Animal` as a generic constraint:

```
func feed<A: Animal>(animal: A) {
    switch animal {
    case let lion as Lion:
        lion.eat(food: Meat())
    case let cow as Cow:
        cow.eat(food: Grass())
    default:
        print("I can't feed...")
        break
    }
}

feed(animal: Cow())
feed(animal: Lion())
```

The next thing you may want to do is to consider all of your animals in a single array:

```
var animals = [Animal]() // Protocol 'Animal' can only be used as a generic
constraint because it has Self or associated type requirements
```

Nope, you can't store the animals altogether; you may want to experiment with a generic class that would hold all of your animals in an array:

```
class AnimalHolder<T> where T: Animal {
    var animals = [T]()
}

let holder = AnimalHolder<# WHAT DO WE PUT HERE#>()
```

In both cases, we're hit by the limitation of PATs, which is that associated types are to be used as generic constraints and not as types.

Is it all lost? Not really; as Swift is an ever-evolving language, this limitation is well documented and you should always have it in the back of your head whenever you're programming with generics. For now, you have multiple options:

- Leverage type erasure pattern, which we'll see later
- Wait for generalized existentials (`https://github.com/apple/swift/blob/master/docs/GenericsManifesto.md#generalized-existentials`), which will allow values to be protocols, even with associated types
- Refactor your code, and stick with object-oriented programming

As we're here to learn about Swift and how to work with Swift 5, let's learn the type erasure pattern and how we can use it to store arrays of animals (or any protocol with associated types or `Self` requirements).

A word on Self requirement

In the previous section, we've seen an example of associated type. Let's see what we mean when mentioning `Self` requirement.

Consider the following protocol:

```
protocol Thing {
    associatedtype AType
}

struct Node: Thing {
    typealias AType = Thing // Self associated type
}
```

Because `Node` conforms to `Thing` and sets its `AType` `associatedtype` to itself via `typealias`, you would probably imagine the following code would work:

```
let thing: Thing = Node()
```

Unfortunately, it doesn't. This is what we call a `Self` requirement and you will be hit by the same problem:

```
Protocol 'Thing' can only be used as a generic constraint because it has
Self or associated type requirements
```

Protocol-oriented programming

In this section, we have covered the following:

- How to define your own protocols
- How to make a type conform to one or many protocol
- How to define protocols in terms of other protocols
- How to leverage protocols with generic types
- What are PATs and their features and limitations

In the next section, we'll go through a comprehensive guide about type erasure. Type erasure is a well known and used design pattern in Swift that helps to work with protocols and generics until generalized existentials are part of the language.

The type erasure pattern

As we've seen in the previous section, protocols cannot be used as types when they are associated with another type, in the form of `Self` or associated type requirements. Indeed, they can only be used as generic constraints.

In this section, we'll discuss the different opportunities that we have in order to overcome this limitation. A common technique is called type erasure.

You may wonder why we want to "erase" a type and what it means to "erase" a type. Let's turn to Wikipedia to answer this question: type erasure refers to the load-time (https://en.wikipedia.org/wiki/Loader_ (computing)) process by which explicit type annotations (https://en. wikipedia.org/wiki/Type_signature) are removed from a program [...] In the context of generic programming (https://en.wikipedia.org/ wiki/Generic_programming), the opposite of type erasure is called reification (https://en.wikipedia.org/wiki/Reification_ (computer_science)).

The goal of type erasure is clear: it's to remove type annotations from a particular program. In particular, we cannot use protocols with associated types as existential, but we can use classes, structures, or enumerations with generics.

Type erasure is a design pattern that helps to represent **protocols** with **associated types** into a **concrete** type with **generics.**

Elements of type erasure

There is a basic implementation of type erasure that is particularly suited if your protocols have few methods. This method is interesting as it requires very few elements, compared to the full erasure pattern. However, it achieves the same goal.

Let's go back to our animal example:

```
struct Grass: Food {}
struct Cow: Animal {
    func eat(food: Grass) {
        print("Grass is yummy! moooooo!")
    }
}

struct Goat: Animal {
    func eat(food: Grass) {
        print("Grass is good! meehhhh!")
    }
}
```

If you remember clearly, we wanted to keep all our grass-eating animals together; however, that wasn't possible:

```
let grassEaters: [Animal] = [Cow(), Goat()] // protocol 'Animal' can only
be used as a generic constraint...
let grassEaters: [Animal<Grass>] = [Cow(), Goat()]  // cannot specialize
non-generic type 'Animal'
```

In order to overcome this, we need to come up with a **generic type**, that can be specialized with the type of `Food`.

As we're implementing the type erasure pattern on the `Animal` type, it's a convention to prefix the name of the concrete object used to wrap the generic with `Any`.

So our type is going be as follows:

- Named `AnyAnimal`
- It's a generic concrete type, so: `AnyAnimal<T>`
- It can be specialized only with `Food`, so: `AnyAnimal<T> where T: Food`

Let's start with this:

```
class AnyAnimal<T> where T: Food {}
```

Now this type will be used as a proxy to the `Animal` type; we want to be able to use all of the same interface as our original protocol. Let's make `AnyAnimal<T>` conform to `Animal`:

```
class AnyAnimal<T>: Animal where T: Food {
    typealias FoodType = T
    func eat(food: T) {}
}
```

Adding the conformance to `Animal` required us to provide the type for `FoodType`; in this case, it will be the generic type, `T`.

Now we can create `AnyAnimal`, for example, `AnyCow` that would be a subclass of `AnyAnimal`:

```
class AnyCow: AnyAnimal<Grass> {}
```

But that's not the point of the type erasure—after all, if we wanted, we could have implemented all of our models as `AnyAnimal` subclasses. If you want to make sure no one does it in your code base, it's good practice to mark the class `final`.

As we have implemented the `AnyAnimal<T>` class as our wrapper, we now have two choices:

- A closure-based implementation
- A box-based implementation

Both implementations have their benefits, so we'll start with the simple closure-based implementation. We'll follow up with the box-based one as this is the "official" type erasure pattern that we see in the Swift code base: `https://github.com/apple/swift/blob/master/stdlib/public/core/ExistentialCollection.swift.gyb#L572`.

Closure-based type erasure

The final step in our closure-based type erasure is to implement the initializer that will be used to wrap `Cows` and `Goats`:

```
final class AnyAnimal<T>: Animal where T: Food {
    typealias FoodType = T

    private let eatBlock: (T) -> Void
```

```
    init<A: Animal>(animal: A) where A.FoodType == T {
        eatBlock = animal.eat
    }

    func eat(food: T) {
        eatBlock(food)
    }
}
```

Let's sum up the changes:

- We marked the class `final` to avoid any wrong usage.
- We added an `eatBlock: (T) -> Void` property to capture the `eat` method from the animal.
- We added an implementation to `func eat(food: T)` to forward the calls to the original method.
- We added the generic initializer that also binds the `T` type to `FoodType` of the provided `Animal` type, `A.FoodType`.

Let's now gather the flock of grass eaters and make let them graze freely in the fields:

```
let aCow = AnyAnimal(animal: Cow())
let aGoat = AnyAnimal(animal: Goat())

let grassEaters = [aCow, aGoat] // it's a small flock but a significant one
assert(grassEaters is [AnyAnimal<Grass>]) // Yay! All grass eaters

grassEaters.forEach { (animal) in // They are quire hungry let them eat
    animal.eat(food: Grass())
}

// Output:
Grass is yummy! moooooo!
Grass is good! meehhhh!
```

This concludes the implementation of the closure based type erasure. Now, let's take a complete look at the box-based type erasure. While more verbose, this implementation should not scare you away.

Boxing-based type erasure

The boxing-based type erasure pattern requires three distinct objects:

- An abstract base class
- A private box, which will inherit the abstract base class
- A public wrapper

As for the public wrapper, we can reuse the one that we wrote above `AnyAnimal<T>`.

In order to make the exercise a bit more interesting, let's change the `Animal` protocol to introduce some complexities such as the animal's preferred food and name:

```
protocol Animal {
    associatedtype FoodType: Food
    var preferredFood: FoodType? { get set }
    var name: String { get }
    func eat(food: FoodType)
}
```

Reflecting the changes in the `Animal` protocol, we need to update `AnyAnimal`. Let's not bother too much with the initializers now, as we'll implement them as we go:

```
final class AnyAnimal<T>: Animal where T: Food {
    typealias FoodType = T
    var preferredFood: T?
    let name: String = ""
    func eat(food: T) {}
}
```

Let's now go over the two new required components that will allow us to achieve the type erasure pattern fully.

The abstract base class

The abstract base class is very similar to the `AnyAnimal` public wrapper due to the following:

- It conforms to our base protocol.
- It's an **abstract** class so provides a top implementation for the private box.
- It defines a generic parameter, `T` or `F`, bound to the associated type.

The convention begs to call this class _Any#MY_PROTOCOL#Base<>. As the design pattern requires the implementation of this class as an abstract class, we implement it with `fatalError()`:

```
private class _AnyAnimalBase<F>: Animal where F: Food {
    var preferredFood: F? {
        get { fatalError() }
        set { fatalError() }
    }
    var name: String { fatalError() }
    func eat(food: F) { fatalError() }
}
```

The private box

The private box will be a type that implements the abstract base class. The goal of the private box is to provide a wrapper around the concrete object implementing the PAT and forward all of the calls to the boxed object.

Following the conventions also suggests that you should use _Any#MY_PROTOCOL#Box as a class name for this component:

```
private final class _AnyAnimalBox<A: Animal>: _AnyAnimalBase<A.FoodType> {
    // The target object, that is an Animal
    var target: A
    init(_ target: A) {
        self.target = target
    }
    // Overrides of the abstract classes's implementation
    // Forward all invocations to the concrete target
    override var name: String {
        return target.name
    }

    override var preferredFood: A.FoodType? {
        get { return target.preferredFood }
        set { target.preferredFood = newValue }
    }
    override func eat(food: A.FoodType) {
        target.eat(food: food)
    }
}
```

As the _AnyAnimalBox class extends _AnyAnimalBase, we will be able to keep references of our boxes as their abstract class type, which successfully bridges the world of protocols and their associated types to the world of generics.

The public wrapper

Now that we have all of the components required to implement our public wrapper, let's have a look at what's left to do:

- Implement an initializer that takes Animal<F>
- Box Animal<F> into _AnyAnimalBox<A>
- Store the boxed animal as _AnyAnimalBase<F> (remember, we can't use A as a generic type, but we can use F)
- Forward all calls to from the public wrapper to the box:

```
final class AnyAnimal<T>: Animal where T: Food {
    typealias FoodType = T
    private let box: _AnyAnimalBase<T>

    init<A: Animal>(_ animal: A) where A.FoodType == T {
        box = _AnyAnimalBox(animal)
    }

    // Call forwarding for implementing Animal
    var preferredFood: T? {
        get { return box.preferredFood }
        set { box.preferredFood = newValue }
    }
    var name: String {
        return box.name
    }
    func eat(food: T) {
        box.eat(food: food)
    }
}
```

Let's have a bit of fun now with our newly implemented type erasure pattern.

First, let's redefine our base types, Cow and Goat:

```
struct Cow: Animal {
    var name: String
    var preferredFood: Grass? = nil
}
```

```
struct Goat: Animal {
    var name: String
    var preferredFood: Grass? = nil
}
```

Then, as these two grass eaters eat the same way, we can provide a conditional default implementation on `Animal`:

```
extension Animal where FoodType: Grass {
    func eat(food: FoodType) {
        if let preferredFood = preferredFood,
            type(of: food) == type(of: preferredFood) {
            print("\(name): Yummy! \(type(of: food))")
        } else {
            print("\(name): I'm eating...")
        }
    }
}
```

Now all of the pieces are together and we can go to the pasture with our flock of grass eaters, and let them enjoy their favorite grass:

```
class Grass: Food {}
class Flower: Grass {}
class Dandelion: Grass {}
class Shamrock: Grass {}

let flock = [
    AnyAnimal(Cow(name: "Bessie", preferredFood: Dandelion())),
    AnyAnimal(Cow(name: "Henrietta", preferredFood: nil)),
    AnyAnimal(Goat(name: "Billy", preferredFood: Shamrock())),
    AnyAnimal(Goat(name: "Nanny", preferredFood: Flower()))
]

let flowers = [
    Grass(),
    Dandelion(),
    Flower(),
    Shamrock()
]

while true {
    flock.randomElement()?
        .eat(food: flowers.randomElement()!)
    sleep(1)
}
```

Running this program should print something similar to the following:

```
Bessie: I'm eating...
Nanny: Yummy! Flower
Henrietta: I'm eating...
Bessie: I'm eating...
Billy: I'm eating...
Henrietta: I'm eating...
Nanny: I'm eating...
Nanny: Yummy! Flower
...
```

The type erasure pattern – a summary

As we've seen in this section, the type erasure pattern helps to use protocols with associated types when the implementation as generic constraints isn't desired. By following this pattern, you'll be able to move from the world of protocols to the world of concrete types with generics.

There are at least two common ways to implement the type erasure pattern. The first implementation lets you get away with simple protocols that are defined simply in terms of functions. As soon as one stored property is required by the protocol, you'll need to implement the fully fledged pattern, with the boxing and abstract classes.

In both cases, you'll need to implement the public wrapper class, so start with that.

In the case of simple protocols that expose only functions, you can benefit from powerful Swift functions and store the wrapped object's functions directly. Otherwise, you'll need to implement the boxing and abstract classes:

- Implement the public wrapper, conforming to your base protocol.
- If the protocol is method-based, store all private functions as properties on the wrapper.
- Otherwise, implement the abstract class and boxing.
- Implement calls forwarding in the public wrapper.

If you have played with Sourcery before, it is also possible to implement the type erasure patterns as a Sourcery stencil in order to reduce the boilerplate. Olivier Halligon maintains a repository of Sourcery stencils (https://github.com/AliSoftware/SourceryTemplates/blob/master/Templates/TypeErase.stencil) where you can find an implementation of it.

Template pattern with protocol-oriented programming

The template design pattern is a popular behavioral design pattern usually implemented with abstract classes. It helps design algorithms at a high level while letting subclasses or implementers modify or provide parts of it.

Protocol-oriented programming is particularly suited to implementing this pattern, as protocol extensions let you provide default implementations. Default implementations are perfect places to design and implement generic algorithms, as those algorithms can later be applied to a slew of concrete types.

To illustrate this design pattern, we'll build a simple recommendation engine that is tailored to the user's need.

A recommendation engine

A recommendation engine can be thought of as a software system that gives you the most relevant answer based on a list of objects:

```
protocol RecommendationEngine {
    associatedtype Model
    var models: [Model] { get }
    func filter(elements: [Model]) -> [Model]
    func sort(elements: [Model]) -> [Model]
}
```

We build our recommendation engine around two core methods—one for filtering out the undesired objects and the other around sorting; the most relevant results are always first.

Thanks to protocol extensions, we're able to provide the default implementation for the matching algorithm:

```
extension RecommendationEngine {
    func match() -> Model? {
        // If we only have 0 or 1 models, no need to run the algorithm
        guard models.count > 1 else { return models.first }

        return sort(elements: filter(elements: models)).first
    }
}
```

Now we have a fully functional protocol with associated types, with our killer and secret algorithm that's hidden from the recommendation engine's implementations.

Let's first make recommendations for restaurants and, to begin with, we want to show the user it's an all time favorite:

```
let restaurants = [
    Restaurant(name: "Tony's Pizza", beenThere: true, score: 2.0),
    Restaurant(name: "Krusty's", beenThere: true, score: 3.0),
    Restaurant(name: "Bob's burger", beenThere: false, score: 4.9)]
```

We added three restaurants into the database and have some information on them:

- The name of the restaurant
- Whether you've visited them or not
- The average score of the restaurant on the platform

See the following code:

```
struct FavoriteEngine: RecommendationEngine {
    var models: [Restaurant]
    // Filter only the restaurants where you've been
    func filter(elements: [Restaurant]) -> [Restaurant] {
        return elements.filter { $0.beenThere }
    }

    // Sort by the best score
    func sort(elements: [Restaurant]) -> [Restaurant] {
        return elements.sorted { $0.score > $1.score }
    }
}

let engine = FavoriteEngine(models: restaurants)
let match = engine.match() // Restaurant(name: "Krusty's"... )
```

Now that we can pull out the favorite restaurant, our users also want to get the best restaurant in town that you haven't visited yet, the one with the best score:

```
struct BestEngine: RecommendationEngine {
    var models: [Restaurant]
    func filter(elements: [Restaurant]) -> [Restaurant] {
        return elements.filter { !$0.beenThere }
    }
    func sort(elements: [Restaurant]) -> [Restaurant] {
        return elements.sorted { $0.score > $1.score }
    }
}
```

```
let engine = BestEngine(models: restaurants)
let match = engine.match() // Restaurant(name: "Bob's burger"... )
```

With the same base matching algorithm, we were able to provides two recommendation engines for restaurants.

You may also have noticed the duplication of the sorting algorithm: restaurants have a score property, and we can use it for the sorting. We can generalize it at protocol level as well, through conditional conformance, and remove the specific implementations in the recommendation engine implementations:

```
extension RecommendationEngine where Model == Restaurant {
    func sort(elements: [Model]) -> [Model] {
        return elements.sorted { $0.score > $1.score }
    }
}
```

With conditional conformance, remember you can conform to any type. As an exercise, you can rewrite part of this algorithm with protocols that expose the filtering or scoring primitives.

Summing up with the template method pattern

The template method pattern in Swift is particularly well implemented with protocols and extensions. Protocols let you efficiently abstract algorithms, their implementations relying on the requirements defined by the protocols themselves.

As we've seen, this pattern is particularly useful when only parts of an algorithm is dynamic and those changes can or should be deferred to subclasses and have no effect on the overall algorithm.

Summary

In this chapter, we jumped deep into Swift and the unique and most advanced features that lie in its powerful type system. Now, protocols with and without associated type and generics, as well as type erasure patterns, should hold no secrets for you.

Now you should be able to effectively employ protocols and their associated types and understand the difference between associated types and generics.

New and powerful features such as conditional conformance should now be mastered and you should be comfortable refactoring your code base to take advantage of it. Lastly, you can use this as a handbook to implement the type erasure pattern and come back to it every time you have a question around this hot topic.

This chapter concludes the second part of this book, which covered most of the well known object-oriented design patterns as well as some Swift specific goodies. As you may have understood now, protocols are a large part of Swift language and are helpful in a variety of situations.

The next part will focus on application architecture and how Swift features help you write better and more maintainable programs.

Using the Model-View-Controller Pattern

9

One of the most fundamental building blocks, when creating apps for iOS or macOS, is the view controller. Sometimes misused, sometimes dreaded, and often misunderstood, this component can be both your best ally and your worst enemy.

We'll go back to the **Model-View-Controller** (**MVC**) pattern in this chapter, looking at its origins and philosophy and exploring in the context of UIKit how we can turn this design pattern to our advantage when designing modern apps.

We'll start by refreshing ourselves on the basics of the MVC pattern, what each component should do, and how they fit together. We'll then revisit view controller life cycles, explore some best practices, and learn some decoupling strategies to keep the view controllers as lean as they should be.

In this chapter, we will look at the following:

- The theory behind the pattern
- An example of pure MVC
- MVC in the context of an iOS app using `UIViewController`
- View controller composition
- How to create model controllers to facilitate decoupling

A refresher on MVC

MVC is a design pattern that encourages separation of concerns. It was invented in 1978, and was generalized in the 80s. Smalltalk was the first language to make extensive use of this design pattern for the creation of user interfaces.

Objective-C, being heavily influenced by Smalltalk, then inherited this design pattern. AppKit and UIKit are also built around it.

While one could argue that other patterns can be just as efficient (or more so), MVC has the benefit of being widely understood by many developers, independent of their language of choice. MVC is widely used and is available in all object-oriented languages.

The theory behind the MVC pattern

Let's go back to the original description of the design pattern:

- **Model** classes are used to represent knowledge and data. A model can be represented as a single object or structures.
- **View** classes are used to represent the data to the user.
- **Controller** classes are used to validate input from the user, passing it to the model layer.

Now, there's a word that isn't properly defined: **user.** Usually, when we program applications and algorithms, the user is the human being at the other end of the program. This definition is misleading, as it perpetuates the idea that there should always be a human being inputting information into the controller, and that views are always graphical interfaces.

I would like to challenge this assumption and from now on, we will define a user as follows: the **program** or **human being** that consumes the output of the view layer. As such, part of the view layer can be a JSON or XML represented view, or a raw view, with pure data printed on-screen.

We can now rewrite the definition as follows:

- **Model** classes provide an internal representation of a component, as well as its ability to be loaded, restored, or persisted.
- **View** classes provide an external representation of a component that is consumable by another entity.
- **Controller** classes provide an entry point for external entities to interact with the model safely, and provide a view representation for feedback.

Finally, I will argue that the MVC pattern can be nested in itself. For example, the view layer can be represented by a **model**, a **controller** and a **view**. This last argument should not surprise you, as iOS and macOS both have `NSViewController` and `UIViewController` classes at the core of their UI frameworks.

A pure MVC example

Without further ado, let's implement a small program using this architectural pattern. It will be a command-line tool independent of AppKit or UIKit.

We'll build a small question/answer game, by decoupling every component in a proper Model-View-Controller manner.

First, we'll implement the model layer, with all of its components, including a model controller, which helps to implement parts of the loading logic.

Second, we'll take a look at the view layer, implemented with the help of a view controller and views. The view controller helps to organize the logic around the views on screen.

Finally, we'll tie the program together, with a controller responsible for organizing the logic between the view layer and the model layer.

The model layer

The model layer of our application will contain the following:

- The `Question` structure, responsible for holding the question string, as well as the expected answer (`true`/`false`)
- The `QuestionController` class, responsible for loading the questions as well as advancing to the next question:

```
// Question.swift
enum BooleanAnswer: String {
    case `true`
    case `false`
}

struct Question {
    let question: String
    let answer: BooleanAnswer
}

extension Question {
    func isGoodAnswer(result: String?) -> Bool {
        return result == answer.rawValue
    }
}

// QuestionController.swift
class QuestionController {
```

```
                    private var questions = [Question]()

                    // Load the questions from memory or disk
                    func load() { /* load from disk, memory or else */ }

                    // Get the next question, if available
                    func next() -> Question? {
                        return questions.popLast()
                    }
            }
```

As you notice, we have implemented our model with a controller, which helps us to perform complex logic at the model layer such as loading the questions from the network or from a local database.

The QuestionController can also be subclassed to accommodate one's needs with regard to specific questions to be loaded, different difficulty levels, and so on.

The view layer

Now that we have the model layer properly defined, let's take a look at the view layer. From here, we'll need to somehow display the current question.

We'll have a QuestionView, responsible for printing the question in the console, but it could also be responsible for a label on-screen in another scenario. We'll also have a PromptView, which will be used to display the prompt for the user to answer.

Finally, we'll have a ViewController, responsible for providing a simple interface that properly displays every question and prompt on-screen, as well as responding to the user on whether their answer was correct:

```
    struct QuestionView {
        func show(question: Question) {
            print(question.question)
        }
    }

    struct PromptView {
        func show() {
            print("> ", terminator: "")
        }
    }

    class ViewController {
        private let questionView = QuestionView()
```

```
        private let promptView = PromptView()

        func ask(question: Question) {
            questionView.show(question: question)
            promptView.show()
        }

        func goodAnswer() { /* implement me */ }
        func badAnswer() { /* implement me */ }
        func finishPlaying() { /* implement me */ }
    }
```

Again we have a controller in our view layer, which is what's expected. A `ViewController` is a general controller, responsible for orchestrating views inside the view layer, which is its only responsibility.

We have no logic around prompting the user, reading their input, and so on. Remember that we're in the view layer, and the view layer's responsibility is to display information, not to gather input. For that, let's look at the controller layer implementation.

The controller layer

The main controller will be called `GameController`, because it manages everything about the current game.

It creates an instance of the `QuestionController` from the model layer, and an instance of a `ViewController` from the view layer:

```
class GameController {
    private let questions = QuestionController()
    private let view = ViewController()

    private func waitForAnswer(question: Question) {
        // Wait for user input
        let result = readLine()
        // Ask the model if answer is good
        if question.isGoodAnswer(result: result) {
            // Update the view
            view.goodAnswer()
        } else {
            view.badAnswer()
        }
    }

    func start() {
        // From the model layer, get the next question
```

```
        while let question = questions.next() {
            // Display the question on screen
            view.ask(question: question)
            waitForAnswer(question: question)
        }
        view.finishPlaying()
    }
}
```

It is now possible to run the game, as follows:

```
// main.swift
GameController().start()
```

With this implementation, we have fully achieved the MVC design pattern:

- A separation of concerns: the model, view, and controller layers are properly separated
- The model layer is responsible for all business logic
- The controller layer is orchestrating
- The view layer is solely responsible for displaying data to the user

With this simple example, we were able to demonstrate the power of the MVC pattern in encouraging proper separation of concerns and isolation of components. We also learned that we can have ViewControllers that don't belong in the controller layer of the application, but in the view layer, instead. They are controllers, but their responsibilities do not extend outside of the view layer.

Often, we see UIViewController and NSViewController suffer from **Massive View Controller** syndrome, as developers fail to realize this small but important detail. When view controllers grow and embed logic for the model layer, as well as take responsibility for complex view hierarchies, we get into the area of Massive View Controllers.

We can now move on to the specificities of UIViewController and NSViewController: how to use them efficiently, and how they fit into Swift programming for iOS and macOS.

UIViewController

Having properly framed the MVC pattern in a general context, we can take a look at the specificities of UIViewController.

The best way to get a proper understanding of view controllers is to consult the official documentation at `https://developer.apple.com/documentation/uikit/uiviewcontroller`:

> *"The UIViewController class defines the shared behavior that is common to all view controllers. You rarely create instances of the UIViewController class directly. Instead, you subclass UIViewController and add the methods and properties needed to manage the view controller's view hierarchy."*

From this quote, we can gather the following:

- `UIViewController` provides shared behaviors
- Those behaviors are intended to be used on view controllers
- You use subclassing in order to benefit from those behaviors
- You use subclassing in order to manage the view controller/views hierarchy

Something interesting about this quote; it doesn't talk about application state, networking, or persistence; the only components that are mentioned are views.

A view controller's responsibilities include the following:

- Updating the contents of the views, usually in response to changes to the underlying data
- Responding to user interactions with views
- Resizing views and managing the layout of the overall interface
- Coordinating with other objects—including other view controllers—in your app

When looking at these responsibilities, we can see that this category of objects doesn't belong to the controller layer, but to the view layer of the MVC pattern.

View controller life cycles

View controllers are responsible for managing a single view hierarchy. The top-level view, containing all of the subviews, is stored in the `view` property of the view controller.

There are multiple ways to provide a `UIViewController` with a view:

- In a storyboard, you can design the complete view hierarchies of multiple view controllers, embed controllers, and use advanced features such as segues and transitions. Storyboards can get very complex quickly, and many developers prefer not to use them. For me, though, they are a very powerful tool, to be used with great care.
- From a nib, which lets you define a single `UIViewController`. Nibs have the advantage of being more lightweight than storyboards, but they are also less powerful, as they don't support controller embedding and references to external nibs.
- Using the `loadView()` method, and creating the complete view hierarchy programmatically. When using `loadView()`, it is possible to load the views from many nibs and assemble them together in a unique view hierarchy.

When displaying a view controller on-screen, whether from a modal presentation, inside a navigation controller, or directly from the application's delegate window, methods will be called to help you manage its life cycle. They are as follows:

- `viewDidLoad()` is called when the view loading has been performed, usually after the first access to the view property
- `viewWillAppear(Bool)` is called just before the view is added to a view hierarchy
- `viewDidAppear(Bool)` is called when the view has been added to a view hierarchy
- `viewWillDisappear(Bool)` is called when the view will be removed from a view hierarchy
- `viewDidDisappear(Bool)` is called when the view has been removed from a view hierarchy

 These methods are called by UIKit. It is recommended that you avoid calling them manually; and when overriding them, you should always call `super`. Try to ensure that the life cycles of your view controllers fit inside the UIKit flow.

Now, let's have a look at some anti-patterns that you should avoid with `UIViewController`.

UIViewController anti-patterns

With great power comes great responsibility, and the UIViewController is a very powerful class. It's important to take care, or you could end up with leaks or other performance issues.

Let's go over some of the most common anti-patterns that we see in iOS applications involving UIViewControllers.

Early view instantiation

Consider the following code snippet:

```
// BadViewController.swift
class BadViewController: UIViewController {
    init() {
        super.init(nibName: nil, bundle: nil)
        self.view = UIView(frame: .zero)
    }

    required init?(coder aDecoder: NSCoder) { fatalError() }
}

// inside another view controller
let badViewController = BadViewController()
present(badViewController, animated: true, completion: nil)
```

While everything looks correct on the surface, we have created the View property at initialization, which is not the way to set the View property on a view controller. Instead, you should use the loadView(), method to do this.

 Never initialize a view in the constructor of a UIViewController—always use loadView() to create them programmatically.

Early view access in initializer

Sometimes, you will want a view controller to always have the same fixed bounds, such as, for example, the width of the screen. Suppose that you have designed a nib with the view defined into it, and you want to make sure that whenever you create a new instance of this controller, the size will always be correct.

You may be tempted to write the following code:

```
class OtherBadController: UIViewController {
    init() {
        super.init(nibName: "OtherBadController", bundle: nil)
        print("before")
        let width = UIScreen.main.bounds.width
        self.view.frame = CGRect(x: 0, y: 0, width: width, height: width)
        print("after")
    }
    override func viewDidLoad() {
        super.viewDidLoad()
        print("loaded")
    }
}

// Output:
before
loaded
after
```

In this example, where we have accessed the view inside the constructor, we can see that the view loading takes place within the constructor, as loaded is logged before after.

You will want to avoid this order at all costs, and ensure that your view controller constructors are properly completed before any view loading occurs. When loading complex view controller hierarchies, this can lead to serious performance problems, and can render your apps unresponsive.

 Always ensure that the view loading mechanisms are triggered in line with other view loading mechanisms, and never during a constructor. Always load or add your subviews in loadView() or viewDidLoad().

Early view access in properties

The preceding example made it clear that we should not load views in the constructor. Now, consider the following generic code that helps us to write controllers with an asynchronous state:

```
enum State<T> {
    case unknown, loading
    case loaded(T)
    case error(Error)
}
```

```
class StateController<T>: UIViewController {
    var state: State<T> = .unknown {
        didSet { updateState() }
    }

    private func updateState() {
        switch state {
        case .loading:
            view.alpha = 0.0 // make it transparent while loading
        case .loaded(_):
            view.alpha = 1.0 // show it when loaded
        default: break;
        }
    }
}

// In another view controller
let controller = StateController<String>()
controller.state = .loading
present(controller, animated: true, completion: nil)
```

This example is a bit trickier, and you may not identify what is wrong at first glance. Here, we have a state property that, when set, will call updateState(), which, in turn, will access the view property in order to toggle its alpha property.

As we know, view is lazily loaded, and the first call to it will be for it to be loaded; therefore, viewDidLoad() is to be called. The problem here is that at the time we set state to .loading, the view controller isn't responsible for any view on the screen. We have again accessed the view outside of UIKit's own life cycle.

Luckily for us, we can solve this problem easily as follows:

1. We need to prevent the view from loading as long as the view isn't on screen
2. As soon as the view is loaded, we should display the current state:

```
class StateController<T>: UIViewController {
    var state: State<T> = .unknown {
        didSet {
            // avoid accessing the view unnecessarily
            guard isViewLoaded else { return }
            updateState()
        }
    }

    override func viewDidLoad() {
        super.viewDidLoad()
        // ensure we show the right state on screen
```

```
                updateState()
        }
        private func updateState() { /* same implementation */ }
}
```

 Always ensure that setting external properties won't trigger a loading cycle for the view. Those issues are among the hardest to detect and identify.

As your project grows, keeping each view controller properly encapsulated and loading within UIKit's or AppKit's life cycles is critical to guaranteeing smooth transitions and efficient memory management.

The issues that we discussed here are common, so check for them in your implementations! In the next section, we'll detail a powerful tool that will help avoid Massive View Controller syndrome, child view controllers, and view controller composition.

Composition and child view controllers

As you saw previously, you should always pay attention to the view life cycle and never rush it. Another thing that we need to pay attention to is the size of our view controller. Smaller view controllers are beneficial for the following:

- **Reusability**: Smaller view controllers are reusable, as they tend to be very specialized.
- **Testability**: A small view controller has a smaller footprint and a smaller API. Having a smaller API makes it easier to test.
- **Maintainability**: Isolating features and components always helps with the separation of concerns.

All of these features come for free when you compose your view controllers accordingly.

Composing view controllers implies using a custom container view controller. The container view controller will be responsible for maintaining the hierarchy of controllers, as well as the views provided by those child view controllers.

Adding child view controllers

Adding a child view controller is possible with the `func addChild(_ childController: UIViewController)` available on `UIViewController` instances. When using this function, you effectively create a strong relationship between the container view controller and the child view controller.

This relationship is necessary, in order to make sure that all the container view controller lifecycle calls are properly forwarded to the children. Doing so will ensure the child view controllers behave like standalone view controllers.

The following is a snippet that will help you safely add a child view controller with animations:

```
extension UIViewController {
    func add(_ childController: UIViewController,
            with animations: (() -> Void)? = nil,
            duration: TimeInterval? = nil) {
        view.addSubview(childController.view)
        addChild(childController)
        if let animations = animations,
            let duration = duration {
            UIView.animate(withDuration: duration, animations:
              animations) { (done) in
                childController.didMove(toParent: self)
            }
        } else {
            childController.didMove(toParent: self)
        }
    }
}
```

The UIKit documentation (https://developer.apple.com/documentation/uikit/uiviewcontroller/1621405-didmove) specifies that you need to manually call `didMove(toParent:)` either right after adding the child view controller, or just after all transitions and animations have been performed.

Removing child view controllers

Once you have added view controllers to a container controller, you may want to remove them if the relationship between those controllers is no longer needed. For example you may want to animate a child view controller through custom transitioning from one view controller to another, and back again. When performing such a transition, you will need to do the following:

- Remove the child controller(s) from their container controller
- Add the child to the next owning controller

When performing the operation on the way back, you will need to perform those steps in the opposite order:

```
extension UIViewController {
    func remove(_ childController: UIViewController,
            with animations: (() -> Void)? = nil,
            duration: TimeInterval? = nil) {
        childController.willMove(toParent: nil)
        if let animations = animations,
            let duration = duration {
            UIView.animate(withDuration: duration, animations: animations)
    { (done) in
                childController.view.removeFromSuperview()
                childController.removeFromParent()
            }
        } else {
            childController.view.removeFromSuperview()
            childController.removeFromParent()
        }
    }
}
```

This extension will help you properly remove a child controller and its view, with or without animations, and will always ensure that all methods are properly called. Note that it's implemented on `UIViewController` but is never itself used. It can be implemented as a static method, or right on the child controller itself.

Using view controller composition

As we have seen in this section, composing view controllers is a powerful design pattern that will help you do the following:

- Keep the view controllers simple
- Reduce the overall complexity
- Encourage reusability

This pattern can be used programmatically or with storyboards. When using this pattern with storyboards, the interface builder lets you reference controllers that are declared in any storyboard of your project. You should prefer the method of splitting your controllers and storyboards, as loading large storyboards can have a dramatic impact on performance at development time or runtime.

The model layer

Now that we have covered view controllers and how they relate to views and controllers, let's take some time to look at the model layer.

Just as your controllers (other than view controllers) should not hold logic relating to views and subviews, they shouldn't hold any logic relating to the model layer. Controllers are simply bridges that get their information from the models, and update the view to reflect the current state.

Using model controllers

Just as we have controllers dedicated to managing views—the view controllers—you should consider using controllers to help communicate with complex model layers. Code bases that suffer from Massive View Controller syndrome often exhibit the following pathologies in their view controllers:

- Network calls, logic, and parsing
- Caches, data stores, or Core Data logic
- Business logic or validators

Let's first start with an interface for a message composer that exhibits Massive View Controller syndrome:

```
class MassiveViewController : UIViewController {
    var textView = UITextView()
    var sendButton = UIButton()

    override func viewDidLoad() {
        super.viewDidLoad()
        /* layout the views */
        /* design the views */
    }

    func sendTapped(sender: UIButton) {
        if textView.text.count == 0 {
            // display error
        } else {
            postMessage(message: textView.text) { (success, error) in
                if success {
                    // all good
                } else if let error = error {
                    // Show an error alert
                }
            }
        }
    }

    struct BooleanResponse: Codable {
        let success: Bool
    }

    struct MessageRequest: Codable {
        let message: String
    }

    private func postMessage(message: String,
                            callback: @escaping (Bool, Error?) -> Void) {
        let messagePayload = MessageRequest(message: message)
        var request = URLRequest(url: postMessageAPIURL)
        request.httpMethod = "POST"
        do {
            try request.httpBody = JSONEncoder().encode(messagePayload)
        } catch let error {
            callback(false, error)
            return
        }

        URLSession.shared.dataTask(with: request) { (data, response, error)
```

```
in
            if let error = error {
                callback(false, error)
            } else if let data = data {
                do {
                    let result = try
JSONDecoder().decode(BooleanResponse.self, from: data)
                    callback(result.success, nil)
                } catch let error {
                    callback(false, error)
                }
            }
        }
    }
}
```

In the preceding code example, we have the following issues:

- The content validation is done at the view controller level
- The network logic, encoding, and decoding
- The error handling

As all the code is set into a view controller, when this controller grows in features and design it will quickly become unmaintainable. Let's refactor with the following goals in mind:

- The view controller should be responsible for view handling and exposing its state
- Network calls should be extracted to their own controller
- Validation should be extracted, as more rules may be added later

Refactoring controllers

In order to properly refactor a Massive View Controller and isolate the model layer, we have to start by refactoring the Massive View Controller. We'll use delegation to communicate whenever the view controller needs an external action to be performed.

View controllers

Let's begin the refactoring of our view controller, as follows:

```
protocol ComposeViewControllerDelegate: AnyObject {
    func composeViewController(_ controller: ComposeViewController,
                              attemptToSend message: String)
}

class ComposeViewController: UIViewController {
    enum State {
    case `default`
    case error(Error)
    case sending
    }
    private var textView = UITextView()
    private var sendButton = UIButton()
    weak var delegate: ComposeViewControllerDelegate?
    var state: State = .default {
        didSet { /* todo handle state */ }
    }
    func sendTapped(sender: UIButton) {
        delegate?.composeViewController(self, attemptToSend: textView.text)
    }
}
```

The view controller is now completely focused on managing views. It is easier to extend and to manage. If we have more actions to add in the future, such as picking a photo or gif, it is easier to add this feature without cluttering the code for the composition message.

Model controllers

The next step is to extract validation and networking logic into their own controllers. That way, we can easily extend their features, while maintaining a simple API surface:

```
class PostMessageNetworking {
    func post(message: String,
            callback: @escaping (Bool, Error?) -> Void) {
        /* original call */
    }
}

class MessageValidator {
    enum ValidationError: Error {
    case emptyMessage
    }
```

```
func validate(message: String) -> ValidationError? {
    if message.count == 0 {
        return .emptyMessage
    }
    return nil
}
```

We extracted both features, validation and networking, into two independent controllers for the model layer. As you can see, none of them interact with the view layer. Their interfaces are simple: one has a callback, the other returns an optional `Error`.

All of the logic is done, and we can test every component independently and easily:

- The view controller can be subjected to UI testing, in order to ensure that the button tap calls the delegate properly, and so on.
- The network controller can be tested against serialization.
- The validator can be unit tested.

The last step is to implement the controller that will tie all those objects together.

The Controller

Tying everything together now is straightforward. We need to port in the message-sending logic, as well as the error handling; and we should be done:

```
class PostMessageController: ComposeViewControllerDelegate {
```

Store references to the view controller, validation controller, and networking controller as follows:

```
let viewController = ComposeViewController()
let validator = MessageValidator()
let networking = PostMessageNetworking()

init() {
    viewController.delegate = self
}
```

The `delegate` method implementation: The implementation here is the core of the logic that ties the *view* layer to the *model* layer (which is the responsibility of the *controller* layer).

This method validates the message, attempts to send it, and updates the view layer to provide feedback to the user through the `state` property of the `ComposeViewController`:

```
func composeViewController(_ viewController: ComposeViewController,
                           attemptToSend message: String) {
    if let error = validator.validate(message: message) {
        viewController.state = .error(error)
        return
    }

    viewController.state = .sending
    networking.post(message: message) { (success, error) in
        if let error = error {
            viewController.state = .error(error)
        } else {
            viewController.state = .default
        }
    }
}
```

`PostMessageController` has been implemented as a true controller, in the MVC sense. It showcases how one controller can and should orchestrate the communication between the view layer and the model layer. Implementing this design pattern will ultimately improve the quality of your code base.

Summary

The MVC pattern should now hold no confusion for you. We have seen in this chapter how this design pattern is widely misunderstood on iOS, and often leads to Massive View Controller syndrome. Hopefully, you should now be able to refactor your code to improve the readability and maintainability of your view controllers, and properly isolate each layer.

We discussed how to use view controller composition with child view controllers, in order to reduce overly complex view controllers or views.

In a nutshell, you should always ensure view controllers only have view layout logic, and increase separation by focusing the responsibilities of each view controller as much as possible. Never forget you can create controllers, model controllers, or other pure objects to help hold your programs together while keeping your view controllers clean.

Following this recommendation should increase the quality of your code base if you're using the MVC pattern across your project.

In the next chapter, we will cover another architectural pattern: the **Model-View-ViewModel** (**MVVM**) pattern. Often presented as a competitive solution to MVC, the MVVM pattern has its own advantages and drawbacks. The following chapter will provide a comprehensive overview of MVVM.

Model-View-ViewModel in Swift 10

In the previous chapter, we detailed how the **Model-View-Controller (MVC)** pattern can be factored in an intuitive and scalable manner. While pervasive in all Cocoa environments, MVC is not the only valid architectural pattern that can be used in Swift. At Microsoft, while working on even driven programming for user interfaces, Ken Cooper and Ted Peters invented the **Model-View-ViewModel (MVVM)** pattern. In the MVVM pattern, views bind on `ViewModels`. Through this binding, `ViewModel` provides objects and methods from the `Model` layer to the `View` layer.

In this chapter, we'll cover the following topics:

- The basics of MVVM
- How to refactor existing MVC code, in order to leverage MVVM
- How to properly use MVVM in complex view controllers
- The advantages and limitations of MVVM

Basics of the MVVM pattern

The MVVM pattern involves three different components. You should be familiar with two of them:

- **Model**: This is the same model as in MVC, and it represents knowledge and data.
- **View**: This is the same as in the MVC pattern; it provides an external representation that is understandable by the user, whether human or machine.
- **ViewModel**: This is the model for a view (duh!). It represents the whole state of the view, and exposes behaviors.

 What about `UIViewControllers` and `NSViewControllers`?

They belong to the `View` layer (think back to the previous chapter). We will inject `ViewModels` in either the views or the `viewControllers`.

Refactoring MVC into MVVM

We will reuse the previous example, the Question/Answer game, but this time, instead of writing it following a pure MVC pattern, we'll use the MVVM pattern.

As with the previous implementation (with the MVC pattern), we'll cover each layer, one after the other, in order to not miss anything.

Model

The model layer still contains the `Question` structure and the `QuestionController` class. We can keep those components as they are. The `ViewModel` pattern is used to bind the model layer to the view layer, and its responsibility is to abstract the details of rendering the model into a view:

```swift
// Question.swift
enum BooleanAnswer: String {
    case `true`
    case `false`
}

struct Question {
    let question: String
    let answer: BooleanAnswer
}

extension Question {
    func isGoodAnswer(result: String?) -> Bool {
        return result == answer.rawValue
    }
}

// QuestionController.swift
class QuestionController {
    private var questions = [Question]()

    // Load the questions from memory or disk
    func load() { /* load from disk, memory or else */ }

    // Get the next question, if available
    func next() -> Question? {
        return questions.popLast()
    }
}
```

Unlike with the MVC design pattern, where we want to design our views before tying everything up with the controllers, we won't jump right into the `View` layer. With this pattern, it is more natural to write the `ViewModel` first.

ViewModel

`ViewModel`, as mentioned previously, is meant to provide a usable representation of `Model` to the `View` layer. It will also provide a way to **bind** itself to events. In Swift, we can use closures, in order to attach the callbacks to `ViewModel`:

```
class ViewModel {
```

Other solutions, including two-way data binding, Observables, and Functional Reactive Programming, provide abstractions over the manual binding example that we'll be performing here. If you were to use MVVM extensively, I'd recommend that you properly leveraged two-way data binding.

Similar to `ApplicationController` in the MVC pattern, we'll keep track of the main `Model` manager, which is the `QuestionController` in `ViewModel`:

```
private let questions = QuestionController()
```

Keeping track of `currentQuestion` is crucial in `ViewModel`, as it should represent the state of `View` at anytime. We'll use the `didSet` feature of Swift members, in order to fire the `onQuestionChanged` callback:

```
private var currentQuestion: Question? = nil {
    didSet { onQuestionChanged?() }
}
```

The next two declarations will make the most of the public API. The `viewModel` exposes two callbacks, to indicate internal changes in `viewModel`. These callbacks will be triggered whenever the program advances to the next question, and when an answer has been given by the user:

```
var onQuestionChanged: (() -> Void)?
var onAnswer: ((Bool) -> Void)?
```

Unlike the MVC example, the `Question` model is not exposed to `View`, as a single parameter is needed to display the question to the user. This is a deliberate design choice; depending on your case, you'll probably resort to an intermediate representation of your model. Using intermediate representations makes your views more flexible to work with:

```swift
func getQuestionText() -> String? {
    return currentQuestion?.question
}
```

The rest of the logic of `ViewModel` exposes the `start()` method, which starts the game and provides a way to read the answer from the command line:

```swift
func start() {
    while let question = nextQuestion() {
        waitForAnswer(question: question)
    }
}
private func waitForAnswer(question: Question) {
    let result = readLine()
    onAnswer?(question.isGoodAnswer(result: result))
}

private func nextQuestion() -> Question? {
    currentQuestion = questions.next()
    return currentQuestion
}
}
```

The `viewModel` is now feature-complete. It abstracts all of the undesired parts of the model away from the `View` layer, and exposes simple callbacks and objects for the view to work with.

 In the `ViewModel`, the `readline()` call is hardcoded, making this `viewModel` unsuitable for use in a context other than the command line. There are multiple ways to refactor it, by subclassing or injection.

As you may have guessed, some refactoring will be needed in the `View` layer, in order to integrate the implementation of `ViewModel`.

View

In the view layer, we originally had a `QuestionView`, responsible for printing the question in the console, as well as a `PromptView`. Both can still live in our new model. They had simple interfaces, and were completely stateless, as follows:

```
struct QuestionView {
    func show(question: Question) {
        print(question.question)
    }
}

struct PromptView {
    func show() {
        print("> ", terminator: "")
    }
}
```

We also have `ViewController`. This class is our main entry point for the `View` layer. It will keep its responsibilities, ask the questions, gain user input features, and bind the `viewModel`. We can call it `MainView`:

```
class MainView {
private let questionView = QuestionView()
private let promptView = PromptView()
```

Initialization will now require to pass `ViewModel`. Often, in the MVVM pattern, the `viewModel` is attached to the following:

```
let viewModel: ViewModel
init(viewModel: ViewModel) {
    self.viewModel = viewModel
    bindViewModel()
}
```

Binding `ViewModel` is the core of the implementation. As it is event-driven, the implementation will require us to set the closures on the `viewModel` object. In response to the events that are sent by `viewModel`, `View` will update and print the appropriate information:

```
func bindViewModel() {
```

The onQuestionChanged handler contains a bit of logic, as viewModel represents the end of the game when it feeds a nil question to the view. It gives the opportunity to view to display a final message:

```
viewModel.onQuestionChanged = { [unowned self] in
    guard let string = self.viewModel.getQuestionText() else {
        // No more questions?
        self.finishPlaying()
        return
    }
    self.ask(question: string)
}
```

The onAnswer handler is very straightforward. A question has been answered by the user, and viewModel has determined that the answer wasn't right. Use isGood: Bool to determine whether the program should congratulate the user or tell them that their answer was inaccurate, as follows:

```
viewModel.onAnswer = { [unowned self] (isGood) -> Void in
    if isGood {
        self.goodAnswer()
    } else {
        self.badAnswer()
    }
}
```

The rest of the implementation for this class is similar to the one in the MVC example:

```
private func ask(question: Question) {
    questionView.show(question: question)
    promptView.show()
}

func goodAnswer() { /* implement me */ }
func badAnswer() { /* implement me */ }
func finishPlaying() { /* implement me */ }
}
```

This completes the refactoring of our game, using the MVVM pattern. As you have seen, the responsibilities have shifted around. The view binds itself on a ViewModel, completely isolating it from the rest of the program. The model layer is still identical, which indicates that we did a great job in our refactoring.

Using the new program is straightforward, as well:

```
// Create a new ViewModel instance
let viewModel = ViewModel()
// Inject the viewModel into the view
let view = View(viewModel: viewModel)
// Start the viewModel
viewModel.start()
```

By starting the `viewModel`, the events will start to fire and the view will update, prompting the user for questions.

Benefits and drawbacks of MVVM

As with any other design pattern, the MVVM pattern has benefits and drawbacks. If we compare it to the MVC pattern, we can clearly see that it dumbed down the view layer, making it merely respond to events from the `viewModel`. This is very important, as it allows us to do the following:

- Test the `ViewModel` independently
- Test the view with a mocked `viewModel`

In the MVC pattern, testing controllers are harder, as the controller holds the logic, as well as references to the model and views. Even if the `ViewModel` makes you feel like it belongs to the view, it really belongs more to the model in the same way, the `ViewController` should be thought of as belonging to the view layer.

Enhanced testing

Because the whole state of the view can be tested externally, thanks to the MVVM pattern, we can write better and more maintainable code. Let's look at how we can properly test the logic of the `ViewModel`, in order to ensure that the views bound to it will react properly.

Ultimately, we need to ensure the following:

- When a question advances to the next one, the `onQuestionChanged` callback is properly called.
- When there are no more questions, `getQuestionText()` returns `nil`:

```
class ViewModelTesting: XCTestCase {
    func testCallsNextQuestion() {
        let questions = QuestionController(questions:
```

```
[Question(question: "OK", answer: .true)])
        let viewModel = ViewModel(questions: questions)
        var called = false
        viewModel.onQuestionChanged = {
            called = true
        }
        let question  = viewModel.nextQuestion()
        XCTAssert(called)
        XCTAssertNotNil(question)
    }
    func testFinished() {
        let viewModel = ViewModel(questions:
QuestionController(questions: []))
        var called = false
        viewModel.onQuestionChanged = {
            called = true
        }
        let question  = viewModel.nextQuestion()
        XCTAssertNil(question)
        XCTAssertNil(viewModel.getQuestionText())
        XCTAssert(called)
    }
}
```

In order to further enable testability, we'd need to remove the strong dependency on the `readline()` call in the `ViewModel` class. This would let us return any string value synchronously, and further test the logic of the `ViewModel`. This technique is called dependency injection, and we'll cover it in depth in the next chapter.

As it is, we can already test large parts of this simple program, as all of the components are properly isolated. By using the MVVM pattern, we were able to further abstract the relationship between a view and its state and behavior.

Improved reusability

As we've seen with testing, the MVVM pattern encourages the proper isolation of the different components. Not unlike MVC, it encourages the following:

- A clean separation of the model layer
- A clean separation of the view layer

We've also seen that most of the views have been reused, between the MVC example and this one. We only needed to refactor the `ViewController` from the MVC example into the `MainView` class.

The refactor was required because the view layer in the MVVM pattern has to be bound to `ViewModel`. In practice, you'll mostly use `UIViewController` and `NSViewController`, in order to hold `viewModel`, as it fits very well into the philosophy of Cocoa, UIKit, and AppKit.

Drawbacks

As with every solution, using the MVVM pattern is not a silver bullet. The pattern can become an anti-pattern and a performance bottleneck if poorly used, due to the following factors:

- It's largely overkill for simple use cases.
- It relies heavily on manual or two-way binding, which isn't Swift-native.
- Large viewModels tend to be very hard to design upfront.
- Stream- and event-based programming can lead to races, and can be hard to debug.

These drawbacks may not be problematic for your use cases, but you have to keep in mind that they will always be a part of the compromises that you make to use MVVM.

MVVM and data binding

While data binding and two-way data binding are not required to use MVVM, you saw in the previous example that binding actions and values is tedious, a source of boilerplate, and prone to errors.

While data binding is usually found in Reactive programming frameworks, it revolves around a simple object: the `Observable` object. The responsibility of an observable is to call the observers whenever a change in the internal value occurs.

Implementing the Observable class

We'll implement `Observable` as a generic class, as it should be able to wrap any kind of object:

```
class Observable<Type> {
    typealias Observer = (Type) -> ()
    typealias Token = NSObjectProtocol
    private var observers = [(Token, Observer)]()
```

```swift
        var value: Type {
            didSet {
                notify()
            }
        }
        init(_ value: Type) {
            self.value = value
        }

        @discardableResult
        func bind(_ observer: @escaping Observer) -> Token {
            defer { observer(value) }
            let obj = NSObject()
            observers.append((obj, observer))
            return obj
        }

        func unbind(_ token: Token) {
            observers.removeAll { $0.0.isEqual(token) }
        }
        private func notify() {
            observers.forEach { (_, observer) in
                observer(value)
            }
        }
    }
}
```

We can demonstrate the capabilities of this `Observer<Type>` object through the following snippet:

```swift
let observable = Observable("")
let token0 = observable.bind {
    print("Changed 0: \($0)")
}
observable.value = "OK"
let token1 = observable.bind {
    print("Changed 1: \($0)")
}
observable.unbind(token1)
observable.value = "NOK"

// Output:
Changed 0:              // initial binding
Changed 0: OK           // the value is set to OK, notifying
Changed 1: OK           // initial binding of second observer
Changed 0: NOK          // The value is set to NOK, notifying
```

With the `Observable<Type>` class, we are able to subscribe to changes occurring at the model layer. The next step is to **bind** the observable to `UIKit` elements, which can have their values change.

Implementing the Binding protocol

`UIControls`, like `UISwitch`, `UITextView`, and `UISlider`, emit events when their underlying values have changed. On the other hand, we have the `Observable` object that also emits events when the underlying value changes. Using what we have learned about protocol-oriented programming, we'll extend `UIControls`, in order to be able to bind them.

First, let's look at the `Bindable` protocol:

```
protocol Bindable: AnyObject {
    associatedtype BoundType
    var boundValue: BoundType { get set }
}
```

We'll use the `boundValue` member as a proxy. The getters should always return the current value of the component, and the setter should update the value:

```
extension Bindable where Self: NSObjectProtocol {
    private var observable: Observable<BoundType>? {
        get {
            return objc_getAssociatedObject(self,
&BindableAssociatedKeys.observable) as? Observable<BoundType>
        }
        set {
            objc_setAssociatedObject(self,
&BindableAssociatedKeys.observable, newValue, .OBJC_ASSOCIATION_ASSIGN)
        }
    }
}
```

 The `Association` type is `OBJC_ASSOCIATION_ASSIGN`; we don't want to extend the life cycle of the observable, as we use it for a backward reference.

The next extension is specific to `UIControl`; it lets us use the `bind()` function, in order:

```
extension Bindable where Self: UIControl {
    private var target: Target? {
```

```
        get {
            return objc_getAssociatedObject(self,
&BindableAssociatedKeys.box) as? Target
        }
        set {
            objc_setAssociatedObject(self, &BindableAssociatedKeys.box,
newValue, .OBJC_ASSOCIATION_RETAIN)
        }
    }
```

The `Association` type is `OBJC_ASSOCIATION_RETAIN`, **as we need to keep the target alive alongside the object:**

```
    mutating func bind(_ observable: Observable<BoundType>) {
        // use a target proxy to get all Objective-C bound events through
the selector.
        // We cannot add a protocol as a target
        let target = Target()
        vew.r this = self
        target.onValueChanged = {
            // set the value to the source
            this.observable?.value = this.boundValue
        }
        observable.bind { (value) in
            // the source has changed, update the current value
            this.boundValue = value
        }
        addTarget(target, action: #selector(Target.valueChanged), for:
[.editingChanged, .valueChanged])
        self.observable = observable
        self.target = target
    }
}
```

The `Target` class is quite simple:

```
internal class Target {
    var onValueChanged: (() -> ())?
    @objc func valueChanged() {
        onValueChanged?()
    }
}
```

Now that we have implemented the `Binding` protocol, as well as the helper functions for `UIControl` types, we can move on to the concrete extension of `UIControl` subclasses.

Two-way binding on UITextField

The only piece of the protocol that isn't implemented is the `var boundValue: BoundType` member. As we're implementing on `UITextField`, `BoundType` will be `String?`, as it is the type of the string property:

```
extension UITextField: Bindable {
    var boundValue: String? {
        get { return self.text }
        set { self.text = newValue }
    }
}
```

We can now use it all, with the following example:

```
let observable = Observable<String?>("Let's get started")
var textField = UITextField(frame: .zero)
textField.bind(observable)
print("1. \(textField.text!)")
observable.value = "Are you Ready?"
print("2. \(textField.text!)")
textField.text = "YES!"
textField.sendActions(for: .valueChanged)
print("3. \(observable.value!)")

// Output:
1. Let's get started       // the text field value has been automatically
set
2. Are you Ready?          // Updating the value in the observable,
updates the text
3. YES!                    // Setting the value in field, updates the
model
```

This concludes the implementation of the `Observable` class and the `Binding` protocol. In the next section, we'll look at how to use two-way binding alongside a complex form.

Using Observables with ViewModels

The `Observable` and `Binding` protocols help to reduce the boilerplate that's necessary when binding a particular view or control to the viewModel's properties.

Let's suppose that we have a simple form for registering users, with their name, password, and age. It can be represented with the following `ViewModel`:

```
class SignupViewModel {
    var username = Observable<String?>(nil)
    var email = Observable<String?>(nil)
    var age = Observable<Double>(0.0)
}

extension SignupViewModel  {
    var description: String {
        return """
username: \(username.value ?? "")
email: \(email.value ?? "")
age: \(age.value)
"""
    }
}
```

With the `ViewModel` configured, we can take a look at `SignupViewController`. It is quite simple, with a few text fields and a stepper to set the age:

```
class SignupViewController: UIViewController {
    @IBOutlet var ageStepper: UIStepper!
    @IBOutlet var ageLabel: UILabel!
    @IBOutlet var usernameField: UITextField!
    @IBOutlet var emailField: UITextField!
    var viewModel: ViewModel! {
        didSet {
            bindViewModel()
        }
    }

    func bindViewModel() {
        // Ensure the view is loaded
        guard isViewLoaded else { return }
        ageStepper.bind(viewModel.age)
        usernameField.bind(viewModel.username)
        emailField.bind(viewModel.email)
        // Bind the viewModel.age value to the label
        // The stepper update the viewModel, which update the label
        viewModel.age.bind { (age) in
            self.ageLabel.text = "age: \(age)"
        }
    }
}
```

The view model will always stay in sync with the view representation. The two-way data binding guarantees that events from the model are properly propagated to the views that display them on screen, and also that each user input is properly stored in the view model.

The view layer is really dumbed down, to the point of simply being responsible for binding the view model. With the help of the `Observable` and the `Binding` protocol, the amount of boilerplate was reduced to a minimum, and the implementation in the view controller is straightforward.

Summary

In conclusion, you should now be able to understand when it makes sense to use the MVVM pattern, and its advantages and limitations over the more native MVC pattern.

We also quickly covered the use of two-way data binding, and how this technique, borrowed from the Reactive world, can help you to bind view models to their views simply and effectively.

 Architectural patterns are not a one-size-fits-all solution. It is appropriate and actually encouraged, to leverage the right solutions for the right problems. Always be mindful when adopting a pattern, as each has its benefits and drawbacks.

We can compare the MVVM philosophy to the dependency injection technique. In this technique, the elements that are required for an object or function to perform a particular task (in the MVVM, it would be the view model) are provided at runtime. We'll jump into the specifics of dependency injection in Swift in the next chapter.

11
Implementing Dependency Injection

In software development, it's always recommended to split the system into loosely coupled modules that can work independently as much as they can. Dependency Injection is a pattern that helps to reach this goal, creating a maintainable and testable system. Dependency Injection is often confused with complex and over-configurable frameworks that permit us to add DI to our code; in reality, it is a simple pattern that can be added without too much effort.

We'll look at different examples of Dependency Injection and the benefits it gives to the code.

In this chapter we will:

- See what Dependency Injection is and how it can make our code more maintainable
- How to implement Dependency Injection in Swift
- The good as well as the anti-patterns for Dependency Injection
- How to use a DI Container in Swift

Dependency Injection, a primer

In this introductory section, we'll see what Dependency Injection is, where it comes, and how it's defined so that we can then discuss various methods to implement it, having a clear understanding of its principles.

We'll also see the benefits it brings to the software, the reasons to apply it, and when to do so.

What is Dependency Injection?

Dependency Injection is one of the most misunderstood concepts in computer programming.
This is because the Dependency Injection borders are quite blurry and they could overlap with other object-oriented programming concepts.
We'll start with a uniform definition of the DI so that we can proceed without confusion.

Definition

Let's start with a formal definition:

"In software engineering, Dependency Injection is a software design pattern that implements inversion of control for resolving dependencies."
- *Wikipedia*

To be honest, this is not really clear: what is *Inversion of Control*? Why is it useful for resolving dependencies?

In procedural programming, each object interacts with all of its collaborators in a direct way and also instantiates them directly. In Inversion Of Control, this flow is managed by a third party, usually, a framework that calls the objects and receives notifications.
An example of this is an implementation of a UI engine. In a UI Engine, there are two parts: the Views and the Models part. The Views part handles all the interaction with the users, such as tapping buttons and rendering labels, whereas the Models part is responsible for business logic. Usually, the application code goes in the Models part, and the connections with the Views are done via callbacks that are called by the engine when the user interacts with a button or a text field. The paradigm changes from an imperative style where the algorithm is a sequence of actions, like in *do this **then do** that*, to an event style, *when the button is tapped **then** call the server*. The control of the actions is thus inverted. Instead of being the model that does things, the model now receives calls.

Inversion of Control is often called **Hollywood Principle**.

The essence of this principle is, "Don't call us, we'll call you," which is a response you might hear after auditioning for a role in Hollywood.

In procedural programming, the flow of the program is determined by the modules that are statically connected together: `ContactsView` talks to `ContactsCoreData` and `ContactsProductionRemoteService`, and each object instantiate its next collaborator. In Inversion of Control, `ContactsView` talks to a generic `ContactsStore` and a generic `ContactsRemoteService` whose concrete implementation could change depending on the context. If it is during the tests, an important role is played by the entity that manages how to create and connect all the objects together.

Martin Fowler, in his 2004 article `https://martinfowler.com/articles/Injection.html` about IoC, says that it can be reached with patterns such as `ServiceLocator` or Dependency Injection, but it can also be done with a Template Pattern or a Strategy Pattern. After having defined the concept of IoC, let's give a simpler definition of DI:

> *"Dependency Injection" is a 25-dollar term for a 5-cent concept. [...] Dependency Injection means giving an object its instance variables. Really. That's it."*
>
> — *James Shore* (`https://www.jamesshore.com/Blog/Dependency-Injection-Demystified.html`)

The first principle of the book *Design Patterns* by the Gang of Four (`https://www.artima.com/lejava/articles/designprinciples.html`), is "Program to an interface, not an implementation" which means that the objects need to know each other only by their interface and not by their implementation.

After having defined how all the classes in software will collaborate with each other, this collaboration can be designed as a graph. The graph could be implemented connecting together the actual implementation of the classes, but following the first principle mentioned previously, we can do it using the interfaces of the same objects: the Dependency Injection is a way of building this graph passing the concrete classes to the objects.

Why DI is useful

As we already mentioned, programming with interfaces permits us to have a loosely-coupled code, permitting us to swap implementation depending on the context, but also to implement the components in a parallel way.

Imagine you have a really big software where multiple teams implement its features in parallel, an effective way of working could be to define the interface, the contract, for each component beforehand, so that they can be worked by different teams at the same time, and each team can mock their collaborators while working at their own component.

Separation of concerns

The Separation of concerns is a principle for separating a computer program into distinct modules, where each module addresses a separate *concern*. A concern can be defined as a set of information or behavior that is part of a computer programming. An example could be persisting data in a store or calculating the discount to apply in an e-commerce app. A program that has an effective and clear separation of concerns is called *modular*.

Dependency Injection helps to reach the modularity of a software defining only the interface of the module so that the details of the implementation don't interfere with the business logic of the module. However, a loosely-coupled code isn't automatically obtained with DI, it needs to be carefully designed and planned.

A loosely-coupled code is easier to maintain, extend, debug, and test. A module could be replaced with a different implementation, changing a store engine from `CoreData` to `Realm`, without the modules having to be changed.

Testability

As already mentioned, another great advantage of using Dependency Injection is improved testability.

We'll deep-dive into the topic of testing in `Chapter 14`, *Testing Your Code with Unit and UI Tests*, where we'll see in great detail how to exploit DI and the technique of Test Doubles to verify code that otherwise would have been impossible to test in an automatic way, such as an interaction with the user or with an external service.

Here, it should be quite intuitive that as we can swap an implementation of a module with a different one with a different technology, we can also replace it with a fake one, a simplified version of the same module to have it under control while testing another component that depends on it.

Dependency Injection by example

After spending a few pages defining and explaining Dependency Injection and its principles, now let's see how to implement it in Swift.

Four ways to use Dependency Injection (with examples)

Dependency Injection is used ubiquitously in Cocoa too, and in the following examples, we'll see code snippets both from Cocoa and typical client-side code. Let's take a look at the following four sections to learn how to use Dependency Injection.

Constructor Injection

The first way to do DI is to pass the collaborators in the constructor, where they are then saved in private properties. Let's have as an example on e-commerce app, whose Basket is handled both locally and remotely.

The `BasketClient` class orchestrates the logic, saves locally in `BasketStore`, and synchronizes remotely with `BasketService`:

```
protocol BasketStore {
    func loadAllProduct() -> [Product]
    func add(product: Product)
    func delete(product: Product)
}

protocol BasketService {
    func fetchAllProduct(onSuccess: ([Product]) -> Void)
    func append(product: Product)
    func remove(product: Product)
}

struct Product {
    let id: String
    let name: String
    //...
}
```

Then in the constructor of `BasketClient`, the concrete implementations of the protocols are passed:

```
class BasketClient {
    private let service: BasketService
    private let store: BasketStore
    init(service: BasketService, store: BasketStore) {
        self.service = service
        self.store = store
    }
```

```
        func add(product: Product) {
            store.add(product: product)
            service.append(product: product)
            calculateAppliedDiscount()
            //...
        }
        // ...
        private func calculateAppliedDiscount() {
            // ...
        }
    }
```

In Cocoa and Cocoa Touch, the Apple foundation libraries, there are a few examples of this pattern.

A notable example is NSPersistentStore in CoreData:

```
    class NSPersistentStore: NSObject {
        init(persistentStoreCoordinator root: NSPersistentStoreCoordinator?,
            configurationName name: String?,
            URL url: NSURL,
            options: [NSObject: AnyObject]?)

        var persistentStoreCoordinator: NSPersistentStoreCoordinator? { get }
    }
```

In the end, Dependency Injection as defined by James Shore is all here: define the collaborators with protocols and then pass them in the constructor.
This is the best way to do DI. After the construction, the object is fully formed and it has a consistent state. Also, by just looking at the signature of init, the dependencies of this object are clear.
Actually, the Constructor Injection is not only the most effective, but it's also the easiest. The only problem is who has to create the object graph? The parent object? The AppDelegate?
We'll discuss that point in the *Where to bind the dependencies* section.

Property Injection

We have already agreed that Construction Injection is the best way to do DI, so why bother finding other methods?

Well, it is not always possible to define the constructor the way want. A notable example is doing DI with ViewControllers that are defined in storyboards. Given we have a `BasketViewController` that orchestrates the `service` and the `store`, we must pass them as properties:

```
class BasketViewController: UIViewController {
    var service: BasketService?
    var store: BasketStore?

    // ...
}
```

This pattern is less elegant than the previous one:

- The `ViewController` isn't in the right state until all the properties are set
- Properties introduce mutability, and immutable classes are simpler and more efficient
- The properties must be defined as *optional*, leading to add question marks everywhere
- They are set by an external object, so they must be writeable and this could potentially permit something else to overwrite the value set at the beginning after a while
- There is no way to enforce the validity of the setup at compile-time

However, something can be done:

- The properties can be set as *implicitly unwrapped optional* and then required in `viewDidLoad`. This is as a static check, but at least they are checked at the first sensible opportunity, which is when the view controller has been loaded.
- A function setter of all the properties prevents us from partially defining the collaborator list.

The class `BasketViewController` must then be written as:

```
class BasketViewController: UIViewController {
    private var service: BasketService!
    private var store: BasketStore!

    func set(service: BasketService, store: BasketStore) {
        self.service = service
        self.store = store
    }

    override func viewDidLoad() {
```

```
        super.viewDidLoad()
        precondition(service != nil, "BasketService required")
        precondition(store != nil, "BasketStore required")
        // ...
    }
}
```

The Properties Injection permits us to have overridable properties with a default value. This can be useful in the case of testing.
Let's consider a dependency to a wrapper around the time:

```
class CheckoutViewController: UIViewController {
    var time: Time = DefaultTime()
}

protocol Time {
    func now() -> Date
}

struct DefaultTime: Time {
    func now() -> Date {
        return Date()
    }
}
```

In the production code, we don't need to do anything, while in the testing code we can now inject a particular date instead of always return the current time. This would permit us of testing how the software will behave in the future, or in the past.

 A dependency defined in the same module or framework is *Local*. When it comes from another module or framework, it's *Foreign*.

A Local dependency can be used as a default value, but a Foreign cannot, otherwise it would introduce a strong dependency between the modules.

Method Injection

This pattern just passes a collaborator in the method:

```
class BasketClient {

    func add(product: Product, to store: BasketStore) {
        store.add(product: product)
        calculateAppliedDiscount()
```

```
        //...
    }
    // ...
    private func calculateAppliedDiscount() {
        // ...
    }
}
```

This is useful when the object has several collaborators, but most of them are just temporary and it isn't worth having the relationship set up for the whole life cycle of the object.

Ambient Context

The final pattern, Ambient Context, is similar to the Singleton.

We still have a single instance as a `static` variable, but the class has multiple subclasses with different behaviors, and each static variable is writeable with a `static` function:

```
class Analytics {
    static private(set) var instance: Analytics = NoAnalytics()
    static func setAnaylics(analitics: Analytics) {
        self.instance = analitics
    }
    func track(event: Event) {
        fatalError("Implement in a subclass")
    }
}

class NoAnalytics: Analytics {
    override func track(event: Event) {}
}

class GoogleAnalytics: Analytics {
    override func track(event: Event) {
        //...
    }
}

class AdobeAnalytics: Analytics {
    override func track(event: Event) {
        //...
    }
}

struct Event {
```

```
    //...
}
```

This pattern should be used only for universal dependencies, representing some *cross-cutting concerns*, such as analytics, logging, and times and dates.

This pattern has some advantages. The dependencies are always accessible and don't need to change the API.
It works well for cross-cutting concerns, but it doesn't fit in other cases when the object isn't unique.
Also, it makes the dependency implicit and it represents a global mutable state that sometimes can lead to issues that are difficult to debug.

Bind the dependencies

At this point of the chapter, it should be clear that Dependency Injection isn't rocket science, but that the main point is where to bind the dependencies and where to create the object graph. In fact, if the objects are created in the previous object, let's say that `ProductListViewController` creates the object for `ProductDetailsViewController`, we are nullifying the advantages of the DI. In this section, we'll see the two ways to address this problem.

Composition Root

A classic solution to the problem of creating the dependencies is using a pattern called **Composition Root**.

The Composition Root is a place in the code where components of different layers are wired together. The reason to have in a separate place is to not mix *configuration logic* and the other different kind of logic, like the *business logic* that defines the behavior of the software. The only responsibility of the Composition Root pattern is to instantiate and configure other components. The Injections of the dependencies, either in the constructor or in properties, must be done in the Composition Root.
In the following diagram, we can see that the Composition Root is a particular layer that has the responsibility of composing the modules.

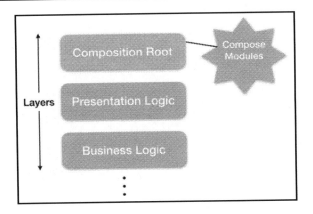

Ideally, only one Composition Root should be present in the app, and be started at the launch of the app. However, it shouldn't be a single class or a single function, but it can be multiple classes with multiple functions; it really depends on the complexity and the preferences of the developers.

Let's use a simple e-commerce app as an example:

```
class AppDependencies {
    private var basketController: BasketController!
    private var productsController: ProductsController!

    init() {
        configureDependencies()
    }

    private func configureDependencies() {
        let configuration = Configuration.loadFromBundleId()
        let apiService = NetworkApi(with: configuration)
        self.basketController = createBasketController(apiService:
apiService, configuration: configuration)
        self.productsController = createProductsController(apiService:
apiService)
    }

    private func createBasketController(apiService: NetworkApi,
configuration: Configuration) -> BasketController {
        let basketService = RestBasketService(apiService: apiService)
        let basketStore = BasketCoreData(with: configuration)
        return BasketController(service: basketService, store: basketStore)
    }

    private func createProductsController(apiService: NetworkApi) ->
ProductsController {
```

```
            let productsService = RestProductsService(apiService: apiService)
            return ProductsController(service: productsService)
        }
    }
```

The `AppDependecies` class creates all the needed objects and links them together. In this case, the objects are created at the start of the app, but if something depends on a product created during the flow, for example, the ID of a product selected from a list, `AppDependencies` could expose the needed functions. Also, `AppDependencies` could inject itself inside the created objects.

However, back in this simple example, now we create the instance of `AppDependencies` in the app delegate:

```
@UIApplicationMain
class AppDelegate: UIResponder, UIApplicationDelegate {
    var window: UIWindow?
    let dependencies = AppDependencies()
    func application(_ application: UIApplication,
didFinishLaunchingWithOptions launchOptions:
[UIApplication.LaunchOptionsKey: Any]?) -> Bool {
        dependencies.installRootViewControllerIntoWindow(window: window)
        return true
    }
}
```

`AppDependencies` **then expose an entry point with** `window` **as an argument:**

```
class AppDependencies {
  //...
    func installRootViewControllerIntoWindow(window: UIWindow?) {
        guard let mainViewController = window?.rootViewController as?
MainViewController else {
            fatalError("The rootViewController must be a
MainViewController")
        }
        mainViewController.basketController = basketController
        mainViewController.productsController = productsController
    }

  //...
}
```

This pattern is simple and effective, but its major downside is that it grows when the app becomes bigger. In general, this solution works well though.

> *"The biggest challenge of properly implementing DI is getting all classes with dependencies moved to Composition Root."*

> —*Mark Seeman, Dependency Injection in NET, 5.3 - Constrained Construction*

DI anti-patterns

When we try to implement a new technique, it is quite easy to lose control and implement it in the wrong way. Let's see then the most common anti-patterns in Dependency Injection.

 An anti-pattern is a description of a commonly-occurring solution to a problem that generates decidedly negative consequences.

Control Freak

The first one is pretty easy to spot: we are not using the Injection at all. Instead of being Injected, the dependency is instantiated inside the object that depends on it:

```
class FeaturedProductsController {
    private let restProductsService: ProductsService

    init() {
        self.restProductsService = RestProductsService(configuration:
Configuration.loadFromBundleId())
    }
}
```

In this example, `ProductsService` could have been injected in the constructor but it is instantiated there instead.

Mark Seeman, in his book *"Dependency Injection in NET"*, Chapter 5.1 - *DI anti-patterns*, calls it *Control Freak* because it describes a class that will not relinquish its dependencies.

The Control Freak is the dominant DI anti-pattern and it happens every time a class directly instantiates its dependencies, instead of relying on the Inversion of Control for that. In the case of the example, even though the rest of the class is programmed against an interface, there is no way of changing the actual implementation of ProductsService and the type of concrete class that it is, it will always be RestProductsService. The only way to change it is to modify the code and compile it again, but with DI it should be possible to change the behavior at runtime.

Sometimes, someone tries to fix the Control Freak anti-pattern using the factory pattern, but the reality is that the only way to fix it is to apply the Inversion of Control for the dependency and inject it in the constructor:

```
class FeaturedProductsController {
    private let productsService: ProductsService

    init(service: ProductsService) {
        self.productsService = service
    }
}
```

As already mentioned, *Control Freak* is the most common DI anti-pattern; pay particular attention so you don't slip into its trap.

Stable and volatile dependencies

However, not always instantiating a dependency in the constructor leads to a *Control Freak* anti-pattern, it depends on the nature of the dependency, as explained in the following.

There are two types of dependencies:

- **Volatile**: A *volatile* dependency is something that depends on the external world, it requires some environment setup, such as a database or network access. If it uses random numbers or depends on time, or when the dependency is not ready because it's still in development, it will eventually be replaced. An effect of a volatile dependency is that it creates strong coupling; if it doesn't let us test or extend the dependent class, it means it is *volatile*.
- **Stable**: A dependency is stable if it's already there, it will not break software depending on it when a new version is installed, and you never need to replace that class with another. A good example of a *stable* dependency is the one in the Foundation framework. Ironically, the dependency containers also fall into this category and they should be considered *stable* dependencies. Only stable dependencies can be initiated in the constructor, whereas volatile dependencies must be injected.

Bastard Injection

Constructor overloads are fairly common in Swift codebases, but these could lead to the *Bastard Injection* anti-pattern. A common scenario is when we have a constructor that lets us inject a Test Double, but it also has a default parameter in the constructor:

```
class TodosService {
    let repository: TodosRepository

    init(repository: TodosRepository = SqlLiteTodosRepository()) {
        self.repository = repository
    }
}
```

The biggest problem here is when the default implementation is a Foreign dependency, which is a class defined using another module; this creates a strong relationship between the two modules, making it impossible to reuse the class without including the dependent module too.

The reason someone is tempted to write a default implementation it is pretty obvious since it is an easy way to instantiate the class just with `TodoService()` without the need of Composition Root or something similar. However, this nullifies the benefits of DI and it should be avoided removing the default implementation and injecting the dependency.

Service Locator

The final anti-pattern that we will explore is the most dangerous one: the Service Locator. It's funny because this is often considered a good pattern and is widely used, even in the famous Spring framework. Originally, the *Service Locator* pattern was defined in *Microsoft patterns & practices' Enterprise Library*, as Mark Seeman writes in his book *"Dependency Injection in NET"*, Chapter 5.4 - *Service Locator*, but now he is advocating strongly against it. Service Locator is a common name for a service that we can query for different objects that were previously registered in it. As mentioned, it is a tricky one because it makes everything seem OK, but in fact, it nullifies all the advantage of the Dependency Injection:

```
let locator = ServiceLocator.instance
locator.register( SqlLiteTodosRepository(),
                  forType: TodosRepository.self)

class TodosService {
    private let repository: TodosRepository

    init() {
        let locator = ServiceLocator.instance
```

```
        self.repository = locator.resolve(TodosRepository.self)
    }
}
```

Here we have a service locator as a singleton, to whom we register the classes we want to resolve. Instead of injecting the class into the constructor, we just query from the service. It looks like the Service Locator has all the advantages of Dependency Injection, it provides testability and extensibility since we can use different implementations without changing the client. It also enables parallel development and separated configuration from the usage.

But it has some major disadvantages. With DI, the dependencies are explicit; it's enough to look at the signature of the constructor or the exposed properties to understand what the dependencies for a class are. With a Service Locator, these dependencies are implicit, and the only way to find them is to inspect the implementation, which breaks the encapsulation. Also, all the classes are depending on the Service Locator and this makes the code tightly coupled with it. If we want to reuse a class, other then that class, we also need to add the Service Locator in our project, which could be in a different module and then adding the whole module as dependency where we wanted just to use one class. Service Locator could also give us the impression that we are not using DI at all because all the dependencies are hidden inside the classes.

To sum up, pay attention to these anti-patterns and if you have any of those, you must refactor them using the Constructor Injection and the Composition Root.

Using a Dependency Injection Container

As already mentioned, most people confuse the Dependency Injection pattern with the use of the DI Container. This is mainly true in other languages, such as Java, where a Framework, such as Spring, has been ubiquitous for a while.
In the Swift ecosystem, DI Containers are less common, but there are a few, and it's worth having a basic idea of how they work since it could be useful in particular projects, such as an enterprise one with several developers.

Why you should use a DI Container

We have seen that Dependency Injection can be achieved by implementing the right constructor and binding the dependencies at the start of the app, without using a third-party framework.

However, sometimes using one of these containers could help to ensure a uniform architecture, which is helpful when you have a really big development team. If the container you choose is used in several apps, you can be sure that it's often more robust than an internally-developed one.

If the dependencies are fixed and don't change during the life of the app, injecting manually is probably better, but if the dependencies are dynamic and change for different reasons, a DI container should permit to have a more flexible code capable to handle this situation. Another advantage of a container is that it can control the life cycle of its service: a service can a be a static, a singleton, it can be recreated for every request, or it can have a *scoped lifetime*. A *scoped lifetime* means the instance is instantiated at the beginning of the scope, or session, and all calls in the same session are done to the same instance; a session could be defined as a transaction flow, buying a flight ticket from the search bar to check out, or from login to checkout.

The Typhoon framework

The Typhoon framework (`http://appsquickly.github.io/Typhoon/`) is probably the most famous DI Container in the Cocoa ecosystem:

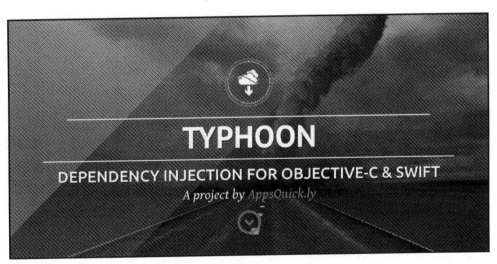

It's full of features, but it isn't too big, just around 3,000 lines of code. It is well-documented because the maintainers are committed to improving it.

The Typhoon building blocks are called *assemblies,* and they look like factories. Let's see the code provided as a sample app on their website (`https://github.com/appsquickly/Typhoon-Swift-Example`):

```swift
public class ApplicationAssembly: TyphoonAssembly {
    //...
    public dynamic func citiesListController() -> AnyObject {
        //...
    }

    public dynamic func weatherReportController() -> AnyObject {
        //...
    }

    public dynamic func weatherReportView() -> AnyObject {
        //...
    }

    public dynamic func addCityViewController() -> AnyObject {
        //...
    }
}
```

In the implementation, instead of returning a concrete instance of the requested type, we return a description of how the instance should be created, which is a `TyphoonDefinition` type:

```swift
public dynamic func citiesListController() -> AnyObject {
    return TyphoonDefinition.withClass(CitiesListViewController.self) {
        definition in

        definition!.useInitializer("initWithCityDao:theme:") {
            initializer in

            initializer!.injectParameter(with:
self.coreComponents.cityDao())
            initializer!.injectParameter(with:
self.themeAssembly.currentTheme())
        }
        definition!.injectProperty("assembly")
    } as AnyObject
}
```

The definition contains the dependencies needed to be injected, and which function must be called to do the Injection, which in this case is a constructor. In the definition, we can set the scope, which is a singleton here:

```
public dynamic func rootViewController() -> AnyObject {
    return TyphoonDefinition.withClass(RootViewController.self) {
        definition in
        //...
        definition!.scope = TyphoonScope.singleton
    } as AnyObject
}
```

The singleton type means that the object is created during the setup of the dependencies and then retained by Typhoon until the end of the app's life cycle. The default scope is `TyphoonScopeObjectGraph`, which means that the instances are retained for the time of the assembly to create the object graph and then passed the ownership to the object graph. This permits us to create a list of the objects retained to a high-level scenario, let's say a view controller.

The assemblies must then be defined in `Info.plist`:

Status bar style	⌄	String	UIStatusBarStyleLightContent
▼ TyphoonInitialAssemblies	⌄	Array	(3 items)
Item 0		String	ApplicationAssembly
Item 1		String	CoreComponents
Item 2		String	ThemeAssembly
▶ App Transport Security Settings	⌄	Dictionary	(1 item)

Using Objective-C runtime inspection, Typhoon then instantiates the assembly and injects it in all the objects.

The object that needs an instance from the assembly then calls the building function in its assembly instance:

```
self.citiesListController = UINavigationController(rootViewController:
self.assembly.citiesListController() as! UIViewController)
```

For the testing, the assembly must be created and activated explicitly:

```
public class CityDaoTests : XCTestCase {
    var cityDao : CityDao!
    public override func setUp() {
        let assembly = ApplicationAssembly().activate()
        self.cityDao = assembly.coreComponents.cityDao() as! CityDao
```

```
        }
        //...
    }
```

As we have seen, Typhoon is quite easy to use, but it relies on Objective-C runtime, and the API isn't really nice to use in Swift. Methods called during the Injection must be *dynamic*, and the class must be subclasses of NSObject. There is a Swift version (https://github.com/appsquickly/TyphoonSwift) with a more Swift-ly API, but it doesn't look as actively maintained.

Swinject

Swinject (https://github.com/Swinject/Swinject) is a lightweight Dependency Injection container written in Swift, which is used in more than 20,000 apps:

Swinject offers pure Swift Type Support, Injection with arguments, constructor and property Injection, object scope, and thread safety. Like Typhoon, in the Swinject repository, you can find a sample app that shows how to use the framework (https://github.com/Swinject/SwinjectSimpleExample).

Swinject's dependency-resolver engine is based on the concept of the container, where the classes and services are registered and then resolved:

```
var container = Container()

// Registrations for the network using Alamofire.
container.register(Networking.self) { _ in Network() }
container.register(WeatherFetcher.self) { r in
    WeatherFetcher(networking: r.resolve(Networking.self)!)
}
//..
```

In the preceding example, the `Networking` and `WeatherFetcher` classes are registered in a container; since `WeatherFetcher` needs the `Networking` instance, it can be resolved by the resolver passed as a parameter of the callback.

Then the instances can be resolved to call the `resolve` function in the container:

```
let fetcher = container.resolve(WeatherFetcher.self)!
fetcher.fetch { cities = $0 }
```

If the objects require more parameters to be passed during the creation process, they can be passed in the resolve function that can later pass inside the callback:

```
container.register(Animal.self) { _, name in
    Horse(name: name)
}
container.register(Animal.self) { _, name, running in
    Horse(name: name, running: running)
}
```

To resolve them, run the following code:

```
let firstAnimal = container.resolve(Animal.self, argument: "Spirit")!

print(firstAnimal.name) // prints "Spirit"
print((firstAnimal as! Horse).running) // prints "false"

let secondAnimal = container.resolve(Animal.self, arguments: "Lucky",
true)!

print(secondAnimal.name) // prints "Lucky"
print((secondAnimal as! Horse).running) // prints "true"
```

Given the Injection process is handled by a callback, how to inject the dependencies is completely in the hands of the developer. It could be a constructor Injection, such as the preceding examples, or a property Injection, as follows:

```
let container = Container()
container.register(Animal.self) { _ in Cat() }
container.register(Person.self) { r in
    let owner = PetOwner()
    owner.pet = r.resolve(Animal.self)
    return owner
}
```

Like in Typhoon, it is possible to define different types of scope:

```
container.register(ProductsFetcher.self) { _ in NetworkProductsFetcher() }
    .inObjectScope(.container)
```

.graph is the scope defined by default one. It means that a new instance is created every time resolve() is called, but if that function is called inside the callback, the previous instance is resolved instead. This permits us to create object graphs with the same life cycle.

.container means that the instance created is owned by that container and it will have the same life cycle of the container. This is equivalent to a singleton in Typhoon.

It is also possible to define a custom scope, as follows:

```
extension ObjectScope {
    static let custom = ObjectScope(storageFactory: PermamentStorage.init)
}
```

Instances in the .custom scope work as in .container, but the container can be cleaned with the following:

```
container.resetObjectScope(.custom)
```

After resetting it, subsequent calls to resolve create a new instance of the objects in the container.

Automatic Storyboard Injection

A really handy extension is the SwinjectStoryboard plugin, which adds Automatic Storyboard Injection to Swinject:

```
extension SwinjectStoryboard {
    class func setup() {
defaultContainer.storyboardInitCompleted(WeatherTableViewController.self) {
r, c in
        c.weatherFetcher = r.resolve(WeatherFetcher.self)
    }
        defaultContainer.register(Networking.self) { _ in Network() }
        defaultContainer.register(WeatherFetcher.self) { r in
            WeatherFetcher(networking: r.resolve(Networking.self)!)
    }
    }
}
```

The SwinjectStoryboard class inherits from UIStoryboard and lets us inject all the dependencies in the view controllers defined in the storyboard. If the setup() class function is present, it will be called during the setup of the app, and it is the place where we'll bind the dependencies. Note that a defaultContainer property is defined in SwinjectStoryboard and this is what we use to set up the dependencies.

As we have seen, Swinject is very friendly and easy to use. Also, it isn't really invasive and it could be used only in certain parts of the app. `SwinjectStoryboard` is then a really nice add-on, which should help us clean the Injection in the view controller, an operation that usually is done in the `prepareForSegue` function of the calling view controller.

Summary

Dependency Injection is a really interesting and useful pattern, but it's often misunderstood. In this chapter, we tried to present every aspect of Dependency Injection, debunking its myths and falsehoods, and showing when and how to use it.

We started the exploration of *Dependency Injection* with its definition, from Martin Fowler's seminal article, and from several other influential sources. A pattern is useless without the context in which it must be applied. We identified two major scenarios where DI is useful: *Separation of concerns*, to help the development of loosely-coupled components and hence create more flexible and maintainable code, and *Testing*, where problematic collaborators could be replaced by Test Double, a simplified and controlled version of the dependencies. There are different ways of implementing DI, such as injecting in the constructor, which is the one to use when possible, injecting using properties, to be used with frameworks such as UIKit, *method Injection*, and *Ambient Context*.

At this point in our journey, we realized that finding a place where we can bind the dependencies is a crucial aspect of the pattern; using the *Composition Root* technique will help us to do it in a clean and effective way. When applying a pattern, we need to take particular care not to slip into applying it in the wrong way. We then explored the most common DI anti-patterns, starting with *Control Freak*, where it looks like we using DI, but actually the code it is strongly coupled, to *Bastard Injection*, where a shortcut we take to make the creation of object easier then creates a dependency between modules, and finally to the Service Locator, the most insidious one, which could lead to creating relationships with the modules that nullify the advantages of DI.

Finally, we explored two DI Containers to use with Swift: *Typhoon*, the most common in the iOS ecosystem, but that still uses the Objective-C runtime libraries, and the more Swift-idiomatic *Swinject*.

In the next chapter, we'll continue our exploration of Swift patterns by moving into sorting asynchronous code, using other languages' common patterns, such as *Futures* and *Promises*, and a more sophisticated solution such as *Reactive Programming*.

12
Futures, Promises, and Reactive Programming

We have already seen a few examples of how Swift makes it possible to handle asynchronous task execution when we introduced **Grand Central Dispatch (GCD)** and HTTP communication using URLSession in Chapter 3, *Diving into Foundation and the Standard Library*. As you may recall from that discussion, when dispatching a task to a GCD queue or passing a callback to an HTTP URLSession, we relied on Swift blocks, also known as closures, as a way to specify what our code was meant to do asynchronously. Closures are not the only way for Swift programmers to write asynchronous code and, while extremely powerful, they may lead to code that is hard to read, prone to leaks and memory issues, and hardly maintainable.

In this chapter, we will do the following:

- Dive deeper into closures and callbacks, showing their power and their shortcomings.
- Explore alternative ways to manage asynchronous computation using futures and promises.
- Get an overview of reactive programming using Signals and Channels.

Callbacks and closures

Callbacks, as mentioned, allow us to handle asynchronous operations by specifying what should happen when that operation is completed. Simply put, a callback is any piece of executable code that is passed to a function that will call it at some later point, either synchronously or asynchronously. As an example of synchronous callback, in Chapter 3, *Diving into Foundation and the Standard Library* we used the forEach method available on Array objects:

```
// Using forEach with a closure:
(1...5).forEach { value in
  print("\(value)")
}
```

This could be equivalently rewritten as follows, where we replace the closure with a function:

```
// The above is equivalente to this:
func printValue<T>(val : T) { print("\(val)") }
(1...5).forEach(printValue)
```

These two examples should help clarify that callbacks and closures correspond to different concepts, although with some overlap, since closures can be used to implement callbacks.

Closures, also known as lambdas in functional languages, and as blocks in C and Objective C, are a very powerful mechanism used to define an anonymous function that carries over a portion of the context where it is defined. In technical terms, a closure implements *lexically scoped name binding,* which means they bind entities belonging to their lexical scope to local identifiers. In less technical terms, a closure can be considered as a function, plus an environment that maps the free variables used in the function to values or references that were bound to the same identifiers in the context where the closure was created. Behaviorally, a closure *closes over* the variables or constants it refers from the context where it was defined.

Actually, in Swift, global functions and nested functions are special cases of closures. The most poignant form of closure, though, are *closure expressions*. Those are unnamed functions that can be written using a lightweight syntax that aims to foster a clean, clear, and clutter-free style. Swift strives to make writing closure expressions as easy as it can be, by supporting the following features:

- **Parameter and return value type inference based on context information**. Let's consider our previous `forEach` example:

```
(1...5).forEach { value in
  print("\(value)")
}
```

As you can see, there was no need to specify the type of the closure `value` parameter, since Swift is able to infer it correctly from the type of the array to which `forEach` is applied. In general, it is always possible to infer the types of a closure's parameters and return type, but it may be good practice to specify them to improve readability and reduce ambiguity when their purpose is not as straightforward as in the present example. In particular, the Swift compiler will require that you always specify closure complex return types.

- **Implicit returns from single-expression closures**. A closure expression can get as complex as good style allows, but, in many cases, a closure can be just made of a single expression. In such cases, a further syntax simplification is possible. For example, consider the following closure expression mapped on to an array element:

```
// No need for return statement in single-expression closures:
let squares1 = (1...5).map { value in
  value * value
}
```

As you can see, the `return` keyword has been omitted. Yet, the Swift compiler is able to handle the return value in a sensible way.

- **Shorthand argument names** allow you to refer to closure arguments by their position, for example, by using names such as `$0`, `$1`, `$2`, and so on. This makes it possible to streamline a single-expression closure even further, as seen here:

```
// Even better:
let squares2 = (1...5).map { $0 * $0 }
```

Shorthand argument names can be used in any closure expression.

- **Trailing closure syntax**. If you recall the first two examples we presented in this section, we showed how you could pass a function to `forEach` in place of a closure. This was possible because `forEach` has the following declaration, where `body` is a function that takes an `Element` and returns `Void`:

```
func forEach(_ body: (Element) throws -> Void) rethrows
```

Now, Swift allows you to replace the last parameter of the function type with a trailing closure after the function call's parentheses. This provides a more natural syntax that makes the closure appear like a block, but it is still just another argument to the function.

Closures and memory management

As we mentioned, a closure closes over the variables and constants it refers from the enclosing context. Now, if the closure is executed synchronously since the caller is blocked waiting for it to return, the closure may safely assume all variables and constants from the enclosing context still exist. On the contrary, when a closure is executed asynchronously, that is, without blocking the caller, there is no such guarantee, and it may happen that the closure is executed when the original enclosing context no longer exists. To ensure, then, that the variables and constants the closure uses outlive the enclosing context, Swift closures are able to *capture* those variables and constants:

```
import Dispatch

struct Book {
    var title: String
    var author: String
    var price: Double
}

func sellBook(_ book: Book) -> () -> Double {
    var totalSales = 0.0
    func sell() -> Double {
        totalSales += book.price
        return totalSales
    }
    return sell
}

let bookA = Book(title: "BookA", author: "AuthorA", price: 10.0)
let bookB = Book(title: "BookB", author: "AuthorB", price: 13.0)

let sellBookA = sellBook(bookA)
```

```
let sellBookB = sellBook(bookB)

sellBookA() //-- book sales for bookA: 10
sellBookB() //-- book sales for bookA: 13

sellBookA() //-- book sales for bookA: 20
sellBookB() //-- book sales for bookA: 26
```

When you pass a closure into another function or method, you should pay attention to whether that closure is executed synchronously or asynchronously, and, in the latter case, add the `@escaping` modifier to the closure parameter declaration. For example, if you define a `delay` function that is meant to execute a function after some time, that is, after the `delay` function exits, then Swift will require you to mark the parameter that takes the closure with `@escaping`:

```
// If you remove @escaping here, the compiler will complain
func delay(_ d: Double, fn: @escaping () -> ()) {
    DispatchQueue.global().asyncAfter(deadline: .now() + d) {
        DispatchQueue.main.async {
            fn()
        }
    }
}
```

For Swift, it is easy to realize the closure may escape the function scope, since you pass it to a dispatch queue. Still, it wants to make sure you know what you are doing and requires you to use `@escaping`.

Swift 3 introduced a fundamental change regarding escaping closures. While all closure parameters were previously escaping by default, since Swift 3 they are non-escaping by default. While breaking source code compatibility, this was a sensible change: non-escaping closure is less taxing on the runtime, since it can be allocated on the stack and can be optimized in more advanced ways.

If you recall our discussion of automatic reference counting in Chapter 2, *Understanding ARC and Memory Management*, it is easy to understand how capturing variables and constants works under the hood. In a simplified view of this process, when a closure captures a variable or constant, it automatically increments its reference count, thus ensuring it is not freed when the enclosing scope exits. After the closure is executed, the reference count of all captured entities is decremented, so they can be freed if need be. This makes capturing values in a closure as transparent and automatic a mechanism as possible, with just one exception: preventing retain cycles.

Cyclic, or circular, dependencies are a general concept in computer programming. A cyclic dependency is a relation between two or more entities that depend on each other, such as when entity A uses another entity, B, that in turns uses entity A. In Swift, due to the use of automatic reference counting, cyclic dependencies may also exist between objects in memory and are called retain cycles. In short, when a retain cycle ensues, ARC cannot free either of the objects. Usually, this issue is to be tackled by carefully deciding which of the two object "owns" the other, which gives a much more desirable unidirectional dependency.

To understand where retain cycles stem from, we may consider two typical scenarios where using a closure may cause a retain cycle:

- An instance O of class C creates a closure, L, and stores it in a member variable of C, so it can be used by other methods of C or from other classes.
- An instance O of class C registers a closure, L, as a KVO observer of one of its strong properties.

In both scenarios, if the closure refers self in its body, then a retain cycle will ensue, since the reference to self from the closure body will make the closure capture self. We can say that the closure holds a strong reference to self.

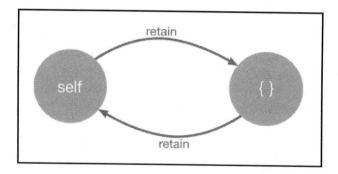

This diagram depicts a typical case of a retain cycle: a closure retaining self

What happens in both cases is that the closure keeps object O alive by increasing its retain count. At the same time, since O owns the property where the closure is stored, O increases the closure's retain count. Thus, the two entities will indefinitely keep each other alive and your program will end up having a memory leak. Indeed, when O's owner is done with O and frees it, O's retain count is decreased; however, this is not sufficient to free the object O, since the closure L is still retaining it.

In case you are interested in looking at the relationship between retaining cycles and closures at a lower level, you might well ask yourself how a closure is affected by being stored into a variable or being used as an observer. The answer is in its simplest form; that is, when you define a closure as a callback to be executed asynchronously or as an inner function, a closure can just be allocated on the stack. This means it is not reference counted and its lifetime is strictly bound to that of the function or method declaring it. On the contrary, when we try to store a closure into a class property or pass it outside the class, the Swift compiler has to copy it over on to the heap, thus making it into a reference counted object.

So, now we know how retain cycles ensue within closures, your question may be: how can we avoid them? The answer is simple: by breaking the cycle. Let's consider the following code:

```
class OperationJuggler {
    private var operations : [() -> Void] = []
    var delay = 1.0
    var name = ""
    init(name: String) {
        self.name = name
    }
    func addOperation(op: (@escaping ()->Void)) {
        self.operations.append { [weak self] () in
            if let sself = self {
                DispatchQueue.global().asyncAfter(deadline: .now() +
sself.delay) {
                    print("Delay: " + String(sself.delay))
                    op()
                }
            }
        }
    }

    func runLastOperation(index: Int) {
        self.operations.last!()
    }
}
```

Here, we have an `OperationJuggler` class that manages a list of operations through an `operations` array. Operations are just functions or closures that, for the sake of this example, take no arguments and have no return value. This code demonstrates the pattern we have described already: `OperationJuggler` stores the closure created by `addOperation` in its `operations` property. The closure refers `self`, so it holds a strong reference to it, but the `operations` array, which is strongly referenced by `self`, also takes a strong reference to the closure. Unfortunately, the preceding code will compile just fine. Even worse, Xcode Analyze command is not able to detect the cycle. Therefore, you will end up knowing that, at runtime, your app may crash due to its memory footprint.

It is not hard to show that the preceding code indeed creates retain cycles that prevent `OperationJuggler` instances from being freed when you are done with them. For example, we could use `OperationJuggler` in a minimal `ViewController`, like in the following snippet:

```
class ViewController: UIViewController {

    var opJ = OperationJuggler(name: "first")
    override func viewDidLoad() {
        super.viewDidLoad()

        opJ.addOperation {
            print("Executing operation 1")
        }
        self.opJ.runLastOperation(index: 0)

        //-- this will release the previous OperationJuggler
        self.opJ = OperationJuggler(name: "replacement")
    }
}
```

In `viewDidLoad`, we added an operation to our `OperationJuggler`, stored in the `opJ` property; then, after one second, we overwrote the `OperationJuggler` in `opJ` with a new instance. We would expect that the original instance is freed when we do it, but this is not the case. You can easily convince yourself of this by adding a `deinit` method to `OperationJuggler` and checking that it is not ever called:

```
class OperationJuggler {

    ...
    deinit {
        print("OperationJuggler freed")
    }
}
```

So, how can we remove this retain cycle? Swift has a special syntax for this that you can use to break the cycle, as shown in the following rewrite of `OperationJuggler`:

```
class OperationJuggler {
    private var operations : [() -> Void] = []
    var delay = 1.0
    var name = ""
    init(name: String) {
        self.name = name
    }
    func addOperation(op: (@escaping ()->Void)) {
        self.operations.append { () in
            DispatchQueue.global().asyncAfter(deadline: .now() +
self.delay) {
                op()
            }
        }
    }

    func runLastOperation(index: Int) {
        self.operations.last!()
    }
    deinit {
        self.delay = -1.0
        print("Juggler named " + self.name + " DEINITIED")
    }

}
```

As you can see, a new [weak self] attribute has made its appearance in the closure body. This will prevent the closure from retaining self, thus not creating the retain cycle. As a consequence of that, it cannot be taken for granted that the closure, to which the self object refers, still exists when it is executed, as it may have been freed. In this case, in accordance with weak ownership, self will be nil. In other words, self is an option type in the closure body, and we need to qualify its use with ?, !, or a guard. In the preceding example, we opted for using the forced unwrapping ! operator, since we are not really interested in preventing our program from crashing, but, in production code, you should be more vigilant. For example, we could write our closure like that shown in the following snippet:

```
func addOperation(op: (@escaping ()->Void)) {
    self.operations.append { [weak self] () in
        DispatchQueue.global().asyncAfter(deadline: .now() +
            (self?.delay ?? 1.0)) {
                op() }
    }
}
```

But more generally, we should prefer a guard:

```
func addOperation(op: (@escaping ()->Void)) {
    self.operations.append { [weak self] () in
        guard let self = self else { return }
        DispatchQueue.global().asyncAfter(deadline: .now() +
self.delay) {
            op()
        }
    }
}
```

The guard let self = self else { return } syntax was introduced in Swift 4.2, so do not try to use it in previous versions of the language. If you are using an older compiler, you can use a somewhat similar syntax, guard let weakSelf = self else { return }, which unfortunately forces you to create a new name to safely refer to self.

The fact that OperationJuggler manages operations that are closures is just a way to make our example richer, but the retain cycle would ensue just the same if it handled integers, as in the following code:

```
class IncrementJuggler {
    private var incrementedValues : [(Int) -> Int] = []
    var baseValue = 100
```

```
func addValue(increment: Int) {
    self.incrementedValues.append { (increment) -> Int in
        return self.baseValue + increment
    }
}
func runOperation(index: Int) {
    //...
}
}
```

Admittedly, retain cycles do not ensue only in the two scenarios mentioned here, nor are they always as easy to spot as in our examples. For example, you will also get a retain cycle when you store a closure in an object, O', which is owned by O, as it happens when you register a closure from your view controller with the view model that the view controller owns. As a general rule of thumb, you should pay special attention every time you are using a closure that refers to self, although it would be overkill to handle all such closure as if they would cause a retain cycle, that is, by using [weak self].

As a matter of fact, [weak self] is not the only means Swift provides to break retain cycles. You could also use [unowned self], which is similar to the former in that it will not retain self, but will not convert self into an optional inside of the closure body (and will not nil it when the object it refers to is freed). So, you can access self inside the closure without concerns about guards or unwrapping it, but, if it ever happens that the object has been freed, your program will crash. So you had better use it when you have alternative means to ensure the object is still there when the closure is executed.

Another approach to not creating retain cycles is passing self as an argument into the closure, as shown in the following example. Notice, though, that in this case, the self in the closure body ceases to be a keyword, becoming just a parameter name.

```
func addOperationAlsoOK(op: (@escaping ()->Void)) {
    self.operations.append { (self) in
        DispatchQueue.global().asyncAfter(deadline: .now() + self.delay) {
            op()
        }
    }
}
```

For the code above to compile, though, you will have to modify our definition of self.operations so stored closures accept an argument. This is left as an exercise for the reader.

The issue with callbacks

After our thorough review of closures, it is time to take a step back and reconsider our original goal for this chapter: showing effective ways to handle concurrency in Swift. We have learned that callbacks provide an architectural building block to write concurrent code, and that closures are a great way to implement callbacks. In this section, we should ask ourselves how callbacks perform in more complex, realistic scenarios.

 We have already met one shortcoming of using callbacks when we implement them through closures, namely, the risk of retain cycles. But there are more fundamental issues with callbacks in general, as we will shortly see.

Let's consider this scenario:

- You want to download a list of items using a REST API. Each item is described using JSON and contains a category name, a URL to retrieve an image representing that category, and an alternate URL to use in case the first one fails.
- For each item, you will want to download an image to be displayed in your UI from its preferred URL or from the alternate URL in case anything fails.
- If both the preferred and alternate URL have problems, you will want to use a default image.

Using callbacks, you could think of writing the following pseudo-code:

```
getListOfItems(listUrl) { list in
  list.forEach { item in
    getImage(url: item.url) { image in
      if let image = image {
        viewModel.addItem(item.categoryName, image)
      } else {
        getImage(url: item.alternateUrl) { image in
        if let image = image {
          viewModel.addItem(item.categoryName, image)
        } else {
          viewModel.addItem(item.categoryName,
            defaultImage(category: item.categoryName))
        }
      }
    }
  }
}
```

Although it solves a pretty trivial problem, this code has some big issues:

- It spans over three nested async callback levels (without counting the `forEach` callback), which makes it obscure and hard to maintain
- It contains replicated code, which is never desirable

The preceding example shows a general property of code that uses callbacks to handle sequences of asynchronous operations when each async operation depends on the result of the previous. It is so widespread that it even has a name: *callback hell*.

Of course, we could rewrite our code using functions to improve its modularity, as in the following example:

```
func useImage(name: String, url: String, onError: () -> Void) {
  getImage(url: url) { image in
    if let image = image {
      viewModel.addItem(name, image)
    } else {
      onError()
    }
  }
}

getListOfItems(listUrl) { list in
  list.forEach { item in
    useImage(item.categoryName, item.url) {
      useImage(item.categoryName, item.alternateUrl) {
        viewModel.addItem(item.categoryName,
          defaultImage(category: item.categoryName))
      }
    }
  }
}
```

As you can see, while nesting has not improved, at least we could write code that expresses more clearly our aim and with less code duplication. This is still far from being a good solution, though, and, indeed, on two accounts:

- Our code design comes to depend on the intricacies of dealing with callbacks. Specifically, you see we decided to coalesce the `getImage` and `addItem` operations within the same function and use a `onError` callback to `useImage` just for the sake of minimizing code duplication. Both design decisions are not driven by any considerations we could relate to our application business logic; rather, it is driven by implementation details of the abstractions we are using to deal with concurrency.

- We could surely try to improve our code even more. For example, we could coalesce the two `useImage` calls into a new function, thus reducing the callback nesting, but you may possibly see clearly that this approach does not scale with the complexity of the `async` workflows we would like to be able to address in our code. In addition, it exacerbates, even further, the design problem we have just mentioned, so it would not be entirely desirable, even if practical.

In the rest of this chapter, we will examine two alternative approaches to deal with concurrent operations, namely futures and promises, and reactive programming, which leverages callbacks with the aim of providing higher-level abstractions to handle concurrency.

Futures and promises

Futures and promises are terms that are used somewhat interchangeably to refer to abstractions representing the idea of a proxy to a value that will be known at some future time. In other words, futures and promises allow you to create objects that encapsulate asynchronous tasks and their result, and use them without waiting for the asynchronous task to finish, as long as you do not need to access the result of that task. When you need to access the task result, either the task has already completed, in which case you can use it without delay; otherwise, you will need to delay the code that wants to use that result until it becomes available. Strictly speaking, a way to differentiate between futures and promises is to say that a future represents a read-only value that may be available or not, while a promise represents the function that is responsible to set that value at some point in time. Thus, in actual fact, futures and promises are two sides of the same coin. The act of setting the value of a future is called *resolving the future* or *fulfilling the promise*.

 Futures and promises originated in functional programming as a way to decouple values and computations, so you could associate one of multiple available promises (that is, ways of calculating a value) to a future.

Futures and promises foster a direct style of handling concurrent operations. For example, our previous callbacks-based code could be rewritten as follows:

```
getListOfItems(url: url)
  .onSuccess { item in useImage(item: item.itemUrl) }
  .onFailure { item in useImage(item: item.itemUrl) }
  .onFailure { useDefaultImage() }
```

As you can see, we get huge improvements in terms of the readability of our code, and can easily extend the promise chain to handle arbitrarily complex sequences of asynchronous operations.

Futures and promises under the hood

A good approach to understand how promises work is to look at a possible, but extremely simplified implementation. So, we could start with something like the following to represent our results and errors, and our generic callbacks:

```
public enum Result<Value> {
    case success(Value)
    case failure(Error)
}

enum SimpleError: Error {
    case errorCause1
    case errorCause2
}

typealias Callback<T> = (Result<T>) -> Void
```

The `Result` generic defined in the preceding snippet is a particular case of a so-called Either type. Usually, Either types are presented at the same time as Option types, since they are related. Indeed, while Option types can represent a value of a given type or the absence of any value, Either types can represent a value of either of two types. Either types are available in many languages, including Haskell and Scala. Either types are frequently used to represent a value that could either be correct, or be an error. A full-fledged definition for a Result type could be enum `Result<V, E>`, which is generic both on the type representing correct outcomes and the type representing an error condition. In our case, we have defined `Result` to be generic on the value only, and will stick to using the Swift `Error` class for the error condition. It is interesting to know that `Result` is likely to be part of the Swift 5 standard library.

Now that we have our basic types in place, let's define what we are trying to achieve. Basically, we need two major classes: a `Future` class representing our read-only, conditionally available value, and a `Promise` class responsible for resolving it with success or failure. Both classes will be generic to be able to represent any kind of outcome from the asynchronous computations. As a start, we would like to be able to use our `Future`, as in the following pseudo-code:

```
// async operation returning a Future
func asyncOperation(...parameters...) -> Future<SomeType>

// get the Future proxying the result of the the async operation
let future : Future<String> = asyncOperation(...arguments...)

// associate a callback to consume the result of our async operation
future.then { result in
  // do something with the result
}
```

A suitable implementation for these requirements is the following:

```
public class Future<T> {

    internal var result : Result<T>? {
        didSet {
            if let result = result, let callback = callback {
                callback(result)
            }
        }
    }
    var callback : Callback<T>?
    init(_ callback: Callback<T>? = nil) {
        self.callback = callback
    }
    func then(_ callback: @escaping Callback<T>) {
        self.callback = callback
        if let result = result {
            callback(result)
        }
    }
}

public final class Promise<T> : Future<T> {
    func resolve(_ value: T) {
        result = .success(value)
    }
    func reject(_ error: Error) {
        result = .failure(error)
```

```
    }
}
```

You will notice we opted for having the `Promise` class derived from `Future`. This is surely not a clean choice, since it is arguable that a `Promise` is not a `Future`: still, it makes our code slightly easier. You will notice, however, that having separate `Promise` and `Future` classes is not mandatory, and we could encapsulate all of our functionality in just one class. This is what happens in many libraries that provide an implementation of promises and futures.

As you can see in the preceding snippet, a Future is essentially made of a result object and a callback. When the `result` is set, the `didSet` property observer will call the callback associated with the future, if any. You can assign a callback to the future either at construction time or passing it to the `then` method.

The Promise class, on the other hand, is really simple, and provides just two methods: `resolve` and `reject`, which have responsibility for setting the future `result` member, thus triggering the execution of the callback.

To use this class, only one last piece of code is required: an asynchronous operation returning a `Future`. We could define one for testing purposes like in the following snippet. This function does not do anything special: it just waits for a configurable `delay`, and then it resolves the `Future` it returns with a fixed string:

```
import Dispatch

func asyncOperation1(_ delay: Double) -> Promise<String> {
    let promise = Promise<String>()
    DispatchQueue.global().asyncAfter(deadline: .now() + delay) {
        DispatchQueue.main.async {
            print("asyncOperation1 completed")
            promise.result = .success("Test Result")
        }
    }
    return promise
}
```

We can test our `Future` implementation by running the following code:

```
let future : Future<String> = asyncOperation1(1.0)
future.then { result in
    switch (result) {
    case .success(let value):
        print(" Handling result: \(value)")
```

```
case .failure(let error):
    print(" Handling error: \(error)")
}
}
```

This will produce the following output:

```
asyncOperation1 completed
  Handling result: Test Result
```

Great! We have our `Future` working, but as it stands, it is not entirely useful, since it does not prevent callback hell at all. Indeed, if we wanted to execute a second asynchronous operation using the result of `asyncOperation1`, we would need to call the second from inside the callback passed to `then`. What we need is a way to chain successive asynchronous operations, so it becomes possible to write:

```
let promise2 = asyncOperation2()
promise2.chain { result in
    return asyncOperation3(result)
}.chain { result in
        return asyncOperation4(result)
}.then { result in
        print("THEN: \(result)")
}
```

We can achieve this by extending our `Future` class and providing a clever implementation for the chain `method`. The first thing we should notice is `chain` will return a `Future`, so we can actually chain any number of calls to `chain`. Since we want to be able to chain `Futures` of different types, the `Future` that chain returns shall have no resemblance to the `Future` it is applied to. Furthermore, the two `Future` classes, the one `chain` is applied to and the one `chain` returns, should actually be *chained*, meaning that, when the former is resolved, the asynchronous operation we want to chain is effectively started, and, when it completes, the latter `Future` is resolved as well. Here, things may get a little dense, since the asynchronous operation triggered when the first `Future` is resolved is itself represented by a `Future`, so we actually have three `Future` classes involved! With this in mind, it should not be entirely obscure what the following implementation is doing:

```
extension Future {
    func chain<U>(_ cbk: @escaping (T) -> Future<U>) -> Future<U> {
        let p = Promise<U>()
        self.then { result in
            switch result {
            case .success(let value): cbk(value).then { r in p.result = r }
            case .failure(let error): p.result = .failure(error)
            }
```

```
        }
        return p
    }
}
```

Once we have our `chain` method in place, we can use it to chain multiple asynchronous operations, in the same vein as `asyncOperation1`:

```
func asyncOperation2() -> Promise<String> {
    let promise = Promise<String>()
    DispatchQueue.global().asyncAfter(deadline: .now() + 1.5) {
        DispatchQueue.main.async {
            print("asyncOperation2 completed")
            promise.resolve("Test Result")
        }
    }
    return promise
}

func asyncOperation3(_ str : String) -> Promise<Int> {
    let promise = Promise<Int>()
    DispatchQueue.global().asyncAfter(deadline: .now() + 1.5) {
        DispatchQueue.main.async {
            print("asyncOperation3 completed")
            promise.resolve(1000)
        }
    }
    return promise
}

func asyncOperation4(_ input : Int) -> Promise<Double> {
    let promise = Promise<Double>()
    DispatchQueue.global().asyncAfter(deadline: .now() + 1.5) {
        DispatchQueue.main.async {
            print("asyncOperation4 completed")
            promise.reject(SimpleError.errorCause1)
        }
    }
    return promise
}
```

Now, run the following code:

```
let promise2 = asyncOperation2()
promise2.chain { result in
    return asyncOperation3(result)
    }.chain { result in
        return asyncOperation4(result)
```

```
    }.then { result in
        print("THEN: \(result)")
}
```

This will give you the following output:

```
asyncOperation2 completed
asyncOperation3 completed
asyncOperation4 completed
THEN: failure(__lldb_expr_55.SimpleError.errorCause1)
```

As you can see, in the last example, we have introduced an error condition. That was just for a change! Granted, our implementation of futures is overly simplified, but it remains true to the general idea behind them, and we hope our discussion helped you understand how futures and promises work under the hood. On the other hand, there is really no need here to implement a production-level futures and promises library, since, as we will see shortly, there are already several open source, fully fledged implementations of futures and promises for Swift!

 Our discourse about futures and promises and the examples we provided made one thing clear: for futures and promises to be useful at all, we need asynchronous operations that return them. This means that all asynchronous operation from any Cocoa or iOS framework cannot be used out of the box with futures and promises. They need to be wrapped in a function that returns a future that proxies their result. This is another very good reason to resort to an open source implementation of futures and promises, since several of them have gone to great lengths to support as many asynchronous operations from Cocoa and iOS frameworks as possible.

Futures and promises frameworks for Swift

As mentioned, a number of frameworks implementing futures and promises for Swift do exist. Instead of reinventing the wheel, the best approach is to choose one of them and start using it in your projects. In this section, we will review a few of them and present their general approaches and syntax.

PromiseKit

`PromiseKit` is among the most successful promise frameworks for Swift, with over 900 forks at the time of writing. It employs a rather custom working for the functions that you use to build an asynchronous workflow, but it also includes a number of extensions that convert most Apple APIs to use promises. This is a big boon since, if the framework you choose does not include such conversion wrappers for you, you will need to create them on your own.

If you want to use `PromiseKit`, the first step is adding it as a dependency to your project. For the Swift Package Manager, this is what you should add to your `Package.swift` file:

```
let package = Package(
  // ...
  dependencies: [
    .package(url: "https://github.com/mxcl/PromiseKit", majorVersion: 6),
  ],
  // ...
)
```

 If you are new to the Swift Package Manager, at this point you might want to take a little detour to `Chapter 13`, *Modularize your apps with Swift Package Manager*, where we provide a short introduction to it.

If you use CocoaPods, just add the following to your `Podfile`:

```
pod "PromiseKit", "~> 6.0"
```

Then, refresh your dependencies by running the following command:

`pod install`

Similarly, for Carthage, add the following to your Cartfile:

```
github "mxcl/PromiseKit" ~> 6.0
```

Then run the following command:

`carthage update`

Once you have added the `Promises` framework dependency to your project, you can import the `Promises` module into your Swift source files as follows:

`import PromiseKit`

If you want to use `PromiseKit` with your app (that is, not solely for testing purposes), then the installation steps should be different. In fact, both the CocoaPods and Carthage packages will include all `PromiseKit` extensions by default. Promise Kit Extensions are the wrappers around Apple asynchronous APIs. A side effect of this is that all of those frameworks, and their corresponding Apple frameworks, will be linked into your app. This is bad for performance, especially at launch time, and Apple discourages having many frameworks linked into your app. For this reason, it is best to just bring the `PromiseKit/Core` package in with your package manager, and then use Git submodules to get only the extensions you are going to use. This involves executing `git init ; git submodule update --recursive --remote` in your project root. Then, you can manually include the frameworks you require in your project.

As an example, let's fetch some data from GitHub using their REST API. This is how our promise-based code could look. To keep things simple, we do not decode the resulting JSON, but simply print it out as a `String`.

```
func testGitHubAPI() {
  if var urlComponents = URLComponents(string:
"https://api.github.com/search/repositories") {
    urlComponents.query = "q=sort=stars;order=desc;per_page=1"
    let url = urlComponents.url!

    URLSession.shared.dataTask(.promise, with: url)
      .then { data -> Promise<(data: Data, response: URLResponse)> in
        let string = String(data:data.data, encoding:String.Encoding.utf8)
        print("Most starred repo: \(string!)")
        urlComponents.query = "q=forks=stars;order=desc;per_page=1"
        return URLSession.shared.dataTask(.promise, with:
urlComponents.url!)
      }
      .then { data -> Promise<Data> in
        let string = String(data:data.data, encoding:String.Encoding.utf8)
        print("Most forked repo: \(string!)")
        return Promise<Data> { seal in seal.fulfill(data.data) }
      }
      .catch { error in
        print("This was unexpected: \(error)")
      }
  }
}
```

Of course, we could have executed the two searches in parallel: PromiseKit even offers a specific when(fulfilled:) function to run multiple async tasks at the same time, but we have done it sequentially for the sake of this example.

Google Promises

Google Promises is a rather recent player among Swift frameworks for async programming using futures and promises. You can add it as a dependency to your project using Swift Package Manager, CocoaPods, or Carthage. If you use Swift Package Manager, you can add the Promises dependency by including it in your Package.swift file, as in the following example:

```
let package = Package(
  // ...
  dependencies: [
    .package(url: "https://github.com/google/promises.git", from: "1.2.3"),
  ],
  // ...
)
```

If you use CocoaPods, just add the following to your Podfile:

```
pod 'PromisesSwift', '~> 1.2.3'
```

Then, refresh your dependencies by running the following:

pod install

Similarly, for Carthage, add the following to your Cartfile:

```
github "google/promises"
```

Then, run this command:

carthage update

If you work at Google, you might find it useful to know that Google Promises supports Bazel, as well—the build tool in use at Google.

Once you have added the Promises framework dependency to your project, you can import the Promises module into your Swift source files as follows:

import Promises

Let's reimplement the same example as used earlier using Google Promises. Contrary to PromiseKit, since the Google Promises framework does not provide a promise-based async wrapper for Swift Foundation APIs, the first bit of code we'll need is such a wrapper for URLSession.dataTask. Let's call it promisedData:

```
func promisedData(_ url: URL) -> Promise<Data> {
    let urlRequest = URLRequest(url: url)
    let defaultSession = URLSession(configuration: .default)
    return wrap { (handler: @escaping (Data, Error?) -> Void) in
        let task = defaultSession.dataTask(with: urlRequest) { (data,
response, error) in
            if let data = data {
                handler(data, error)
            } else {
                handler(Data(), error)
            }
        }
        task.resume()
    }
}
```

As you can see, all the heavy lifting is done by the Promises' wrap function, and we just have to provide a proper callback adapter. Once that function is available, we can set out to use GitHub REST API to retrieve the most starred repository first, followed by the most forked one:

```
func testGitHubAPI() {
        if var urlComponents = URLComponents(string:
"https://api.github.com/search/repositories") {
            urlComponents.query = "q=sort=stars;order=desc;per_page=1"
            let p : Promise<Data> = promisedData(urlComponents.url!)
            p.then { data -> Promise<Data> in
                let string = String(data:data,
encoding:String.Encoding.utf8)
                print("Most starred repo: \(string!)")
                urlComponents.query = "q=forks=stars;order=desc;per_page=1"
                return promisedData(urlComponents.url!)
            }.then { data -> Promise<Data> in
                let string = String(data:data,
encoding:String.Encoding.utf8)
                print("Most forked repo: \(string!)")
                return Promise(data)
            }.catch { error in
                print("This was unexpected: \(error)")
            }
        }
}
```

Besides supporting the basic chaining `then` and `catch` functions, Google Promises provides a number of other functions that aim to make it easy to write complex asynchronous workflows, including the following:

- **all**: An `all` promise is fulfilled when all of the promises passed to its constructor are.
- **any**: Similar to `all`, but will be rejected only if all the composing promises are.
- **always**: An `always` block that will always be executed in a promise workflow, even if some previous step is rejected.
- **await**: The `await` function will wait for a promise to be fulfilled on a different thread. This makes it possible to use promises in a complete sync style.
- **recover**: Similar to `catch`, but it will handle an error condition without breaking the workflow.
- **retry**: Attempts multiple times to fulfill a Promise if it is rejected.

As mentioned, there exist several open source frameworks for promise-based asynchronous operation handling. What you learned in this section will allow you to pick up any of them and get up to speed quickly.

Reactive programming

In the previous section, we looked at promises and futures, trying to get a thorough understanding of the way they work and presenting two popular promises frameworks that help you use promises in your programs. Here, we will consider a completely different approach to asynchronous computation, **Reactive Programming** (**RP**). The basic idea behind RP is that of *asynchronous data streams*, such as the stream of events that are generated by mouse clicks, or a piece of data coming through a network connection. Anything can be a stream; there are really no constraints. The only property that makes it sensible to model any entity as a stream is its ability to change at unpredictable times. The other half of the picture is the idea of *observers*, which you can think of as agents that subscribe to receive notifications of new events in a stream. In between, you have ways of transforming those streams, combining them, creating new streams, filtering them, and so on.

A related but ultimately deeply different idea to RP is **Functional Reactive Programming (FRP)**. In somewhat abstract terms, you could think of FRP as a declarative approach to describing the relationship between timed entities, that is, entities whose value changes continuously. For example, you could use FRP to describe the relationship $a = b + c$. You may see some similarity between RP and FRP. Indeed, in this example, you could think of having a subscribe to both b and c for any change to their values, so a can recalculate its own value accordingly. In fact, RP and FRP are not the same, since RP lacks a declarative notation and works in discrete time, generated by the arrival of discrete events.

In the remaining part of this section, we will give a light introduction to one popular framework for RP in Swift, RxSwift, and its Cocoa counterpart, RxCocoa, to make Cocoa ready for use with RP. RxSwift is not the only RP framework for Swift. Another popular one is ReactiveCocoa, but we think that, once you have understood the basic concepts behind one, it won't be hard to switch to the other.

You could look at RP as a generalization of **Key-Value Observing (KVO)**, a mechanism that is present in the macOS and iOS SDKs since their inception. KVO enables objects to receive notifications about changes to other objects' properties to which they have subscribed as observers. An observer object can register by providing a keypath, hence the name, into the observed object. Unfortunately, KVO is partially broken in Swift, at least up to Swift 4.2, and your app may crash when the KVO keyPathsForValuesAffectingValue method is run on a background thread while the main thread is attempting to register an observer, for example, to update a UI element. See this radar issue (https://bugs.swift.org/plugins/servlet/mobile#issue/SR-6795) for more details.

RxSwift

RxSwift aims to be fully compatible with Rx, Reactive Extensions for Microsoft .NET, a mature reactive programming framework that has been ported to many languages, including Java, Scala, JavaScript, and Clojure. Adopting RxSwift thus has the advantage that it will be quite natural for you to use the same approach and concepts in another language for which Rx is available, in case you need to.

It may be interesting to know that Rx.NET came into existence thanks to the work of Erik Meijer and others at Microsoft, which also led to the creation of LINQ, a popular query language for .NET, and to the introduction of `async`/`await` primitives to handle asynchronous calls on all .NET languages.

If you want to play with RxSwift, the first step is creating an Xcode project and adding the SwiftRx dependency. If you use the Swift Package Manager, just make sure your `Package.swift` file contains the following information:

```
let package = Package(
  ...
  dependencies: [
    .package(url: "https://github.com/ReactiveX/RxSwift.git", "4.0.0" ..<
"5.0.0")
  ],
  targets: [
    .target(name: "TestTarget", dependencies: ["RxSwift", "RxCocoa"])
  ]
)
```

If you use CocoaPods, add the following dependencies to your `podfile`:

```
pod 'RxSwift', '~> 4.0'
pod 'RxCocoa', '~> 4.0'
```

Then, run this command:

pod install

Finally, if you use Carthage, add this to `Cartfile`:

```
github "ReactiveX/RxSwift" ~> 4.0
```

Then, run this command to finish:

carthage update

As you can see, we have also included RxCocoa as a dependency. RxCocoa is a framework that extends Cocoa to make it ready to be used with RxSwift. For example, RxCocoa will make many properties of your Cocoa objects observable without requiring you to add a single line of code. So if you have a UI object whose position changes depending on some user action, you can observe its `center` property and react to its evolution.

Observables and observers

Now that RxSwift is set up in our project, let's start with a few basic concepts before diving into some code:

- A stream in SwiftRx is represented through `Observable<ObservableType>`, which is equivalent to `Sequence`, with the added capability of being able to receive new elements asynchronously.
- An observable stream in Rx can emit three different events: `next`, `error`, and `complete`.
- When an observer registers for a stream, the stream begins to emit `next` events, and it does so until an `error` or `complete` event is generated, in which case the stream stops emitting events.
- You subscribe to a stream by calling `ObservableType.subscribe`, which is equivalent to `Sequence.makeIterator`. However, you do not use that iterator directly, as you would to iterate a sequence; rather, you provide a callback that will receive new events.
- When you are done with a stream, you should release it, along with all resources it allocated, by calling `dispose`. To make it easier not to forget releasing streams, SwiftRx provides `DisposeBag` and `takeUntil`. Make sure that you use one of them in your production code.

 One way to look at reactive extensions is as a mix of the iterator and observer design patterns. Now, while the former is intrinsically associated with a sequential, synchronous view of things, the latter is an asynchronous, callback-based paradigm. Rx acts as a bridge across those two worlds, ensuring you can go from one view to the other without losing any information. This property actually has a mathematical proof (`https://repository.tudelft.nl/islandora/object/uuid:bd900036-40f4-432d-bfab-425cdebc466e/datastream/OBJ/download`), and, although maybe not immediately interesting, this only adds to the beauty of the paradigm.

All of this can be translated into the following code snippet:

```
let aDisposableBag = DisposeBag()
let thisIsAnObservableStream = Observable.from([1, 2, 3, 4, 5, 6])

let subscription = thisIsAnObservableStream.subscribe(
  onNext: { print("Next value: \($0)") },
  onError: { print("Error: \($0)") },
  onCompleted: { print("Completed") })

// add the subscription to the disposable bag
// when the bag is collected, the subscription is disposed
subscription.disposed(by: aDisposableBag)
// if you do not use a disposable bag, do not forget this!
// subscription.dispose()
```

Usually, your view controller is where you create your subscriptions, while, in our example `thisIsAnObservableStream`, observers and observables fit into your view model. In general, you should make all of your model properties observable, so your view controller can subscribe to those observables to update the UI when need be. In addition to being observable, some properties of your view model could also be observers. For example, you could have a `UITextField` or `UISearchBar` in your app UI and a property of your view model could observe its `text` property. Based on that value, you could display some relevant information, for example, the result of a query. When a property of your view model is at the same time an observable and an observer, RxSwift provides you with a different role for your entity—that of a `Subject`. There exist multiple categories of subjects, categorized based on their behavior, so you will see `BehaviourSubject`, `PublishSubject`, `ReplaySubject`, and `Variable`. They only differ in the way that they make past events available to their observers.

Before looking at how these new concepts may be used in your program, we need to introduce two further concepts: transformations and schedulers.

Transformations

Transformations allow you to create new observable streams by combining, filtering, or transforming the events emitted by other observable streams. The available transformations include the following:

- `map`: This transforms each event in a stream into another value before any observer can observe that value. For example, you could map the `text` property of a `UISearchBar` into an URL to be used to query some remote service.

- `flatMap`: This transforms each event into another Observable. For example, you could map the `text` property of a `UISearchBar` into the result of an asynchronous query.
- `scan`: This is similar to the `reduce` Swift operator on sequences. It will accumulate each new event into a partial result based on all previously emitted events and emit that result.
- `filter`: This enables filtering of emitted events based on a condition to be verified.
- `merge`: This merges two streams of events by preserving their ordering.
- `zip`: This combines two streams of events by creating a new stream whose events are tuples made by the successive events from the two original streams.

Schedulers

Schedulers allow you to control to which queue RxSwift operators are dispatched. By default, all RxSwift operations are executed on the same queue where the subscription was made, but by using schedulers with `observeOn` and `subscribeOn`, you can alter that behavior. For example, you could subscribe to a stream whose events are emitted from a background queue, possibly the results of some lengthy tasks, and observe those events from the main thread to be able to update the UI based on those tasks' outcomes. Recalling our previous example, this is how we could use `observeOn` and `subscribeOn` as described:

```
let aDisposableBag = DisposeBag()
let thisIsAnObservableStream = Observable.from([1, 2, 3, 4, 5, 6])
  .observeOn(MainScheduler.instance).map { n in
     print("This is performed on the main scheduler")
  }

let subscription = thisIsAnObservableStream
  .subscribeOn(ConcurrentDispatchQueueScheduler(qos: .background))
  .subscribe(onNext: { event in
     print("Handle \(event) on main thread? \(Thread.isMainThread)")
  }, onError: { print("Error: \($0). On main thread?
\(Thread.isMainThread)")
  }, onCompleted: { print("Completed. On main thread?
\(Thread.isMainThread)") })

subscription.disposed(by: aDisposableBag)
```

Asynchronous networking – an example

Now we can take a look at a slightly more compelling example, showing off the power of reactive programming. Let's get back to our previous example: a UISearchBar collects user input that a view controller observes, to update a table displaying the result of a remote query. This is a pretty standard UI design. Using RxCocoa, we can observe the text property of the search bar and map it into a URL. For example, if the user inputs a GitHub username, the URLRequest could retrieve a list of all their repositories. We then further transform the URLRequest into another observable using flatMap. The remoteStream function is defined in the following snippet, and simply returns an observable containing the result of the network query. Finally, we bind the stream returned by flatMap to our tableView, again using one of the methods provided by RxCocoa, to update its content based on the JSON data passed in record:

```
searchController.searchBar.rx.text.asObservable()
  .map(makeURLRequest)
  .flatMap(remoteStream)
  .bind(to: tableView.rx.items(cellIdentifier: cellIdentifier)) { index,
record, cell in
    cell.textLabel?.text = "" // update here the table cells
  }
  .disposed(by: disposeBag)
```

This looks all pretty clear and linear. The only bit left out is the networking code. This is pretty standard code that we've already seen in this and other chapters of the book, with the major difference that it returns an observable wrapping a URLSession.dataTask call. This following code shows the standard way to create an observable stream by calling observer.onNext and passing the result of the asynchronous task:

```
func remoteStream<T: Codable>(_ request: URLRequest) -> Observable<T> {

    return Observable<T>.create { observer in
        let task = URLSession.shared.dataTask(with: request) { (data,
response, error) in
            do {
                let records: T = try JSONDecoder().decode(T.self, from:
data ?? Data())
                for record in records {
                    observer.onNext(record)
                }
            } catch let error {
                observer.onError(error)
            }
            observer.onCompleted()
        }
```

```
        task.resume()

        return Disposables.create {
            task.cancel()
        }
    }
}
```

As a final bit, we could consider the following variant: we want to store the `UISearchBar` `text` property value in our model, instead of simply retrieving the information associated with it in our remote service. To do so, we add a `username` property in our view model and recognize that it should, at the same time, be an observer of the `UISearchBar` `text` property as well as an observable, since it will be observed by the view controller to retrieve the associated information whenever it changes. This is the relevant code for our view model:

```
import Foundation
import RxSwift
import RxCocoa

class ViewModel {
    var username = Variable<String>("")
    init() {
        setup()
    }
    setup() {
        ...
    }
}
```

The view controller will need to be modified as in the following code block, where you can see we bind the `UISearchBar` `text` property to our view model's `username` property; then, we observe the latter, as we did previously with the search bar:

```
searchController.searchBar.rx.observe(String.self, "text")
  .bindTo(viewModel.username)
  .disposed(by: disposeBag)

viewModel.username.asObservable()
  .map(makeURLRequest)
  .flatMap(remoteStream)
  .bind(to: tableView.rx.items(cellIdentifier: cellIdentifier)) { index,
record, cell in
    cell.textLabel?.text = "" // update here the table cells
  }
  .disposed(by: disposeBag)
```

With this last example, our short introduction to RxSwift is complete. There is much more to be said, though. A whole book could be devoted to RxSwift/RxCocoa and how they can be used to write Swift apps!

Summary

In this chapter, we have reviewed three main paradigms to handle concurrent tasks in Swift: using callbacks and closures; using futures and promises; using reactive programming. The aim of this chapter has mainly been to provide readers with solid foundations to understand why callbacks are a low-level mechanism not entirely suitable to write complex programs, to understand what futures and promises really are under the hood, and to appreciate the beauty of reactive programming. We have also provided a necessarily short introduction to a few frameworks that will make using futures and promises of reactive streams with Swift a breeze.

In the next chapter, we are going to focus on Swift Package Manager, which can be a great companion through the task of refactoring your code and extracting frameworks from it that you can easily share.

13

Modularize Your Apps with Swift Package Manager

Released alongside Swift 3, Swift Package Manager (SPM) is Swift's native response to attempt to solve the dependency-management problem. SPM is native in the sense that it is written in Swift, and you will use Swift to interact with it. If you are not familiar with dependency management, it can be defined as tools and techniques that enable to share and integrate external (or internal) libraries in a structured manner.

In this chapter, we will cover the following topics:

- Creating a library package as well a command-line tool that consumes the library
- Adding third-party dependencies and integrating your packages in iOS and macOS Xcode projects
- Refactoring an existing app to extract a reusable framework out of it and sharing it using a git repository

Creating a library package

In order to create a package, you will use the `swift package` command.

Running the command without any argument will print in the terminal the different options and subcommands you can run. As we are getting started, here are the most important ones:

- `swift package init`: Initializes a new package.
- `swift package update`: Updates package dependencies.
- `swift package generate-xcodeproj`: Generates an Xcode project.
- `swift package describe`: Describes the current package.

As we are getting started with SPM, the command we are the most interested in is `swift package init`.

 Swift Package Manager is designed to build command-line tools and libraries for Linux and macOS targets. You will not be able to depend on Apple's proprietary frameworks, such as UIKit. Note that swift web apps (Kitura- or Vapor-based) are a perfect scenario to use SPM.

For the example, we'll recreate a popular HTTP client library, inspired by the popular node.js **request** library.

As the library's goal is to be able to call URLs, and will be similar to cURL, let's call it **swURL**:

```
$ mkdir swURL # create the swURL folder
$ cd swURL
$ swift package init --type library # create the library in the current
folder

Creating library package: swURL
Creating Package.swift
Creating README.md
Creating .gitignore
Creating Sources/
Creating Sources/swURL/swURL.swift
Creating Tests/
Creating Tests/LinuxMain.swift
Creating Tests/swURLTests/
Creating Tests/swURLTests/swURLTests.swift
Creating Tests/swURLTests/XCTestManifests.swift
```

```
$ tree
.
├── Package.swift              // 1
├── README.md
├── Sources
│   └── swURL                  // 2
│       └── swURL.swift
└── Tests
    ├── LinuxMain.swift        // 3
    └── swURLTests
        ├── XCTestManifests.swift
        └── swURLTests.swift
```

If your OS does not have the `tree` command available, you can use `find . -not -path '*/\.*'`, which provides equivalent information. Alternatively, if you have Homebrew or MacPorts available, you can easily install by executing `brew install tree` or `port install tree`.

Swift Package manager created the directory structure and files for us. Here are some are notable ones:

- `Package.swift`: This is the package manifest.
- The `swURL` folder in `sources`: This is the main folder in which we'll put the sources for our library.
- `LinuxMain.swift`: This is required to run the tests on Linux.

Without any modifications to the current sources, we can `build` and `test` the project:

```
$ swift build
Compile Swift Module 'swURL' (1 sources)

$ swift test
Compile Swift Module 'swURLTests' (2 sources)
Linking ./.build/x86_64-apple-
macosx10.10/debug/swURLPackageTests.xctest/Contents/MacOS/swURLPackageTests
Test Suite 'All tests' started.
Test Suite 'swURLPackageTests.xctest' started
Test Suite 'swURLTests' started.
Test Case '-[swURLTests.swURLTests testExample]' started.
Test Case '-[swURLTests.swURLTests testExample]' passed (0.160 seconds).
Test Suite 'swURLTests' passed.
 Executed 1 test, with 0 failures (0 unexpected) in 0.160 (0.160) seconds
Test Suite 'swURLPackageTests.xctest' passed.
 Executed 1 test, with 0 failures (0 unexpected) in 0.160 (0.160) seconds
Test Suite 'All tests' passed.
 Executed 1 test, with 0 failures (0 unexpected) in 0.160 (0.160) seconds
```

Now you are all set up, and your new library is ready to be actively developed.

Adding features to the library

Now we are ready to add the first few methods to our library. The first thing we want to do is add the GET HTTP method. To this aim add the following code to the Sources/swURL/swURL.swift file that SPM created for you:

```
public func get<T: Decodable>(url: URL,
                completion: @escaping(_ data: T?, _ error: Error?) -> Void)
-> Void {
    jsonRequest(urlRequest: URLRequest(url: url), completion: completion)
}
```

Let's also add a simple implementation to the POST request:

```
public func post<T: Encodable, U: Decodable>(url: URL, body: T,
                                    completion: @escaping (_ data:
U?, _ error: Error?) -> Void) -> Void {
    var request = URLRequest(url: url)
    request.httpMethod = "POST"
    request.httpBody = try? JSONEncoder().encode(body)
    jsonRequest(urlRequest: request, completion: completion)
}
```

Finally, let's add a small executor in order to perform the requests and return the responses:

```
private func jsonRequest<T: Decodable>(urlRequest: URLRequest,
                                completion: @escaping (_ data: T?, _ error:
Error?) -> Void) -> Void {
    let task = URLSession.shared.dataTask(with: urlRequest) { (data,
response, error) in
        let d = try? JSONDecoder().decode(T.self, from: data!)
        completion(d, error)
    }
    task.resume()
}
```

This code work but its testability is not great as it is highly dependant on the following:

- JSONEncoder and JSONDecoder, which we can improve
- URLSession

Now, you could add dependency injection to these functions, along the lines we saw in Chapter 11, *Implementing Dependency injection*. This is left as an exercise for the reader.

Now, we can add a unit test in `Tests/swURLTests/swURLTests.swift`. Simply replace the boilerplate code that SPM created for you with this:

```
import Foundation
import XCTest
@testable import swURL

struct Todo: Decodable {
    let userId: Int
    let id: Int
    let title: String
    let completed: Bool
}

final class swURLTests: XCTestCase {
    func testGet() {

        var todo : Todo = Todo(userId:0, id: 0, title:"", completed:false)
        let expectation = self.expectation(description: "URLTest")

        swURL.get(url: URL(string:
"https://jsonplaceholder.typicode.com/todos/1")!) {
        (result : Todo?, error: Error?) -> Void in
            todo = result!
            expectation.fulfill()
        }
        waitForExpectations(timeout: 10, handler: nil)
        XCTAssertEqual(todo.id, 1)
    }
    static var allTests = [
        ("testGet", testGet),
    ]

}
```

In the preceding test, we make use of the great `jsonplaceholder` project, which provides a simple API that will allow us to test against a real web server our library.

Running the tests with `swift test` at the root of our package should produce the following:

```
Compile Swift Module 'swURL' (2 sources)
Compile Swift Module 'swURLTests' (2 sources)
Linking ./.build/x86_64-apple-
macosx10.10/debug/swURLPackageTests.xctest/Contents/MacOS/swURLPackageTests
Test Suite 'All tests' started
Test Suite 'swURLPackageTests.xctest' started
Test Suite 'swURLTests' started
```

```
Test Case '-[swURLTests.swURLTests testGet]' started.
Test Case '-[swURLTests.swURLTests testGet]' passed (0.265 seconds).
Test Suite 'swURLTests' passed.
 Executed 1 test, with 0 failures (0 unexpected) in 0.265 (0.265) seconds
Test Suite 'swURLPackageTests.xctest' passed.
 Executed 1 test, with 0 failures (0 unexpected) in 0.265 (0.265) seconds
Test Suite 'All tests' passed.
 Executed 1 test, with 0 failures (0 unexpected) in 0.265 (0.265) seconds
```

Now that we have a fully-functional library for making GET and POST JSON requests, we can integrate the library into an executable target.

Adding more targets

To add an executable target to our package, we will edit the `Package.swift` file to add a new short section under `targets` (the new target definition in bold):

```
.target(
    name: "swURL",
    dependencies: []),
.target(
    name: "swURLCli",
    dependencies: ["swURL"]),
.testTarget(
    name: "swURLTests",
    dependencies: ["swURL"]),
```

Then, we create a new `swURLCli` directory under the `Sources` directory to contain the new `swURLCli` executable source files. Finally, add a `main.swift` file in `swURLCli` with the following content:

```
import Foundation
import swURL

struct Todo: Decodable {
    let userId: Int
    let id: Int
    let title: String
    let completed: Bool
}

func doTask(completion: @escaping (_ data: Todo?, _ error: Error?) -> Void)
{

    let group = DispatchGroup()
    group.enter()
```

```
        swURL.get(url: URL(string:
"https://jsonplaceholder.typicode.com/todos/1")!,
                            completion: { (result : Todo?, error: Error?) in
                                completion(result, error)
                                group.leave()
                        })

        group.wait()
    }

    doTask { (result : Todo?, error: Error?) -> Void in
        print("Hello, world!")
    }
```

As you can see, we made sure to synchronize our main thread with the asynchronous network operation using a dispatch group. Had we not done this, the main thread would exit before the asynchronous task had a chance to finish. To double-check that everything is fine, this is how your directory hierarchy should look:

```
$ tree
.
├── Package.swift
├── README.md
├── Sources
│   └── swURL
│   └── swURL.swift
│   └── swURLCli  // new directory
│   └── main.swift // new file
└── Tests
    ├── LinuxMain.swift
    └── swURLTests
        ├── XCTestManifests.swift
        └── swURLTests.swift
```

Now you can run `swift build`, which should output the following information:

```
$ swift build
Compile Swift Module 'swURLCli' (1 sources)
Linking ./.build/x86_64-apple-macosx10.10/debug/swURLCli
```

The `./.build/x86_64-apple-macosx10.10/debug/swURLCli` file is your new executable, which you can run from the command line. Now that we have an executable, let's link it to an external library to understand how dependency management works in SPM.

As soon as you add an executable target to your SPM package, it will stop generating a framework that you can use in iOS applications. This is because you cannot include executables in iOS apps, so Xcode will complain about the lack of a binary targeting the ARM platform within your SPM package.

Adding third-party dependencies

Now that we have learned the basics of using SPM to create a simple library, let's have a look at how to work with external dependencies. So, let's add one to our package. For this example, we will work with Google Promises, which we covered in Chapter 12, *Futures, Promises, and Reactive Programming.* So, open Package.swift in your preferred editor and make sure the dependencies section looks like this (the text you should add is in bold):

```
dependencies: [
    // Dependencies declare other packages that this package depends
on.
    // .package(url: /* package url */, from: "1.0.0"),
    .package(url: "https://github.com/google/promises.git",
.exact("1.2.3")),
],
```

When it comes to editors, every programmer has their inalienable preferences. Swift is supported by most text editors, including Sublime Text, Atom, and Emacs. You may find, though, that the level of Swift support varies across editors, and Xcode provides unequivocally the best Swift support. This state of things could be about to change, though. Indeed, the Swift team recently released their initial implementation of the Language Protocol Server for Swift. This is still a work in progress, but as it becomes more stable and rich in features, you might see that most editors will provide the same level of support for Swift, hopefully it's the same level as for Xcode. So, stay tuned!

After saving the file, run swift package resolve to get the dependency installed under .build/repositories/:

```
Fetching https://github.com/google/promises.git
Completed resolution in 1.81s
Cloning https://github.com/google/promises.git
Resolving https://github.com/google/promises.git at 1.2.3
```

The `swift package resolve` command also creates a `Package.resolved` file in your package root, which contains a list of all installed dependencies along with their repository URL, version, and commit hash. If you want to get a shortened version of the same information, just run `swift package show-dependencies`, which will show the following:

```
warning: dependency 'Promises' is not used by any target
.
└── Promises<https://github.com/google/promises.git@1.2.3>
```

SPM supports a number of different commands. If you want to get an overview, or if you forgot how a specific command is called or its arguments, you can run `swift package --help` to be reminded.

Now, we could import Promises in our executable `main.swift` file and refactor our code to use that library. Instead, we will leave that as an exercise to the reader and will focus on another important feature in SPM: its ability to automatically update dependencies when new versions are available.

In our current example, we pinned Google Promises down to version 1.2.3. Say we now want to remove that restriction and accept any version of that library starting with 1.2.3. To do that, we modify our `Package.swift` dependency section to look like this, where we replaced `.exact("1.2.3")` with `from:"1.2.3"`:

```
    dependencies: [
        // Dependencies declare other packages that this package depends
on.
        // .package(url: /* package url */, from: "1.0.0"),
        .package(url: "https://github.com/google/promises.git", from:
"1.2.3"),
    ],
```

After that, whenever you want to make SPM update your package dependencies, just run `swift package update`:

```
$ swift package update
Updating https://github.com/google/promises.git
Completed resolution in 1.14s
Resolving https://github.com/google/promises.git at 1.2.4
```

Besides specifying the exact version you want to use, or a starting version, SPM supports a number of additional possibilities:

```
.package(url: "https://github.com/google/promises.git",
        .upToNextMajor(from: "1.2.3")),
.package(url: "https://github.com/google/promises.git",
        .upToNextMinor(from: "1.2.4")),
.package(url: "https://github.com/google/promises.git",
        "1.2.3"..<"1.2.6"),
.package(url: "https://github.com/google/promises.git",
        "1.2.3"..."1.2.8"),
.package(url: "https://github.com/google/promises.git",
        .branch("develop")),
.package(url: "https://github.com/google/promises.git",
        .revision("e74b07278b926c9ec6f9643455ea00d1ce04a021"))
```

This is all great! But let's see how we can leverage SPM in a workflow aimed at the creation of a full-fledged iOS or macOS app written in Xcode.

 If you ever get a sense that SPM is not doing what you expect it to, such as not updating a dependency after you changed its version number in `Package.swift`, the `swift package reset` command can come to your rescue. It will completely empty your package's build/cache directory and force SPM to get and build any dependencies from scratch.

Using SPM with Xcode

As mentioned, SPM currently only supports creating libraries and command-line executables. So you will not be able to write your next macOS app entirely using SPM – you will still need Xcode. Yet, SPM can be extremely useful in collaboration with Xcode as a tool to manage your dependencies and keep them up to date. Indeed, SPM is able to generate an Xcode project containing all the targets and dependencies you specified in Package.swift, which you can include within your macOS app Xcode project or workspace. Let's look at this in more detail.

If you want to create an Xcode project with the same definition of your SPM package, just run `swift package generate-xcodeproj`, which will output the following information:

```
$ swift package generate-xcodeproj
generated: ./swURL.xcodeproj
```

If you ran `generate-xcodeproj` on the last version of your SPM package, you will also see this warning: `warning: dependency 'Promises' is not used by any target`. No worries, that only means that the Google Promises library was not required and therefore SPM did not include it in the Xcode project.

If you open in Xcode the generated project, you will see it contains all of the files we created previously.

```swift
import Foundation
import swURL

struct Todo: Decodable {
    let userId: Int
    let id: Int
    let title: String
    let completed: Bool
}

func doTask(completion: @escaping (_ data: Todo?, _ error: Error?) -> Void) {

    let group = DispatchGroup()
    group.enter()

    swURL.get(url: URL(string: "https://jsonplaceholder.typicode.com/todos/1")!,
              completion: { (result : Todo?, error: Error?) in
                   completion(result, error)
                   group.leave()
              })

    group.wait()
}

doTask { (result : Todo?, error: Error?) -> Void in
    print("Hello, world!")
}
```

Usually, you will not want to make any changes to this auto-generated project, since you are going to generate it anew every time you have new dependencies. Instead, you'll include it as a subproject within your main Xcode project or workspace.

Do not forget to remove the executable target we added in the *Adding more targets* section, otherwise, you will not be able to compile the Xcode project that we are going to build in the remainder of this section. In this case, just create a macOS project instead of an iOS project and you will be fine.

To try this out, let's walk through the following steps:

1. Create a new iOS project in Xcode using the Single View App template.
2. Locate the swURL.xcodeproj we just created using the Finder, but do not open it.
3. Drag and drop swURL.xcodeproj from the Finder into your project Navigator area (the leftmost column with a listing of your files).
4. Go to your iOS app target Build Phases editor and add a new **Link Binary With Library** phase. Click the "+" button and select swURL.framework in the ensuing dialog.
5. Modify your ViewController.swift file so it contains the following code:

```
import UIKit
import swURL

struct Todo: Decodable {
    let userId: Int
    let id: Int
    let title: String
    let completed: Bool
}


class ViewController: UIViewController {

    func doTask(completion: @escaping (_ data: Todo?, _ error:
Error?) -> Void) {
        swURL.get(url: URL(string:
"https://jsonplaceholder.typicode.com/todos/1")!,
                completion: { (result : Todo?, error: Error?) in
                    completion(result, error)
        })
    }
    override func viewDidLoad() {
        super.viewDidLoad()
        // Do any additional setup after loading the view,
typically from a nib.

        doTask { (result : Todo?, error: Error?) -> Void in
            print("Hello, world!")
        }
    }
}
```

Finally, you can run your app and check the Xcode console to verify it contains "Hello, world!"

As you will notice, the code we used in ViewController is similar to what we used in our command-line target that created previously. The only difference is the absence of the dispatch group synchronization. Indeed, an iOS app is based on a run loop – it will be there until the user decides to quit it – so there is no need to make you main thread wait for the asynchronous task to complete.

Congratulations! You have just created an iOS app with a dependency that you can easily manage using SPM. Whenever new versions of your dependencies will be available, you will just need to run `swift package update` and `swift package generate-xcodeproj` to update your dependencies in your iOS app.

Extracting and sharing a framework

Now that we know a little more about SPM and what it brings to developing with Xcode, it's time to rewind our story and go back to our initial aim of using SPM to break our apps down into separate, reusable modules. When you extract some code from an existing project to create a framework out of it, it is usually the case you will need to refactor the code to improve its modularity. This is the focus of the next section, while the following one will focus on creating the framework.

You may find it a bit confusing, but we should take care of differentiating between modules and modularity when using Swift. On the one hand, indeed, modules and frameworks are almost the same in Swift parlance. In Swift, in fact, modules are the representation of frameworks at the language level. Or, if you prefer, frameworks are binary entities that Swift represents through modules. Modularity, on the other hand, is a more general concept, which extends to using frameworks to encapsulate and share code, as well as to organizing your code across multiple files to keep it more structured. In the preceding paragraph, we were referring to the latter meaning of modularity.

Refactoring your code

As you know, in Chapter 12, *Futures, Promises, and Reactive Programming,* we created a streamlined implementation of futures and promises packaged as an Xcode playground. That code is certainly a good candidate for extracting a framework that we can reuse in other projects. The playground mixed the futures and promises implementation with the code using it. So our first refactoring step is keeping just the futures and promises implementation and removing the rest, which is highlighted in italics in the following snippet (to keep the listing short, we have left only the signatures of the functions to be removed):

```swift
public enum Result<Value> {
    case success(Value)
    case failure(Error)
}

enum SimpleError: Error { ... }

typealias Callback<T> = (Result<T>) -> Void

public class Future<T> {

    internal var result : Result<T>? {
        didSet {
            if let result = result, let callback = callback {
                callback(result)
            }
        }
    }
    var callback : Callback<T>?
    init(_ callback: Callback<T>? = nil) {
        self.callback = callback
    }
    func then(_ callback: @escaping Callback<T>) {
        self.callback = callback
        if let result = result {
            callback(result)
        }
    }
}

public final class Promise<T> : Future<T> {
    func resolve(_ value: T) {
        result = .success(value)
    }
    func reject(_ error: Error) {
        result = .failure(error)
```

```
        }
}

import Dispatch

func asyncOperation(_ delay: Double) -> Promise<String> {
...
}

let future : Future<String> = asyncOperation(1.0)
future.then { result in
...
}

func asyncOperation2() -> Promise<String> {
...
}

func asyncOperation3(_ str : String) -> Promise<Int> {
...
}

func asyncOperation4(_ input : Int) -> Promise<Double> {
...
}

extension Future {
    func chain<Z>(_ cbk: @escaping (T) -> Future<Z>) -> Future<Z> {
        let p = Promise<Z>()
        self.then { result in
            switch result {
            case .success(let value): cbk(value).then { r in p.result = r }
            case .failure(let error): p.result = .failure(error)
            }
        }
        return p
    }
}

let promise2 = asyncOperation2()
promise2.chain { result in
...
}
```

As you can see, we have a couple of types, ResultValue<T> and Callback<T>; two classes, Future<T> and Promise<T>; and an extension to the Future<T> class. Admittedly, the amount of code for all that is not much, but we want to separate the three classes across different files to better support their evolution. Additionally, it seems a good idea to have all of our shared types in their own modules. So we may want to create the following four files using our preferred text editor: Types.swift, Future.swift, Promise.swift, and Future+Chain.swift. One thing we should be really careful about is specifying the correct protection level for all types, classes, and methods. In fact, it is not enough to mark as public all the classes you want as part of your framework API, since according to Swift default protection rules, public classes default to having internal protection. This works great when you are writing your code for a monolithic app, but is not necessarily what you want when writing libraries, since, if you do not declare a method as public, it will not be accessible from the outside. Keeping this in mind, here is the content of the four files in our package:

```swift
// FuturesAndPromises
// Types

public enum Result<Value> {
    case success(Value)
    case failure(Error)
}

public typealias Callback<T> = (Result<T>) -> Void

// FuturesAndPromises
// Future

public class Future<T> {

    internal var result : Result<T>? {
        didSet {
            if let result = result, let callback = callback {
                callback(result)
            }
        }
    }
    var callback : Callback<T>?
    public init(_ callback: Callback<T>? = nil) {
        self.callback = callback
    }
    public func then(_ callback: @escaping Callback<T>) {
        self.callback = callback
        if let result = result {
            callback(result)
        }
```

```
        }
}

// FuturesAndPromises
// Promise

public final class Promise<T> : Future<T> {
    public func resolve(_ value: T) {
        result = .success(value)
    }
    public func reject(_ error: Error) {
        result = .failure(error)
    }
}

// FuturesAndPromises
// Future+Chain

extension Future {

    public func chain<Z>(_ cbk: @escaping (T) -> Future<Z>) -> Future<Z> {
        let p = Promise<Z>()
        self.then { result in
            switch result {
            case .success(let value): cbk(value).then { r in p.result = r }
            case .failure(let error): p.result = .failure(error)
            }
        }
        return p
    }
}
```

One of the benefits of Swift being a static, strongly-typed language is its great support for refactoring. When you refactor some code, the compiler will flag any mistake you might have made even before attempting to run your refactored code. This does not mean, though, that you do not need tests for successful refactoring. On the contrary, it is a good practice to refactor your code only once you have a decent unit-test suite in place. We will cover unit testing specifically in Chapter 14, *Testing Your Code with Unit and UI Tests*.

One additional refactoring that could help to make our code more easily reusable is replacing our actual `Result` definition – which is tied to using `Error` to represent an error condition – with a new definition that is on the error type. This task is left as an exercise to the reader. As a hint, you could consider the following definition for your new `Result` type:

```
public enum Result<Value, Err> {
    case success(Value)
    case failure(Err)
}
```

One further thing we should never forget when creating a framework is providing an extensive unit-testing suite. We already looked into how you can define unit tests using SPM in the *Adding features to the library* section, so the task of extracting a test from our initial playground is also left as an exercise to the reader.

Extracting a framework

Now that we have our code properly and satisfactorily refactored, we can move on to the next step: making the actual framework and using it in a project.

To create our new `FuturesAndPromises` framework, perform the following steps:

1. Create a new directory, called `FuturesAndPromises`
2. Run `cd FuturesAndPromises` and then `swift package init --type library`
3. Copy the four source files you created into `Sources/FuturesAndPromises`
4. Run `swift build` to check that your code compiles correctly; if not, fix all the errors until it compiles successfully
5. If you have created a test file, copy it to `Tests/FuturesAndPromisesTests` and run `swift test`

If your `swift build` step completed without errors, you have successfully created your `FuturesAndPromises` framework. Now, you can use it in other projects. For example, we could modify our previous `swURL` example so it uses `FuturesAndPromises` to manage its network operations instead of relying on callbacks. To do so, we need to perform the following:

- Add `FuturesAndPromises` as a dependency to `swURL`
- Rewrite parts of `swURL` to use `FuturesAndPromises` instead of `URLSession`

We saw earlier that adding a dependency to an SPM package is as easy as listing it in `Package.swift`, where you can add its Git repository URL under the dependencies section. In our current case, we do not have any Git URL available, since `FuturesAndPromises` is a local framework we have just created that has not been pushed yet to, for example, GitHub. It turns out, though, that SPM also supports local Git repositories, so this will not be a big problem. But, we will need to create a Git repository for our FuturesAndPromises framework and create a version tag for it, so SPM can retrieve it.

Creating a Git repository for FuturesAndPromises is quite an easy task. Just cd to the directory containing FuturesAndPromises files and run the following commands:

- `git init`: Initializes your repo
- `git add .`: Adds all required files to the repository
- `git commit -m "initial commit" -a`: Commits your changes
- `git tag 1.0.0`: Creates a version tag

Now, you can open the `Package.swift` file in `swURL` and add the dependency to `FuturesAndPromises`. Open that file in your preferred editor and make sure its dependencies section looks similar to the following, where you will take care of setting the correct relative or absolute path to your `FuturesAndPromises` location:

```
dependencies: [
    .package(url: "../FuturesAndPromises", from: "1.0.0"),
],
```

Now, if you run `swift build`, you will see the following output:

```
Updating https://github.com/google/promises.git
Fetching /Users/sergio/tmp/packt-book/Chap13-code/FuturesAndPromises
Completed resolution in 0.43s
Removing https://github.com/google/promises.git
Cloning /Users/sergio/tmp/packt-book/Chap13-code/FuturesAndPromises
Resolving /Users/sergio/tmp/packt-book/Chap13-code/FuturesAndPromises at
1.0.0
warning: dependency 'FuturesAndPromises' is not used by any target
```

You may be puzzled by the references to the Google Promises framework. As you may remember, we added it as a dependency to our initial `swURL` implementation. The latest changes to `Package.swift` we just outlined removed that dependency, so SPM cleaned it up!

The final line in the output of `swift build` is a warning telling us we are not using `FuturesAndPromises` anywhere. This will be fixed when we will complete our swURL implementation. This will require creating a wrapper for `URLSession.dataTask` and rewriting the `swURL.jsonRequest` method so it uses a promise. We already did something very similar in `Chapter 12`, *Futures, Promises, and Reactive Programming*, so we will leave this as exercise to the reader.

Once you are done rewriting `swURL` to use `FuturesAndPromises`, the next step is to generate a convenience Xcode project out of it. As you know, we mentioned that this is required if you want to integrate your Swift package into another Xcode project. In our case, having modified the `swURL` framework, this step will have the effect of bringing all of those changes to any Xcode project that uses it. This is another benefit of using SPM with Xcode.

Of course, you can also integrate the `FuturesAndPromises` framework into a new Xcode project independently from `swURL`. The steps to do so are the same as those outlined when we integrated `swURL` into an Xcode project, so you should have no trouble carrying this through as an exercise.

As a final note, with SPM, there is an easy way to share your frameworks across your project, within your organization, or with the open source community. Indeed, all is needed is publishing them to GitHub, BitBucket, or any other cloud-based Git provider. Of course, you will need your account with that provider to be private if you do not want your framework to become available to the whole open source community.

Summary

In this chapter, we encountered Swift Package Manager and reviewed its main features. Then, we used it to create a package that contains a simple Swift framework, a command-line tool using it, and some unit tests. Swift Package Manager makes it easy to add external dependencies to your packages, whether they are remote or local Git repositories, and we showed how you can add and remove them. The last step in an SPM-based development cycle is generating a convenience Xcode project that will makes it easy for you to use your Swift package in another project.

Often, creating libraries is not an organic process where you start off with the idea for a new library. In fact, it's usually the opposite, and you see the chance to create a library from a monolithic codebase once you find a second use for some piece of code. So, we looked at how you can extract that code from an existing app and refactor it to create a package that you can reuse elsewhere.

In the next chapter, we will address another fundamental aspect of developing Swift programs, that is, defining unit tests to provide a solid foundation for your app's quality and development process.

14
Testing Your Code with Unit and UI Tests

For a long time, automatic testing wasn't as widely practiced in the iOS development community as it was in other software communities, such as Java or general backend development. However, doing automatic testing is now an accepted mainstream practice. I would even say it's a necessary method for anyone who aims to release sound and robust software.

In this chapter, even an inexperienced developer will find all the needed information for testing their app using different techniques, such as TDD to design it or just adding tests at the end of the development.

The following topics will be covered in this chapter:

- Unit testing using XCTest
- Advanced testing techniques for testing in isolation using test doubles
- UI testing with XCTUITest
- A few tips and tricks to improve the effectiveness of our tests

Unit testing using XCTest

The traditional way of testing software encompasses a long phase of manual testing at the end of the software development cycle. This approach has been proven ineffective because manual testing is a long and non-scalable process, and also because the more efficient way is to have short release cycles—two or three weeks—and have a part of the iteration dedicated to the manual testing which, simply isn't affordable. Also, as developers, we realized that the best way of making our code testable is to write simple, granular, and automatic tests while we are still in development. This method, called **Test-Driven Development (TDD)**, was made famous by Kent Beck in his work on *Extreme Programming*, a revolutionary software programming methodology, revolutionary for its time.

It's based on writing the tests before writing the production code, such as tests that must run automatically using a testing framework. The first framework for doing this was called SUnit because it was for a programming language called Smalltalk. We could define a unit such as a chunk of software that implements a functionality. Using SUnit, the developer could implement a test to verify that functionality automatically, without the need of verifying it manually. Even though TDD was rarely used in the iOS community until a few years ago, it is currently widely accepted as a mainstream practice. There are several testing frameworks in Swift or Objective-C that can be used in Swift code, however, Apple provides a good solution for it as a default in Xcode, called XCTest. We'll start exploring it in this section.

Testing an RPN Calculator app

One of the challenges we face when we want to test our apps is to separate the different parts of it in a meaningful way. In general, we want to separate the UI from the rest of the app, and it would be better to test all the business logic, leaving a few high-level integration tests to cover the connection between the UI and the rest of the app. In this section, we'll see how to do this separation, and how to grow a functionality driven by tests. However, before proceeding with the code, we must define how to do it using automatic tests, with TDD.

TDD

unit testing is usually associated with *TDD*, a famous technique for developing software. In TDD, tests are written before implementing the actual production code, in small steps, to help the system grow organically.

The TDD is performed in a cycle:

1. Write a test
2. Make the test pass
3. Refactor the code to remove the duplication and prepare for the next test

There is more to it than that, but let's see an example of how to do TDD in Swift. As a simple example, we'll implement a basic RPN Calculator.

What is an reverse polish notation calculator?

Reverse Polish Notation (RPN), and it is also known as postfix notation. In RPN, the operators follow their operands, and mathematical operations such as 3 + 4 or 4 * 3 + 2 are written as 3 4 + and 4 3 * 2 +. At first glance, it might look counterintuitive, but it's really handy once you get used to it. One useful advantage of an RPN calculator is that it's easier to solve nested operations with it. It's easier because it doesn't need to use parentheses to resolve the logical priority between operations.
For example:

3 * (2 + 5) must be written as 3 2 5 + *

The mechanic is based on the concept of stacking: each operand is added to a stack. When an operator is inserted, like *add*, *multiply*, *divide* or *subtract*, it is applied to the two topmost operands. The result is put on the top of the stack.

Let's look at a graphical example for solving the previous operation. Before the first operator, we have the following stack:

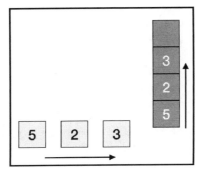

When we insert the +, we sum the two operands on top and push the result on the stack:

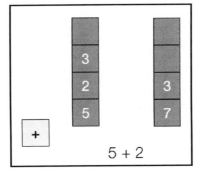

5 + 2

Then, for the multiplication, we do the same thing and we finally have our result on the top of the stack:

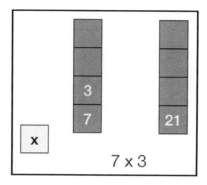

A simple RPN Calculator app

The app we are going to implement is a simplified version of an RPN Calculator. The UI will have an upper section, which will show the four upper values in the stack in reversed order, and a lower part with the numbers 0 to 9, the four basic operations, and an *Enter* key, which will put the value in the stack.

When we create the app using the wizard in Xcode, we must remember to check the two boxes to add Unit and UI tests.

The view in the storyboard mimics a simple calculator with the basic operations and four entries for the stack; as we mentioned earlier, the stack is upside down, with the topmost element at the bottom. The button with the e represents Enter, which will push the elements in the stack up and insert an empty value in the topmost place:

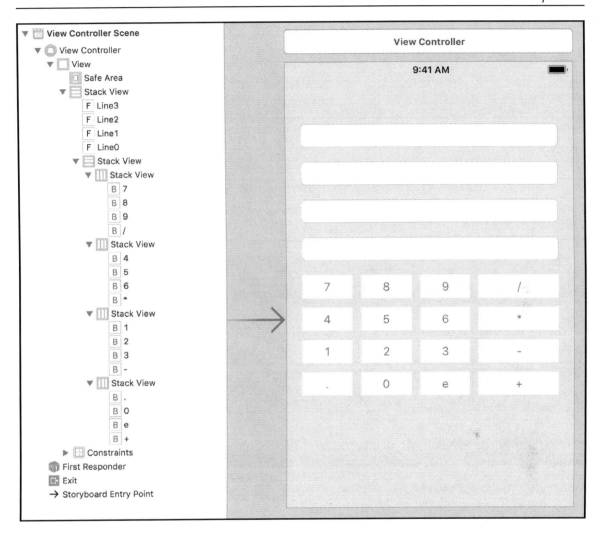

In Chapter 11, *Implementing Dependency Injection*, we stressed the importance of separating the UI from the business logic so that our view controller just connects the UI elements and action to a business logic object, which we model with a protocol:

```
class ViewController: UIViewController {
    @IBOutlet var line3: UITextField!
    @IBOutlet var line2: UITextField!
    @IBOutlet var line1: UITextField!
    @IBOutlet var line0: UITextField!
    private let rpnCalculator:RpnCalculator = FloatRpnCalculator()

    @IBAction func buttonDidTap(button: UIButton) {
```

```
        guard let token = button.title(for: .normal) else {
            return
        }
        rpnCalculator.new(token: token)
        line0.text = rpnCalculator.line0
        line1.text = rpnCalculator.line1
        line2.text = rpnCalculator.line2
        line3.text = rpnCalculator.line3
    }
}
```

The code in the action takes the text from the button that has raised the action and passes it to RpnCalculator, which changes its status; then the status, represented by the first four elements in the stack, is shown in the UI.

As you can see, we use an implementation of RpnCalculator, called FloatRpnCalculator, that converts the result into a float.

Given the way ViewController calls the calculator, we already know how to define its interface:

```
protocol RpnCalculator {
    var line3: String { get }
    var line2: String { get }
    var line1: String { get }
    var line0: String { get }
    func new(element: String)
}
```

Before writing the first test, we need at least to have the project compiling, and the simplest way to implement a compilable FloatRpnCalculator is as follows:

```
class FloatRpnCalculator: RpnCalculator {
    var line3: String = ""
    var line2: String = ""
    var line1: String = ""
    var line0: String = ""

    func new(element: String) {
    }
}
```

We already know that this isn't the code that can satisfy our requirements, but we want to be driven by the tests without planning too much how to write the production code.

The first test

Now that the project is compilable, let's move to the test file, called something similar to `RpnCalculatorTests`.

As you can see, Xcode already implemented a few tests using a template; however we don't need any of those, so we delete all the template code and start from scratch.

The first test we want to write is to check that when we insert the number 2, we have that number in the `line0` property of the model. An important piece of information to know when using `XCTest` is that all the tests must start with the *test* prefix; this is the way Xcode understands how to run the tests – using inspection it searches for all the functions in a subclass of `XCTestCase` whose names start with *test*. Apart from that, we are free to call the test functions what we want.

There are several testing naming conventions, and it is, in general, a matter of taste. We'll use one where we specify the context of the test and the expected result, such as a short story of the test:

- WHEN Two is inserted THEN we see Two At The Top
- WHEN Two and Enter And Three are inserted THEN we see Three and Two in the stack

However, some words don't give any information, such as WHEN and THEN, so we can omit them and assume they are there. Every time we are reading a test description, we can assume there is a WHEN after `test_` and a THEN after the double underscore, for example:

```
func test_TwoIsAddedToTwo__FourIsTheResult()
```

The preceding code can be read as testing that WHEN Two Is Added To Two THEN Four Is The Result.

However, this is only one possible convention on writing test names, and there are several others, but describing them is beyond the scope of this chapter.

The only important thing is to select one method and then stick to it so that all the test names are uniformly named and can be read in the same way.

Getting back to our first test, we can write it as follows:

```
import XCTest
@testable import RpnCalculator

class RpnCalculatorTests: XCTestCase {
    var rpnCalculator: RpnCalculator = FloatRpnCalculator()

    func test_Two__TwoOnTopMostPlace() {
```

```
        rpnCalculator.new(element: "2")
        XCTAssertEqual(rpnCalculator.line0, "2")
    }
}
```

We introduce here the function that `XCTest` uses to verify whether a value is something we expect: `XCTAssert`.

There are many of those, and we'll describe them in another section; however, the most used is `XCTAssertEqual(par1, par2)`, which passes if both the parameters are equal, and fails if not. We'll now run the tests, either via the **Product | Test** menu, or with the ⌘ + *u* keyboard shortcut, and we get a failure.
Following the rules of TDD, let's make it pass in the simplest way possible:

```
class FloatRpnCalculator: RpnCalculator {
  // ...
    func new(element: String) {
        line0 = element
    }
}
```

When we run the test now, it passes. Congratulations on your first green test!

I know that it looks like cheating, since this code cannot be part of the production, but the first trivial test is important to implement the structure and infrastructure that we'll use to build the real code.

More tests

In the second test we write, we'll show that we need to change the internal representation of the calculator.

The scenario we want to test is that when we tap on *Enter*, the number we just entered moves from the first to the second position: WHEN we select the two AND we tap on *Enter* THEN the stack first position is empty AND the second contains the number 2.

With this scenario, we want to introduce *Enter* as a way to add multiple operands. The test could be written as follows:

```
func test_TwoEnter__TwoOnSecondPlace() {
    rpnCalculator.new(element: "2")
    rpnCalculator.new(element: "e")
    XCTAssertEqual(rpnCalculator.line0, "")
    XCTAssertEqual(rpnCalculator.line1, "2")
}
```

We must now introduce an implementation of `Stack`. The Swift standard library, unlike many of the other languages, doesn't provide a default Stack implementation, however, it is easy to implement it backed with an array:

```
struct Stack {
    private var data: [String] = []

    mutating func push(_ element: String) {
        data.append(element)
    }

    mutating func pop() -> String {
        return data.popLast() ?? ""
    }

    subscript(idx: Int) -> String {
        guard idx < data.count else {
            return ""
        }
        return data[data.count - idx - 1]
    }
}
```

Other than push and pop, we also need a way to inspect the value of the elements using an index, so we added a subscript. Since we push on the tail and we pop on the head, our stack is upside down, and in the subscript, we must invert the index, ensuring that we do not exceed the boundaries.

With the implemented stack, the calculator is now as follows:

```
class FloatRpnCalculator: RpnCalculator {
    private var stack: Stack = Stack()
    var line3: String {
        get { return stack[3] }
    }
    var line2: String {
        get { return stack[2] }
    }
    var line1: String {
        get { return stack[1] }
    }
    var line0: String {
        get { return stack[0] }
    }

    func new(element: String) {
        if element == "e" {
            stack.push("")
```

```
        } else {
            stack.push(element)
        }
    }
}
```

We run the tests, and voilà, green again:

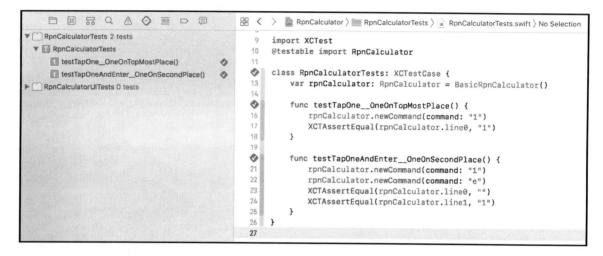

Moving on to the third test, we want to ensure that we can add multiple operators.

This how we write the test:

```
func test_TwoEnterFour__FourTwoOnTheStack() {
    rpnCalculator.new(element: "2")
    rpnCalculator.new(element: "e")
    rpnCalculator.new(element: "4")
    XCTAssertEqual(rpnCalculator.line0, "4")
    XCTAssertEqual(rpnCalculator.line1, "2")
}
```

Since we have already implemented Enter, we might be lucky, and this could just pass.

If we run the tests now, we get red.

This is how Xcode will present the failing error:

```
func test_TwoEnterFour__FourTwoOnTheStack() {
    rpnCalculator.new(element: "2")
    rpnCalculator.new(element: "e")
    rpnCalculator.new(element: "4")
    XCTAssertEqual(rpnCalculator.line0, "4")  ◇ XCTAssertEqual failed: ("") is not equal to ("2") -
    XCTAssertEqual(rpnCalculator.line1, "2")
}
```

This is because we push a new element every time we add a new element, but in this case what we want is to append it to the element at the topmost place.

We need to add to our stack implementation, a feature to append a value to the topmost element:

```
struct Stack {
  // ...
    mutating func appendAtTopmost(_ element: String) {
        guard !data.isEmpty else {
            return push(element)
        }
        data[data.count - 1] += element
    }
  // ...
}
```

The calculator changes accordingly:

```
class FloatRpnCalculator: RpnCalculator {
  // ...
    func new(element: String) {
        if element == "e" {
            stack.push("")
        } else {
            stack.appendAtTopmost(element)
        }
    }
}
```

Refactoring the tests

If we look now at the tests, we can see that all the tests start with the same instruction, which adds a 2.

Let's refactor the tests removing the common instruction from each test. In the XCTestCase class, a function named setup() is called before each test, and it looks like we can move that instruction in that function:

```
override func setUp() {
    super.setUp()
```

```
        rpnCalculator.new(element: "2")
    }
```

However, now the test names are a bit misleading and it would be better to express the fact that all these tests have one thing in common. The thing they have in common is that the first element is the number 2: this defines the context of the suite. It could be helpful to use a trick to name the class to express that context:

```
class RpnCalculator_WithTwo: XCTestCase {
    var rpnCalculator: RpnCalculator = FloatRpnCalculator()
    override func setUp() {
        super.setUp()
        rpnCalculator.new(element: "2")
    }

    func test_TwoOnTopMostPlace() {
        XCTAssertEqual(rpnCalculator.line0, "2")
    }

    func test_Enter__TwoOnSecondPlace() {
        rpnCalculator.new(element: "e")
        XCTAssertEqual(rpnCalculator.line0, "")
        XCTAssertEqual(rpnCalculator.line1, "2")
    }

    func test_EnterFour__FourTwoOnTheStack() {
        rpnCalculator.new(element: "e")
        rpnCalculator.new(element: "4")
        XCTAssertEqual(rpnCalculator.line0, "4")
        XCTAssertEqual(rpnCalculator.line1, "2")
    }
}
```

Now the Tree Test View is even more expressive:

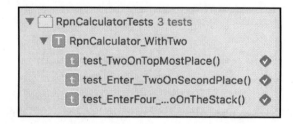

It probably doesn't help much in this simple app, however, it's a nice trick to know when you have hundreds of tests in the same area.

Adding operations

We can now safely add the test for the operations, starting from the addition. Using the same trick, we create a TestCase called RpnCalculator_Operations, where we are going to assert that adding 1 and 2 gives us 3.00.
Since the calculator is a Float calculator, the result must be 3.00:

```
class RpnCalculator_Operations: XCTestCase {
    var rpnCalculator: RpnCalculator = FloatRpnCalculator()

    func test__OneEnterTwoAdd__ThreeOnFirstPlace() {
        rpnCalculator.new(element: "1")
        rpnCalculator.new(element: "e")
        rpnCalculator.new(element: "2")
        rpnCalculator.new(element: "+")
        XCTAssertEqual(rpnCalculator.line0, "3.00")
    }
}
```

The code used to make it pass is as follows:

```
func new(element: String) {
    if element == "e" {
        stack.push("")
    } else if element == "+" {
        if let secondOperand = Float(stack.pop()),
            let firstOperand = Float(stack.pop()) {
            let result = firstOperand + secondOperand
            stack.push(String(format: "%.2f", result))
        }
    } else {
        stack.appendAtTopmost(element)
    }
}
```

The test's descriptions are now starting to get a bit too long and too similar to each other. Before moving on to the next one, let's take the opportunity to create a custom assertion to test a long list of elements. To do that, we create a protocol and we add the assertion in its extension:

```
protocol CalculatorAsserting {
    var rpnCalculator: RpnCalculator { get }
}
extension CalculatorAsserting {
    func assertThatEntering(elements: [String],
                           resultShouldBeEqualTo result: String) {
        elements.forEach { rpnCalculator.new(element: $0) }
```

```
            XCTAssertEqual(rpnCalculator.line0, result)
        }
    }
```

The test case becomes the following:

```
class RpnCalculator_Operations: XCTestCase, CalculatorAsserting {
    var rpnCalculator: RpnCalculator = FloatRpnCalculator()

    func test__OneEnterTwoAdd__ThreeOnFirstPlace() {
        assertThatEntering(elements: ["1", "e", "2", "+"],
                           resultShouldBeEqualTo: "3.00")
    }
}
```

This works fine for this already-passing test, but when we add the multiplication test, we can see that something isn't right:

```
func test__TwoEnterThreMultiply__SixOnFirstPlace() {
    assertThatEntering(elements: ["2", "e", "3", "*"],
                       resultShouldBeEqualTo: "6.00")
}
```

Running the test, the failure indication is not inside the test as we expect, but inside the custom assertion:

```
    func test__TwoEnterThreMultiply__SixOnFirstPlace() {
        assertThatEntering(elements: ["2", "e", "3", "*"],
                           resultShouldBeEqualTo: "6.00")
    }
}

extension CalculatorAsserting {
    func assertThatEntering(elements: [String],
                            resultShouldBeEqualTo result: String) {
        elements.forEach {
            rpnCalculator.new(element: $0)
        }
        XCTAssertEqual(rpnCalculator.line0, result)    ◇ XCTAssertEqual failed: ("3*") is not equal to ("6.00") -
    }
}
```

If we look at the XCTAssertEqual signature, we can see that there are two parameters for file and line with the #file and #line default arguments:

```
func XCTAssertEqual<T>(_ expression1: @autoclosure () throws -> T, _
expression2: @autoclosure () throws -> T, _ message: @autoclosure () ->
String = default,
file: StaticString = #file,
```

```
line: UInt = #line
) where T : Equatable
```

Knowing that, if we pass those from the assertion function name to XCTAssertEqual, we'll restore the expected behavior:

```
func assertThatEntering(elements: [String],
                        resultShouldBeEqualTo result: String,
                        file: StaticString = #file,
                        line: UInt = #line) {
    elements.forEach { rpnCalculator.new(element: $0) }
    XCTAssertEqual(rpnCalculator.line0, result, file: file, line: line)
}
```

Moving on to the code for the multiplication, we just duplicate the code we have written for the addition:

```
func new(element: String) {
    if element == "e" {
        stack.push("")
    } else if element == "+" {
        if let secondOperand = Float(stack.pop()),
            let firstOperand = Float(stack.pop()) {
            let result = firstOperand + secondOperand
            stack.push(String(format: "%.2f", result))
        }
    } else if element == "*" {
        if let secondOperand = Float(stack.pop()),
            let firstOperand = Float(stack.pop()) {
            let result = firstOperand * secondOperand
            stack.push(String(format: "%.2f", result))
        }
    } else {
        stack.appendAtTopmost(element)
    }
}
```

It's pretty obvious that the code is duplicated and we'll proceed in the same manner for the missing operations.
We refactor it, then, extracting a function that accepts a closure and converting the if chain to a switch:

```
func new(element: String) {
    switch element {
    case "e":
        stack.push("")
    case "+":
        return doOperation { $0 + $1 }
```

```
    case "*":
        return doOperation { $0 * $1 }
    default:
        stack.appendAtTopmost(element)
    }
}

private func doOperation(operation: (Float, Float) -> Float) {
    if let secondOperand = Float(stack.pop()),
        let firstOperand = Float(stack.pop()) {
        let result = operation(firstOperand, secondOperand)
        stack.push(String(format: "%.2f", result))
    }
}
```

The two final operations are pretty simple to add.

Here are the tests:

```
func test__SixEnterTwoDivision__ThreeOnFirstPlace() {
    assertThatEntering(elements: ["6", "e", "2", "/"],
        resultShouldBeEqualTo: "3.00")
}

func test__SixEnterTwoSubctract__FourOnFirstPlace() {
    assertThatEntering(elements: ["6", "e", "2", "-"],
        resultShouldBeEqualTo: "4.00")
}
```

And here is the code:

```
func new(element: String) {
    switch element {
    case "e":
        stack.push("")
    case "+":
        return doOperation { $0 + $1 }
    case "*":
        return doOperation { $0 * $1 }
    case "/":
        return doOperation { $0 / $1 }
    case "-":
        return doOperation { $0 - $1 }
    default:
        stack.appendAtTopmost(element)
    }
}
```

Learnings from our first TDD code

We easily implemented a complete app driven by a test pretty quickly. XCTest demonstrated itself to be a really solid test engine and the results are quite good.

UI is completely separated by the business logic, the test is terse and readable, and the code is quite neat.
Another interesting thing is that with TDD, at the beginning you feel slowed down, but when the infrastructure is in place, you are actually faster than without tests.

Assertions

In all the tests of the previous example, we used only one assertion, but XCTest comes with several types of assertions. Let's have a look at the most important ones.

All the assertions are based on a fundamental one:

```
XCTAssert(expression: Bool)
```

This checks whether the expression is true, otherwise, it stops and makes the test fail. In theory, we could use only this one to cover all the possible types of tests, but the other assertions help the reader understand the semantics of the test and what the developer wanted to express. Hence, a good rule is to use the more specific assertion needed for the test we are currently writing.

Slightly more precise assertions are the Boolean assertions, which check whether a value is true or false:

```
XCTAssertTrue(expression: Bool)
XCTAssertFalse(expression: Bool)
```

XCTAssert is equivalent to XCTAssertTrue.

When we want to test whether two objects or scalars are equal, we must use the equality assertions:

```
XCTAssertEqual(expression: Equatable)
XCTAssertNotEqual(expression: Equatable)
```

For float or double, a series of assertions allows to pass an accuracy, otherwise, because of the rounding, we could have a false negative, as follows:

```
XCTAssertEqual(expression1: FloatingPoint, expression2: FloatingPoint,
accuracy: FloatingPoint)
XCTAssertNotEqual(expression1: FloatingPoint, expression2: FloatingPoint,
accuracy: FloatingPoint)
```

We can also assert whether a value is greater than another:

```
XCTAssertGreaterThan(expression1: Comparable, expression2: Comparable)
XCTAssertLessThan(expression1: Comparable, expression2: Comparable)
```

To check whether a value is `nil`, we use the following:

```
XCTAssertNil(expression: Any?)
XCTAssertNotNil(expression: Any?)
```

The Swift way of handling errors is to throw exceptions, so we must have a way to check whether an expression throws an exception:

```
XCTAssertThrowsError(expression: T)
XCTAssertNoThrow(expression: T)
```

Finally, sometimes we have to fail the test without checking anything, as a body of a `guard` for example. In this case, we can use the following:

```
XCTFail(message: String)
```

As a final note, all the previous assertions also have a format where you can pass a message to the `Assert` function, a message that will be shown by Xcode if the assertion fails, like in the following example:

```
class MessagingTests: XCTestCase {
    func sum(_ a: Float, _ b: Float) -> Float {
        return a*b
    }

    func testSum() {
        XCTAssertEqual(sum(2, 3), 5, "2 + 3 must be equal to 5")
    }
}
```

⊗ XCTAssertEqual failed: ("6.0") is not equal to ("5.0") - 2 + 3 must be equal to 5

Advanced testing with mocks, spy, and others

As we have seen, testing part of the software when it doesn't depend on other parts of the same app is quite straightforward:

1. Create an instance of the class
2. Set an initial context
3. Trigger some behavior to change the state or to return a new set of values

This is even easier if the class being tested is well-designed and has only a single well-defined responsibility. However, it's not common to have a class that depends on other classes, or, even more complicated, a class that depends on external collaborators, such as databases, a network service, or user input.

In the next section, we'll see a technique to test this scenario. The nomenclature we use is the one defined by Gerard Meszaros in his seminal book *Xunit test Patterns, Chapter 11, Using Test Doubles*, and now widely used in the industry.

Testing in Isolation

When the class we want to test depends on other classes, we have two choices: test all the classes it depends on, or try to isolate it and test it in isolation. Generally, the piece of software we want to test is called **system under test (SUT)**. Even though sometimes it makes sense to test all the dependencies together, we'll explore here a technique, called **test double**, to test in isolation.

The idea is to replace the dependencies with something that resembles the dependent collaborator, but that doesn't have all the logic and dependencies of the real one. The SUT has two kinds of relationships: **indirect input** and **indirect output**.

While the test itself creates the direct input and verifies the direct output, the collaborator can generate an indirect input to the SUT or receive indirect output from the SUT. The way the indirect input and output are handled defines the different type of test double.

Dummy test double: when we don't need to test the collaborator

Let's consider a `TaskManager` class that has `NetworkService` as a collaborator; the tasks are stored locally until the user decides to save them on a server by tapping on a synchronization button.

Basically, we have two different behaviours in the class, and we want to test them in different scenarios.

However, when we test one of these behaviors, we need to take the other into account somehow.

The code could be something similar to this:

```swift
class TaskManager {
    private var tasks = [Task]()
    private let service: TaskManagerService
    init(service: TaskManagerService) {
        self.service = service
    }
    func add(task: Task) {
        tasks.append(task)
    }
    var count: Int {
        return tasks.count
    }
    func sync() {
        service.sync(tasks: [Task])
    }
}

protocol TaskManagerService {
    func fetchAllTasks(completion: ([Task]) -> Void)
    func sync(tasks: [Task])
    // ...
}

struct Task {
    // ---
}
```

When we want to test, for example, that the count of the tasks is equal to the task we add, we don't need to consider the network service, but it's needed to compile the class. Remembering what we saw in `Chapter 11`, *Implementing Dependency Injection* about Dependency Injection, we defined the collaboration using a protocol, so that we could replace it with a dummy service:

```
struct TaskManagerServiceDummy: TaskManagerService {
    func fetchAllTasks(completion: ([Task]) -> Void) {}
    func sync(tasks: [Task]) {}
}
```

The test can be easily written like this:

```
func testNumberOfTasks() {
    let taskManager = TaskManager(service: TaskManagerServiceDummy())
    taskManager.add(task: Task())
    taskManager.add(task: Task())
    XCTAssertEqual(taskManager.count, 2)
}
```

A **dummy object** is a placeholder passed to the SUT that is never called during the test.

Fake test double: a simplified collaborator

A fake object is a simplified version of a collaborator, with similar or partial functionalities, but implemented in a simpler way. Considering a version of `TaskManager` that stores the tasks locally, using a store object as a collaborator, whose implementation is unknown to the `TaskManager`, it might be implemented as file-persistent on file or database-persistent with `CoreData`.

`TaskManager` relies on the store to persist the tasks:

```
class TaskManager {
    private let store: TaskStore

    init(store: TaskStore) {
        self.store = store
    }
    func add(task: Task) {
        store.add(task: task)
    }
    var count: Int {
        return store.allTasks.count
    }
}
```

`TaskStore` has the following interface:

```
protocol TaskStore {
    var allTasks: [Task] { get }
    func add(task: Task)
}
```

The fake implementation of the store, instead of using `CoreData`, will use a simple array, which we can write as follows:

```
class FakeTaskStore: TaskStore {
    private(set) var allTasks = [Task]()

    func add(task: Task) {
        allTasks.append(task)
    }
}
```

Similarly to the previous one, the test is simply as follows:

```
func testNumberOfTasks() {
    let taskManager = TaskManager(store: FakeTaskStore())
    taskManager.add(task: Task())
    taskManager.add(task: Task())
    XCTAssertEqual(taskManager.count, 2)
}
```

Stub test double: a predefined collaborator

A **test stub** is a collaborator that has canned returns so that we can control the indirect input of the **SUT**.

Considering the example of the fake, we create a Stub that already has two tasks:

```
class StubTaskStoreWithTwoTasks: TaskStore {
    private(set) var allTasks = [Task(), Task()]

    func add(task: Task) {
        allTasks.append(task)
    }
}
```

The test is as follows:

```
func testAddATaskToPreloadedTasks() {
    let taskManager = TaskManager(store: StubTaskStoreWithTwoTasks())
    taskManager.add(task: Task())
    XCTAssertEqual(taskManager.count, 3)
}
```

Spy test double: verifying collaboration

As Stub verifies the indirect input, a Test Spy permits us to verify the indirect output, exposing a way that indicates whether the functions in the Spy were called during the test. Let's consider a variation of the `TaskManager` that we implemented in the Dummy example, *Dummy test double: when we don't need to test the collaborator*, that manages the tasks in a remote server. We want to verify that the tasks are refreshed, fetching them from the server when `TaskManager` is constructed.

The code for the manager is the following:

```
protocol TaskManagerService {
    func fetchTask(completion: ([Task]) -> Void)
    func sync(tasks: [Task])
}

class TaskManager {
    private let service: TaskManagerService
    private var tasks = [Task]()

    init(service: TaskManagerService) {
        self.service = service
        self.service.fetchTask { [weak self] tasks in
            self?.tasks = tasks
        }
    }
}
```

To verify the call, the Spy has a Boolean property that is set to `true` when the fetch function is called:

```
class SpyTaskManagerService: TaskManagerService {
    private(set) var fetchHasBeenCalled = false

    func fetchTask(completion: ([Task]) -> Void) {
        fetchHasBeenCalled = true
    }
```

```
    func sync(tasks: [Task]) { }
}
```

The test is as follows:

```
func testTasksAreFetchedInStartup() {
    let service = SpyTaskManagerService()
    _ = TaskManager(service: service)
    XCTAssertTrue(service.fetchHasBeenCalled)
}
```

Mock test double: asserting collaboration

When someone is talking about **Mock**, they probably mean test double—as you have seen, the differences between the types of test double are really subtle. However, test mock is a well-defined test double. The goal here is to verify the indirect input and generate the indirect output in a precise way.

In the test, we set the expectations, which are the function invocations with the exact parameters, and at the end of the test, we verify the actual versus the expected invocation in the mock. For this example, we still use `TaskManager` with a store, modifying it to returning the number of tasks after adding one.

Since we need to check the exact parameter passed in the invocation, we add an `id` property to the task, and we make it `Equatable`:

```
struct Task: Equatable {
    let id = UUID().uuidString
}

class TaskManager {
    private let store: TaskStore

    init(store: TaskStore) {
        self.store = store            .
    }
    func add(task: Task) -> Int {
        store.add(task: task)
        return store.count
    }
    var count: Int {
        return store.count
    }
}
```

```
protocol TaskStore {
    func add(task: Task)
    var count: Int { get }
}
```

The test will become slightly more verbose because we are setting the expectations at the beginning, and, depending on the number of the interactions with the mock, it could be quite a long list:

```
func testAddAnCountTasks() {
    let firstTaskToBeAdded = Task()
    let secondTaskToBeAdded = Task()
    let mockTaskStore = MockTaskStore()
    mockTaskStore.callAdd(with: firstTaskToBeAdded)
    mockTaskStore.callCount(returning: 1)
    mockTaskStore.callAdd(with: secondTaskToBeAdded)
    mockTaskStore.callCount(returning: 2)

    let taskManager = TaskManager(store: mockTaskStore)
    _ = taskManager.add(task: firstTaskToBeAdded)
    _ = taskManager.add(task: secondTaskToBeAdded)

    mockTaskStore.verify()
}
```

In other languages, such as Java or C#, that have more dynamic characteristics compared to Swift, mocks are usually implemented by libraries that use introspection to generate from a protocol, the functions to implement the verification and the expectations. Due to the static nature of Swift, this isn't possible yet. There have been a few attempts to do it by generating code from protocols, but these are very cumbersome to use, and making manual mocks is still the best option.

Let's see here how to do it for the `TaskStore`:

```
class MockTaskStore: TaskStore {
    private enum FunctionType {
        case add, count
    }

    private struct FunctionInvocation {
        let type: FunctionType
        let params: [Any]
    }

    private var expected = [FunctionInvocation]()
    private var actual = [FunctionInvocation]()
    private var nextCall: Int = 0
```

```
        var count: Int {
            let currentCall = expected[nextCall]
            let returningValue = (currentCall.params[0] as? Int) ?? 0
            actual.append(FunctionInvocation(type: .count, params:
[returningValue]))

            nextCall = expected.index(after: nextCall)
            return returningValue
        }

        func add(task: Task) {
            actual.append(FunctionInvocation(type: .add, params: [task]))
            nextCall = expected.index(after: nextCall)
        }

        func callAdd(with task: Task) {
            expected.append(FunctionInvocation(type: .add, params: [task]))
            nextCall = expected.startIndex
        }

        func callCount(returning value: Int) {
            expected.append(FunctionInvocation(type: .count, params: [value]))
            nextCall = expected.startIndex
        }

        func verify() {
            XCTAssertEqual(expected.count, actual.count)
            zip(expected, actual).forEach { (expected, actual) in
                XCTAssertEqual(expected.type, actual.type)
                switch (expected.type, actual.type) {
                case (.add, .add):
                    if let expectedParam = expected.params.first as? Task,
                        let actualParam = actual.params.first as? Task {
                            XCTAssertEqual(expectedParam, actualParam)
                    } else {
                        XCTFail("Wrong parameter for call of type
\(expected.type)")
                    }
                default:
                    break
                }
            }
        }
    }
}
```

As you can see, the code for the Mock is very long, and it would be even longer if we'd added more functions to the store. Also, it is a kind of test that rigidly defines the contract between the SUT and the collaborators, not only in the functions that can be called but also on the sequence of the calls; in this way, we are in a certain sense blocking the implementation of the SUT, and we can easily break the encapsulation of the SUT, making it more difficult to refactor and extend the software. For this reason, test mocks must be used sparingly, and you should use other kinds of less invasive test doubles.

UI testing with Xcode

As you may recall, when we created the project for `RpnCalculator`, we toggled on UI testing too, giving us the ability to run a full suite test using the UI of the app, as if the app were run by a user.

In this section, we'll explore the surface of UI testing, the reasons to do UI testing, when to stop, and how to write the tests.

The importance of UI testing

It's common thinking that the tests that use the UI are generally slow and brittle, and difficult to write and maintain. Nevertheless, UI testing is a practice that is useful to consider when designing the test strategy for developing a software.

A few years ago, Mike Cohn defined the Agile Testing Pyramid in his book *Succeeding with Agile: Software Development Using Scrum*, which describe the types of tests, and how many are required for each type of implement action to be effective:

- **Unit tests**: These are the basement, they are quick to run, can be exhaustive, can cover all the classes in the app, and we should write as many as possible.
- **Service tests**: In the middle, these are connected to a service layer, the RPN `calculator` in our simple case. This layer offers all the features or services to the UI.
- **UI tests**: At the top, this uses the elements of the app as if it were a user. The problems of the fragility and slowness of this kind of test remain, but still, they carry value, and, if written in a clean way, and if written only for the ones that touch as many parts as possible, they give us the confidence that all the layers are connected together correctly.

The following diagram depicts the testing pyramid:

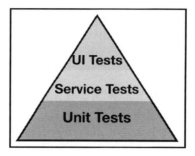

Recording a UI test

In Xcode 6, Apple released a framework based on XCTest for UI testing called XCUITest. Not only can we write UI tests as we do for unit testing, but we can also record the keystrokes while using the app. To activate it, we need to open the UI test case and select a test, moving the cursor in the body of any test function. Doing that, the **Red** button at the left bottom, becomes selectable and we can record the session:

```
class RpnCalculatorUITests: XCTestCase {
    override func setUp() {
        continueAfterFailure = false
        XCUIApplication().launch()
    }

    func testAddition() {
        // Use recording to get started writing UI tests.
        // Use XCTAssert and related functions to verify your tests produce the correct results.
    }
}
```

Let's record a simple addition, as follows:

```
class RpnCalculatorUITests: XCTestCase {
    override func setUp() {
        continueAfterFailure = false
        XCUIApplication().launch()
    }

    func testAddition() {
        // Use recording to get started writing UI tests.
```

```
        // Use XCTAssert and related functions to verify your tests
        //produce the correct results.
        let app = XCUIApplication()
        app.buttons["2"].tap()
        app.buttons["e"].tap()
        app.buttons["3"].tap()
        app.buttons["+"].tap()
    }
}
```

The structure is the same as the normal unit test and in the `setUp()` method, the application is launched.

Running the test, the simulator will launch the app, as activated in `setUp`, and it will tap in the buttons as specified in the test. However, without an assertion phase, we are not testing anything. In the next section, we'll expand the test by adding the missing assert, and we'll see what else we can do with UI `XCTest`.

Writing UI tests in code

Being based on `XCTest`, we are already familiar with the assert functions, so that we'll use an `XCTAssertEqual` function.

In order to retrieve the value in the topmost place, we have to find the right text field. `XCUIApplication` is a proxy to the interface of our app and it contains helper functions to access the elements.

`XCUITest` is based on the concept of queries; every element in the screen can be reached via a query and the script can send any kind of interaction, which will be executed at runtime. As we used `app.buttons` to reach the buttons, we'll use `app.textFields`. Being the text field we want to check, in the last position, we need to calculate its index position in the array, so we need to calculate its exact position:

```
func testAddition() {
    let app = XCUIApplication()
    app.buttons["2"].tap()
    app.buttons["e"].tap()
    app.buttons["3"].tap()
    app.buttons["+"].tap()

    let line0 = app.textFields.element(boundBy: app.textFields.count - 1)
    XCTAssertEqual(line0.value as! String, "5.00")
}
```

However, relying on the position is fragile and not maintainable, and it also tightly couples the tests to the layout of the page, risking that changing the layout for some reason would break the tests. A better approach is to name the elements for the accessibility with an identifier, such as `ui.textfield.line0`. Every `UIKit` control has an `accessibilityIdentifier` property for this purpose, and the value can be set either in the storyboard or in the code. If we add it in the code, `ViewController` becomes the following:

```
class ViewController: UIViewController {
  //..
  @IBOutlet var line0: UITextField! {
      didSet {
          line0.accessibilityIdentifier = "ui.textfield.line0"
      }
  }
  private let rpnCalculator:RpnCalculator = FloatRpnCalculator()
  //..
}
```

The test now can search for the identifier:

```
func testAddition() {
    let app = XCUIApplication()
    // ...

    let line0 = app.textFields["ui.textfield.line0"]
    XCTAssertEqual(line0.value as! String, "5.00")
}
```

Identifying the elements makes the definition of the tests more robust and more maintainable, and it should be the first practice to adopt when preparing the code for a full testing strategy. Another improvement we could make to our test is to change the level of abstraction. The test relies on low-level elements, such as buttons or text fields, but it should use higher level concepts, such as `tapOnZero`, `tapOnEnter`, or `valueOnTopMostPlaceOfTheStack`. In this way, the code will be more readable, concise, and it will be easier to extend. To reach this goal, we can use the `PageObject` pattern, a useful testing pattern where each screen is wrapped in a class that exposes the service of the page.

In our example, a page object could be similar to this:

```
class CalculatorScreen {
    private let app = XCUIApplication()
    //...
    func tapOnTwo() {
        tapOnButton(title: "2")
```

```
    }
    func tapOnThree() {
        tapOnButton(title: "3")
    }
    //...
    func tapOnAdd() {
        tapOnButton(title: "+")
    }
    func tapOnEnter() {
        tapOnButton(title: "e")
    }
    //...
    var valueOnTopMostPlaceOfTheStack: String {
        guard let value =
            app.textFields["ui.textfield.line0"].value as? String
            else {
                return ""
        }
        return value
    }

    private func tapOnButton(title: String) {
        app.buttons[title].tap()
    }
}
```

Using the `CalculatorScreen` object, the test is now written in a clearer way:

```
func testAddition() {
    let calculator = CalculatorScreen()
    calculator.tapOnTwo()
    calculator.tapOnEnter()
    calculator.tapOnThree()
    calculator.tapOnAdd()

    XCTAssertEqual(calculator.valueOnTopMostPlaceOfTheStack, "5.00")
}
```

We just scratched the surface of XCUITest, but with this basic information, we are ready to implement a full testing strategy for our apps.

Tips and tricks

So far, we've seen how to test the code properly in the cleanest way possible. However, it's not always possible to find the code in the perfect state – testable and isolated – so this section will cover a few helpful tips.

Testing singletons

The singleton is one of the most controversial designing patterns. Its aim is to have one, and only one, instance of a particular class in our code base, but what happens is that we abuse the global nature of the singleton to have all the dependencies at hand when we need them. In this way, however, we are losing the power of DI as we have seen in Chapter 11, *Implementing Dependency Injection*.

Since a Singleton cannot be instantiated, it cannot be replaced with a test double. In his blog (https://www.swiftbysundell.com/), John Sundel demonstrates a few steps to make a singleton replaceable at testing time.

Let's try some code that relies on URLSession.instance to work:

```
class DataFetcher {
    enum Result {
        case data(Data)
        case error(Error)
    }

    func fetch(from url: URL, completionHandler: @escaping (Result) ->
Void) {
        let task = URLSession.shared.dataTask(with: url) { (data, response,
error) in
            if let error = error {
                return completionHandler(.error(error))
            }

            completionHandler(.data(data ?? Data()))
        }

        task.resume()
    }
}
```

If we want to mock URLSession to verify the calls from FetcherLoader, we cannot do it. The first step is to define a protocol for the mock that defines the only function of URLSession that is used from the singleton:

```
protocol NetworkSession {
    typealias CompletionHandler = (Data?, URLResponse?, Error?) -> Void

    func performRequest(for url: URL, completionHandler: @escaping
CompletionHandler)
}
```

Then, implement this as a URLSession extension:

```
extension URLSession: NetworkSession {
    typealias CompletionHandler = NetworkSession.CompletionHandler

    func performRequest(for url: URL, completionHandler: @escaping
CompletionHandler) {
        let task = dataTask(with: url, completionHandler:
completionHandler)
        task.resume()
    }
}
```

Having made URLSession conform to NetworkSession, we can inject it instead of using the shared global instance in the code. Also, the injected object is defaulted to URLSession.instance, so that the code that relies on FetcherLoader doesn't need to be changed:

```
class DateFetcher {
    enum Result {
        case data(Data)
        case error(Error)
    }
    private let session: NetworkSession

    init(session: NetworkSession = URLSession.shared) {
        self.session = session
    }

    func fetch(from url: URL, completionHandler: @escaping (Result) ->
Void) {
        session.performRequest(for: url) { (data, response, error) in
            if let error = error {
                return completionHandler(.error(error))
            }
```

```
                    completionHandler(.data(data ?? Data())))
            }
        }
    }
```

And now, we can finally write the test that injects a mock in a determinable way:

```
func testFetchingData() {
    class MockNetworkSession: NetworkSession {
        typealias CompletionHandler = NetworkSession.CompletionHandler

        var requestedURL: URL?

        func performRequest(for url: URL, completionHandler: @escaping
CompletionHandler) {
            requestedURL = url

            let data = "Hello world".data(using: .utf8)
            completionHandler(data, nil, nil)
        }
    }

    let session = MockNetworkSession()
    let loader = DataFetcher(session: session)

    var result: DataFetcher.Result = .data("".data(using: .utf8)!)
    let url = URL(string: "test/api")!
    loader.fetch(from: url) { result = $0 }

    XCTAssertEqual(session.requestedURL, url)
    switch result {
    case .data(let data):
        XCTAssertEqual(data, "Hello world".data(using: .utf8)!)
    case .error:
        XCTFail()
    }
}
```

One of the arguments against using singletons is that it makes the code difficult to test. This is certainly true, but we don't always have the freedom to get rid of singletons, maybe because they are provided by external libraries, such as in this case, or because they are developed by another team working on the same app.

However, using the technique we just experimented with, we can test the code thoroughly even with a lot of singletons in our code base.

Testing Async code

A common problem every developer encounters when adding tests to their software is how to test asynchronous code. Why is it a problem? It's because the flow of a test is expecting synchronous code.

Let's consider, for example, testing a file loader that loads the content of a JSON file in an asynchronous way:

```
class FileLoader {
    func loadContent(fromFilename: String,
                     onSuccess: @escaping (Any) -> Void) {
        guard let path = Bundle.main.path(forResource: fromFilename,
                                          ofType: "json") else {
            return
        }

        DispatchQueue.global(qos: .background).async {
            guard let data = try? Data(contentsOf: URL(fileURLWithPath:
path),
                                       options: .alwaysMapped) else {
                print("Error: Couldn't decode data")
                return

            }

            guard let decodedJSON = try? JSONSerialization.jsonObject(
                with: data, options: []) else {
                    print("Error: Couldn't decode data")
                    return
            }
            DispatchQueue.main.async {
                onSuccess(decodedJSON)
            }
        }
    }
}
```

If we want to test it, we could write a test such as this:

```
func testLoadingFile() {
    let fileLoader = FileLoader()

    fileLoader.loadContent(fromFilename: "FixturePlayers") { result in
        guard let array = result as? [[String: Any]] else {
            return XCTFail()
        }
        XCTAssertEqual(5, array.count)
```

```
        }
    }
```

If we run it, the test is immediately green, but it is a false positive; the code with the assertion is never run. We can verify this by changing the number of players in the assert to 10 for example, and we see that the tests are still passing. The reason for this is because the test runs in a synchronous way, and after calling the `loadContent` function, it finishes without waiting for the closure to be called. To execute this kind of test, Xcode introduced the concept of expectation, which is a way for the execution to wait until something fulfills the expectation or a timeout arrives:

```
func testLoadingFile() {
    let fileLoader = FileLoader()

    let expectation = self.expectation(description: "Loading")

    fileLoader.loadContent(fromFilename: "FixturePlayers") { result in
        defer {
            expectation.fulfill()
        }
        guard let array = result as? [[String: Any]] else {
            return XCTFail()
        }
        XCTAssertEqual(5, array.count)
    }

    waitForExpectations(timeout: 5)
}
```

This is a useful addition that Apple made in Version 6 of Xcode, which makes testing asynchronous code straightforward, giving us no excuses for not testing it.

Run only the test with the cursor

If you're already inside the TDD, you'll end up using the ⌘ + *u* shortcut to run all the tests, hundreds of times every day. But as your test base starts to grow, running all the tests can take a long time. So, you may start to have the habit to run only the test you selected with the cursor, using the mouse and the checkbox next to the name of the test; this, however, means you break your flow to move the mouse there.

There is a shortcut for running only the current test: *alt* + ⌘ + *u*. It's just a shortcut, but knowing it will increase your productivity.

Summary

We spent a lot of time exploring the default test library provided by Swift. Testing is an important practice during the development of an app; the strategy we want to follow must be clear so that we can produce the best and most robust app possible. We must put a lot of effort into unit and UI tests, without forgetting to test the app in the ways that it will be used by the customer. We can't always test in isolation, so the test double technique will help us to separate the different parts we want to verify in a practical way.

Now that we've covered all these techniques for testing the software, we are ready to go open source, which means releasing our software in the wild, as we'll see in the next chapter.

Going Out in the Open (Source) **15**

We all rely on open source; our software ecosystem is built on open source. It's time for you to get started and publish your first package. In this chapter, we'll discuss the steps that you should consider taking before you can release your project. This will require a deep understanding of all the concepts we've discussed in this book.

From a great architecture to properly used design patterns, open sourcing a project is an exciting endeavor. Not for the faint of heart, it's full of traps and mistakes that can be easily avoided.

Great projects exhibit great documentation, and documentation starts with documenting the public and private API appropriately. Documenting the internals of your project is a great way to ensure a smooth onboarding of contributors, but how do you validate that their contributions are working properly? Continuous integration services, such as Travis, Circle and `bitrise.io`, offer free tiers for open source projects. GitLab is also a strong contenter as they offer free private projects as well as CI and CD pipelines. Every now and then, as an iOS developer, you will want to publish updates to your beta testers. Fastlane can automate this process and usually works flawlessly on the CI services. Lastly, from your first commit to your first contributor, you will meet various individuals with questions, bugs, feature requests, and more. Being prepared for this is a great way to get all of these tedious project management aspects off your plate.

In this chapter, we will cover the following topics:

- Learning to document your code, generate documentation, and use GitHub Pages to publish it
- Configuring Travis and GitLab to build, run, and test your app automatically
- Using fastlane to automate the delivery of your app to the testflight, fabric, or hockey app
- Tips and tricks about maintaining open source projects

Documenting Swift

Your code is meant to be read and written by humans. While it should be syntactically correct to compile, your naming conventions, comments, and other artifacts of your coding style are of no importance to the compiler. The level of detail and attention you will put into documenting your code can make all the difference to internal or external contributors.

If you honed your craft on Objective-C, you're not in luck. Apple, which for the longest time used `HeaderDoc`, switched to a Markdown-flavored documentation engine. This is for the better, as Markdown is a widely used markup language and you will feel right at home if you have any experience with it.

The Markdown language

Yes, this is still a book about Swift, but let's take a minute to have a look at the Markdown language.

Language is a big word. Unlike with other programming languages, you can become proficient in Markdown in a few minutes.

Markdown allows for a lightweight annotation of your text so it can be structured and rendered without impeding the readability of the raw code:

```
A Simple Tomato Sauce

This is a simple tomato sauce recipe

You can add a title with the # sign or by underlining with = or -

# List of ingredients

Below is a simple unordered list, any one of the -, + • or * character will
make for a new list item

- Tomatoes
- Garlic
- Basil
- Pecorino romano

Using more than one # character lets you add a sub level to your titles.

## From your pantry

- Olive oil
```

```
- Salt, pepper
```

Lastly, you can create ordered lists using regular numbers. You do not have to count the number, always using 1 works perfectly well

```
# Recipe

1. Cook the garlic over medium heat
1. Once golden, add the sliced tomatoes and a cup of water
1. Bring to a boil, and reduce to a simmer
1. Add salt, pepper, basil
```

There is one gotcha: if you are familiar with Markdown already, you know that tables are not supported.

The anatomy of a documentation block

The documentation blocks come in a predetermined structure. Most of your documentation will use the following five sections:

- **Summary**: What your function does, always at the top of the documentation. This is also the first paragraph of your documentation comment.
- **Discussion**: Additional information about your function. This will be rendered with all other paragraphs, except the first one.
- **Returned values**: You can add more information about what your function returns by starting your line with `Returns:`.
- **Parameters**: Each parameter of your function can be described with `Parameter <name>:`.
- **Thrown errors**: You can provide additional information about the errors your method can throw by using `Throws:`.

The **Parameters** section also supports more than one parameter, as you may imagine. To document them all, you can use an unordered list as in the following example:

```
/**
 Compute the slope between two points

 This function calculate the slope between two points in a carthesian plane

 - Returns:
 the slope between the points (x0, y0) and (x1, y1)

 - Parameters:
```

```
    - x0: the x coordinate for the first point
    - y0: the y coordinate for the first point
    - x1: the x coordinate for the second point
    - y1: the y coordinate for the second point

  - Throws: SlopeError.infinite when y1 - y0 === 0: ie the slope is infinite

 */
func slope(x0: Double, y0: Double, x1: Double, y1: Double) throws -> Double
{
    guard y1 - y0 != 0 else {
        throw SlopeError.inifinite
    }
    return x1 - x0 / y1 - y0
}
```

Keeping example usages for each methods, when not obvious or complicated, is also a good idea. Luckily, Markdown has us covered with different techniques to delimit blocks of code. The best of all? You get free a gorgeous rendering of your code examples for everyone to read during their implementation – for free! Code samples come in two flavours:

- For simple lines or single elements, you can use `` ` ``, which will render within your current block but with a monospace font.
- For multiline code examples, you can use two formats:
    - Four-spaces indents
    - Triple backticks `` ``` ``

My personal preference is the triple backticks, as I find them more readable and predictable compared to the four-space indents. Try to determine what fits your needs and preferences.

Have a look at the following example from the preceding code:

```
/**
 Compute the slope between two points

 This function calculate the slope between two points in a carthesian plane

 - Returns:
 the slope between the points (x0, y0) and (x1, y1)

 - Parameters:
    - x0: the x coordinate for the first point
    - y0: the y coordinate for the first point
    - x1: the x coordinate for the second point
    - y1: the y coordinate for the second point
```

```
- Throws: SlopeError.infinite when y1 - y0 === 0: ie the slope is infinite

` ` `
const flat = try! slope(x0: 2, y0: 1, x1: 5, y1: 1)
flat == 0
` ` `

*/
func slope(x0: Double, y0: Double, x1: Double, y1: Double) throws -> Double
{
    guard x1 - x0 != 0 else {
        throw SlopeError.inifinite
    }
    return y1 - y0 / x1 - x0
}
```

The preceding example will render nicely in the Quick Help:

Summary
Compute the slope between two points

Declaration
```
func slope(x0: Double, y0: Double, x1: Double, y1: Double) throws
-> Double
```

Discussion
This function calculate the slope between two points in a carthesian plane

```
const flat = try! slope(x0: 2, y0: 1, x1: 5, y1: 1)
flat === 0
```

Parameters

x0   the x coordinate for the first point

y0   the y coordinate for the first point

x1   the x coordinate for the second point

y1   the y coordinate for the second point

Throws
SlopeError.infinite when y1 - y0 === 0: ie the slope is infinite

Returns
the slope bewteen the points (x0, y0) and (x1, y1)

Declared In
15 - Documentation.playground

Rich content

You can format your documentations with bold, italics, as well as with the inline code style.

```
The **rich** capabilities of markdown help your render text *nicely*.
You can mention `code` inline with the single backtick.
```

This is rendered here as follows:

> The **rich** capabilities of markdown help your render text *nicely*. You can mention code inline with the single backtick.

Now that we can format our code nicely, let's have a look at all the callouts Xcode documentation offers in order to structure your help.

Additional callouts

Reading through the Apple documentation you may have encountered more keywords in documentation structure than the five we described previously. Apple has us covered again with many more supported callouts.

	Available in Comments	Available in Playgrounds	Remarks
Attention	✓	✓	
Author	✓	✓	
Authors	✓	✓	
Bug	✓	✓	
Complexity	✓	✓	Use this to indicate the space/time complexity of your method
Copyright	✓	✓	
Custom Callout		✓	Used as - `Callout(My Custom Callout):`
Date	✓	✓	
Example		✓	
Experiment	✓	✓	
Important	✓	✓	
Invariant	✓	✓	
Note	✓	✓	
Precondition	✓	✓	
Postcondition	✓	✓	

Remark	✓	✓	
Requires	✓	✓	
See Also	✓	✓	Used as – `SeeAlso`, use it to point to related features
Since	✓	✓	
Version	✓	✓	
Warning	✓	✓	

 All callouts are rendered in order of declaration and in the description section of the Quick Help module.

Structural annotations

With Objective-C, we were able to mark different sections of the code with the help of the `#pragma` mark directive.

Swift exposes three straightforward keywords you can use in your code base. Those markers appear in the symbols list dropdown, which you can bring up by default with the *Ctrl + 6* shortcut:

```
// MARK: renders with a blue list
// MARK: - (inserts an empty line)
// TODO: renders with a blue bullet list
// FIXME: renders with an orange band-aid
```

Generating HTML docs

Now that you know how to write properly formatted documentation so that it can be used within Xcode's Quick Help infrastructure, you will likely want to publish this documentation online for consulting later, and encourage people to use your library.

Apple's toolchain falls short in this matter and there is no official documentation generator that will make it look and feel like Apple's own docs. However, there is a very popular and healthy project that can take care of it: Jazzy.

Jazzy is an open source project, written in Ruby, whose goal is to generate documentation for Swift and Objective-C.

Jazzy is maintained by Realm and you can find all the documentation, use cases, and more information about the project at `https://github.com/realm/jazzy`.

Getting started with Jazzy should not be complicated if you are running macOS, as Ruby comes preinstalled:

```
$ gem install jazzy
$ jazzy
```

Publishing to GitHub Pages

GitHub is a company that offers Git hosting as a service. They also offer a static website-hosting service. Hosting a static website is often the only thing you need to publish your documentation online. One of the great features of GitHub is that we can publish documentation in the same repository as our code.

Configuring GitHub Pages is straightforward, as it sits right in the general settings of your repository.

GitHub offers multiple options for publishing your documentation to a static website:

- The `master` branch
- The `master` branch `docs` folder
- The `gh-pages` branch

 The `gh-pages` option does not appear if you do not have a `gh-pages` branch.

As you will likely use the master branch for your codebase, you are left with two options: using the `docs` folder or the `gh-pages` branch. Each has its own advantages and drawbacks, but no one solution is better than the other in all scenarios.

The best is to try to find the solution that works for you.

If you select the `docs` folder solution, use the `--output docs` option with Jazzy, commit your changes and added files, and push.

Using the `gh-pages` branch is a bit trickier and will probably require some force-pushing:

```
# Clone the gh-pages branch in to the docs folder
git clone -b gh-pages --single-branch $REPO ./docs
```

```
# Pull the latest changes
cd docs
git pull origin gh-pages

# go back to the root folder
cd ..

# Generate the docs
jazzy —output docs_tmp

# Copy the docs in to the docs folder
cp —R docs_tmp/* "docs/"
cd docs
git add —A

# Commit your changes
git commit —am "Updates documentations..."

# push the changes to the gh-pages branch
git push
```

As you can see, the gh-pages solution involves more work, but in the long run, your code base is not polluted by artifacts that can be generated (or regenerated) by any commit.

 Jazzy does not support API versioning, so if you want to publish versioned APIs you are out of luck.

In this first section, you have learned how to format the comments above your code properly in order to generate valid documentation for Xcode's internal Quick Help as well as for Jazzy, the powerful documentation generator. You have also seen that GitHub can be used to publish your documentation alongside your code.

Documentation generation is something that should be automated, first because we don't want contributors to bother with it, but mostly because machines are great at doing things over and over again.

In the next section, we will investigate how it is possible to use Travis or Circle, two continuous integration services, to run tests automatically, report the status of the tests, and ultimately ensure you, and your contributors, never introduce any bad commits!

Continuous integration

Open source relies a lot on free and available continuous integration services. I will expose the use of Travis and Circle not because I am paid by them, but because both are trusted by thousands of open source developers and are industry leaders.

 You can also explore GitLab's offering as their services cover git-repository management, CI, CD, and more. We will not cover this service in this book.

In this section, we will cover using those services for building apps and libraries with Xcode on macOS as well as using Linux builds for pure Swift projects.

 Continuous integration is the art of merging developers' working copies as quickly as possible in the mainline. In open source projects, this means merging contributors code into the master or default branch. We devise a set of practices like automated testing, and pull request reviews in order to achieve continuous delivery. Services like Travis help achieve those goals as they can run your unit tests on each pull request, therefore ensuring your project is always up to spec.

Travis CI

Travis CI is run by a Berlin-based company, and is the de facto build tool of many projects and maintainers. Travis offers free build hours for open source projects, so it would be silly not to enjoy it!

Configuring simple projects

Travis requires us to have a special file, the `.travis.yml` file, in our repository in order to give instructions for building the project.

Working with simple projects or libraries, you can leverage Travis configuration settings that allow you to build and test a project.

The basic file should have the following values:

```
language: objective-c
osx_image: xcode10.1
xcode_project: MyNewProject.xcodeproj # path to your xcodeproj folder
xcode_workspace : MyNewWorkspace.xcworkspace # use this instead of your
```

```
project if you have a workspace
xcode_scheme: MyNewProjectTests # scheme for the tests
xcode_destination: platform=iOS Simulator,OS=12.0,name=iPhone XS
```

 `language: objective-c` indicates the build will occur on macOS-based servers, and not on Linux-based ones.

For more information about the build configuration, head over to the Travis documentation at https://docs.travis-ci.com/user/languages/objective-c/.

Configuring more complex build scenarios

As your project grows, you may want to test on more simulators, different targets, or you may simply want more control over the build; you can always not use the default configuration suggestions and configure the different build steps on your own.

The command you will want to run on Travis should most probably use `xcodebuild`, the command-line tool that can build and test any Xcode project.

This is what the `.travis.yml` file should look like now:

```
language: objective-c
 osx_image: xcode10.1
 script:
     - xcodebuild clean test -project MyNewProject.xcodeproj \
         -scheme MyNewProject \
         -destination "platform=iOS Simulator,OS=12.0,name=iPhone XS" \
         CODE_SIGN_IDENTITY="" CODE_SIGNING_REQUIRED=NO ONLY_ACTIVE_ARCH=NO
 | xcpretty
```

Now that you are able to build any Xcode project, let's see how to work with pure Swift projects.

Configuring pure Swift projects

As you know, pure Swift projects are meant to run on any platform. The Swift team is maintaining development snapshots as well as downloadable builds of the Swift toolchain.

We can use this in order to install Swift on Linux and macOS.

Travis offers great configuration capabilities through its build matrix and stages. A build matrix is defined by multiple environment variables, and each environment variable defines a different configuration for your continuous integration scripts. A build stage defines a step in your continuous integration process. If a stage fails, any subsequent stage will be cancelled. Mixing matrices and stages allows your builds to run multiple commands in parallel while minimizing the amount of resources you will consume if any stage fails.

```
env:
  - SWIFT_BRANCH=swift-4.2.1-release
  - SWIFT_VERSION=swift-4.2.1-RELEASE
jobs:
  include:
  - stage: OSX
    os: osx
    osx_image: xcode10.1
    language: objective-c
    sudo: required
    install:
    - wget
https://swift.org/builds/$SWIFT_BRANCH/xcode/$SWIFT_VERSION/$SWIFT_VERSION-
osx.pkg
    - sudo installer -pkg $SWIFT_VERSION-osx.pkg -target /
    - export
PATH="$PATH:/Library/Developer/Toolchains/$SWIFT_VERSION.xctoolchain/usr/bi
n"
    script:
    - swift package update
    - swift test

  - stage: Linux test
    os: linux
    language: generic
    dist: trusty
    sudo: required
    install:
    - sudo apt-get install clang libicu-dev
    - mkdir swift
    - curl
https://swift.org/builds/$SWIFT_BRANCH/ubuntu1804/$SWIFT_VERSION/$SWIFT_VER
SION-ubuntu18.04.tar.gz -s | tar xz -C swift &> /dev/null
    - export PATH="$(pwd)/swift/$SWIFT_VERSION-ubuntu18.04/usr/bin:$PATH"
    script:
    - swift package update
    - swift test
```

In this section, we covered usage of Travis to test and build your projects hosted on GitHub. In the next section, we will explore how we can use `gitlab.com` in order to build, test, and lint your projects.

GitLab.com

GitLab is a direct competitor to GitHub. While GitHub's focus is on repository-hosting and open source communities, GitLab has built a strong and independent spirit. After all, all of GitLab's offerings are notably open sourced!

In this section, I will assume you have created an account on GitLab and a project. You are able to upload your code to GitLab with git by adding it as a remote to your local repository.

 GitLab does not support building macOS or iOS applications on their infrastructures. If you are interested in using GitLab in conjunction with your build machine or servers, have a look at the `gitlab-runner` project: `https://docs.gitlab.com/runner/install/osx.html`.

Instead, we will focus on building Swift package manager apps.

Building and testing

As we saw in the *Travis CI* section, it is possible to build and test pure Swift programs on Linux systems. We will use this capability in GitLab. With the help of the official prebuilt Docker images, we can quickly set up the free, continuous integration on GitLab.

In your project, add a `.gitlab-ci.yml` file and insert the following into it:

```
test:
    image: swift:4.2.1
    script:
    - swift package update
    - swift test
```

Line by line, here is what the code is doing:

- `image`: Indicates we will use the official Swift Docker image, with Swift Version 4.2.1.
- `script`: Indicates the list of scripts to run; each step should succeed and exit with code 0.

Push those changes to your GitLab repository and you will see that your project will be tested, as you would do locally.

> The tests that are run are the ones exposed in `LinuxMain.swift`.

Adding a linter, SwiftLint

Linting your code is an essential step in ensuring the style is consistent across contributors but also over time. Alongside Jazzy, realm also maintains the excellent SwiftLint tool. It is written in Swift and installable through **Swift Package Manager (SPM)**. Now, SPM is not able to install CLI tools. We often turn to Gems or Homebrew to install those. Luckily, thanks to the vibrant Swift community, we can use Mint, the pure SPM for CLI tools.

1. In the `.gitlab-ci.yml` file, you can add the following to create a lint step:

```
test:
    image: swift:4.2.1
    script:
    - swift package update
    - swift test

## Add linter step
lint:
    image: swift:4.2.1
    before_script:
        # Keep the current directory in a variable
    - export PWD=$(pwd)
        # Install mint with the Swift PM method
    - git clone https://github.com/yonaskolb/Mint.git /tmp/Mint
    - cd /tmp/Mint
    - swift run mint install yonaskolb/mint
        # Install SwiftLint with mint
    - mint install realm/SwiftLint
    - cd $PWD
    script:
    - swiftlint
```

2. You can see that the important part of the script is actually in `before_script`, where `mint` will be installed, and we'll use `mint` to install `swiftlint` from `realm/SwiftLint`.

3. The script phase will be simply using `swiftlint`.

4. Commit those changes, and push your code to GitLab: both `lint` and `test` will run, and will succeed if your code is appropriately written.

 You can find more information about GitLab's CI configuration at `https:/ /docs.gitlab.com/ee/ci/yaml/README.html`

What you will encounter now is that the build is quite slow, stretching into minutes, as it is always pulling and building Mint and SwiftLint from scratch, from their GitHub repositories.

In order to overcome the newly added slowness, you should consider creating a custom Docker image that contains the full toolchain. One of the great benefits of Docker is in ensuring the consistency of a particular environment. I went through that exercise and published a `swift-ci` image on Docker hub that contains both `SwiftLint` and `Mint`.

The `Dockerfile` is straightforward:

```
FROM swift:4.2.1
RUN git clone https://github.com/yonaskolb/Mint.git /tmp/Mint
WORKDIR /tmp/Mint
RUN swift run mint install yonaskolb/mint
RUN mint install realm/SwiftLint
```

We moved all the commands from the CI `before_script` step into a single `docker` image.

Following this, you can run the build's tag and push commands:

```
$ docker build .
Sending build context to Docker daemon  2.048kB
Step 1/5 : FROM swift:4.2.1
 ---> e863e310b19f
Step 2/5 : RUN git clone https://github.com/yonaskolb/Mint.git /tmp/Mint
 ---> Using cache
 ---> 9b3d8ae04db2
Step 3/5 : WORKDIR /tmp/Mint
 ---> Running in 38496a152ac9
Removing intermediate container 38496a152ac9
 ---> 40203dfb1956
Step 4/5 : RUN swift run mint install yonaskolb/mint
 ---> Running in 544d333228ea
Fetching https://github.com/onevcat/Rainbow.git
Fetching https://github.com/kylef/Spectre.git
Fetching https://github.com/jakeheis/SwiftCLI
```

```
Fetching https://github.com/apple/swift-package-manager.git
Fetching https://github.com/kylef/PathKit.git
Completed resolution in 7.10s
Cloning https://github.com/jakeheis/SwiftCLI
Resolving https://github.com/jakeheis/SwiftCLI at 5.1.3
Cloning https://github.com/apple/swift-package-manager.git
Resolving https://github.com/apple/swift-package-manager.git at 0.2.0
Cloning https://github.com/kylef/Spectre.git
Resolving https://github.com/kylef/Spectre.git at 0.8.0
Cloning https://github.com/kylef/PathKit.git
Resolving https://github.com/kylef/PathKit.git at 0.9.1
Cloning https://github.com/onevcat/Rainbow.git
Resolving https://github.com/onevcat/Rainbow.git at 3.1.4
Compile clibc libc.c
Compile Swift Module 'SwiftCLI' (20 sources)
Compile Swift Module 'Rainbow' (11 sources)
Compile Swift Module 'SPMLibc' (1 sources)
Compile Swift Module 'PathKit' (1 sources)
Compile Swift Module 'POSIX' (11 sources)
Compile Swift Module 'Basic' (37 sources)
Compile Swift Module 'Utility' (19 sources)
Compile Swift Module 'MintKit' (9 sources)
Compile Swift Module 'MintCLI' (9 sources)
Compile Swift Module 'Mint' (1 sources)
Linking ./.build/x86_64-unknown-linux/debug/mint
  Finding latest version of mint
  Resolved latest version of mint to 0.11.2
  Cloning https://github.com/yonaskolb/mint.git 0.11.2...
  Building Mint Package with SPM...
  Installing Mint...
  Installed Mint 0.11.2
  Linked mint 0.11.2 to /usr/local/bin.
Removing intermediate container 544d333228ea
 ---> 0e205b06c84b
Step 5/5 : RUN mint install realm/SwiftLint
 ---> Running in 0cc1b6f74d82
  Finding latest version of SwiftLint
  Resolved latest version of SwiftLint to 0.28.2
  Cloning https://github.com/realm/SwiftLint.git 0.28.2...
  Building SwiftLint Package with SPM...
  Installing SwiftLint...
  Installed SwiftLint 0.28.2
  Linked swiftlint 0.28.2 to /usr/local/bin.
Removing intermediate container 0cc1b6f74d82
 ---> 0da15117fc71
Successfully built 0da15117fc71
$ docker tag 0da15117fc71 flovilmart/swift-ci:4.2.1
$ docker push flovilmart/swift-ci:4.2.1
```

With this published module, we can now have a very lean `.gitlab-ci.yml`:

```
lint:
  image: flovilmart/swift-ci:latest
  script:
    - swiftlint
test:
  image: swift:4.2.1
  script:
    - swift package update
    - swift test
```

It is only a matter of time before popular tools such as SwiftLint and Jazzy (which, at the time of writing, don't support generation on Linux) jump on the Docker bandwagon and provide fully featured images that ultimately help to speed up the development flow.

 In the `swift-ci` Docker image lives Mint, which can help install tools such as Sourcery, which was discussed in earlier chapters.

With this configuration, the linter step is down to a much faster time, purely the time to clone the code and lint, as we saved all the compilation time by migrating to Docker.

Some final words on Travis and GitLab

Continuous integration is an important part of any modern development workflow, whether you're professionally developing or pushing your first package on an open source repository, having a continuous integration step is something you often cannot work around. It gives you the confidence, as a maintainer, to merge foreign code and features to your code base while ensuring you and other contributors do not introduce regressions.

That being said, we can use continuous integration servers to automate the delivery of your apps and packages. We have seen that GitLab is limited to running only pure Swift packages in an easy way, so we'll go back to using Travis and fastlane in the next section. There, we'll cover how to use fastlane to automate and simplify the delivery of your apps to the app store, manage your certificates, and more.

Using fastlane for automated delivery

Fastlane is a very popular tool that was born from the need to automate communications with the App Store. It was originally written to overcome the burden of renewing developer and push certificates. Now, Xcode can be configured to generate certificates automatically, but at the same time, fastlane grew as a full-fledged automation suite with a pluggable system.

The original features for synchronizing certificates and uploading to `testflight` are still alive and well, but they have been joined by a slew of plugins that would be too long to list! Just look here: `https://docs.fastlane.tools/plugins/available-plugins/`.

Hopefully you won't need them all, so getting started with fastlane is still straightforward.

 Fastlane is written in Ruby, and uses `xcodebuild` under the hood, so this will require a macOS machine to run. If you want to use it with GitLab, you can use the `gitlab-runner`: `https://docs.fastlane.tools/best-practices/continuous-integration/#gitlab-ci-integration`.

Getting started with fastlane

There are multiple ways to get fastlane installed for your project.

You can use `ruby gems`:

```
sudo gem install fastlane
```

Or you could use `Homebrew`:

```
brew cask install fastlane
```

It is a good practice to use `Gemfile`, as this will ensure that all the collaborators use the same version of fastlane.

In the `root` directory, create `Gemfile`:

```
source "https://rubygems.org"

gem "fastlane"
```

You will then use bundler-related commands such as the following:

- `bundle update`: Updates your dependencies
- `bundle install`: Installs fastlane on the CI and developer's machines
- `bundle exec fastlane [action]`: Executes the fastlane actions

For the rest of this section, we'll use the `fastlane` command without the fastlane exec bundle for the sake of brevity. Please ensure it adapts to your use case.

Your first lane

Now that fastlane is installed on your system, you can run the following:

```
fastlane init
```

This will create a folder in fastlane, with many files.

 There is a fastlane Swift support in beta that will **not** be covered in this section. It features a Swift-based `Fastfile`.

We will focus on the `Fastfile` located in `fastlane/Fastfile`. It is in this file that you will declare all your lanes or actions.

Each action is a series of commands, written in Ruby; actions can depend on other actions or invoke plugins.

Now that the required files are created, you can create your first lane:

```
lane :test do
  run_tests(scheme: " MyNewProjectTests",
         devices: ["iPhone XR", "iPhone XS"])
end
```

To run this lane, use the following command:

```
$ fastlane test
```

You can then replace your `.travis.yml` configuration with this:

```
language: objective-c
osx_image: xcode10.1
install: bundle install
script: fastlane test
```

As you can see, the structure of the Travis configuration is tremendously simplified, as we moved all the logic into `Fastfile`.

Fastlane beta

Now that we've migrated our tests with `fastlane`, we can automate the deployment of our app.

Before we can get into the code for `Fastfile`, you need to configure your project's provisioning profiles. If you wish to share provisioning profiles with your CI with the minimum configuration, it's best to use **match**, a tool part of `fastlane` that securely stores your provisioning profiles and signing certificates. We will not do a complete tutorial on match as the online documentation is awesome and worth digging into. `fastlane` on its own is moving fast. You can find the recommendations for configuring your Xcode project on the `fastlane` docs repository: `https://docs.fastlane.tools/codesigning/xcode-project/`.

Deploying a beta version of your app requires as little code as running the tests:

```
# If you deploy with travis
# keep this line to unlock the keychain for match
setup_travis

lane :beta do
  build_app(scheme: "MyNewProject",
            workspace: "MyNewWorkspace.xcworkspace")
  # upload to crashlytics
  crashlytics(api_token: ENV['FABRIC_API_TOKEN'],
              build_secret: ENV['FABRIC_API_SECRET']) if
ENV['FABRIC_API_TOKEN'] && ENV['FABRIC_API_SECRET']
  # Upload to apple testflight
  upload_to_testflight

  # Upload to hockey app
  hockey(api_token: ENV['HOCKEY_API_TOKEN']) if ENV['HOCKEY_API_TOKEN'
end
```

By default, this beta lane will deploy to `testflight` with the default configuration. If you happened to set FABRIC_API_TOKEN and FABRIC_API_SECRET, the build would also be uploaded to `crashlytics`, and setting HOCKEY_API_TOKEN would enable uploading to the hockey app.

As always, please do refer to the official documentations if you encounter any issues using those code samples. Open source projects can move fast, and those references may be out of date.

Using Travis to upload on tags

Now that we have both a test and a beta lane, you will likely want to run tests on all pull requests and changes, and deploy to `testflight` when it reaches the `master` branch or when a tag is created on the repository.

This configuration can be simply set in the `.travis.yml` configuration file:

```
language: objective-c
osx_image: xcode10.1
install: bundle install
jobs:
  include:
  - stage: tests
    script: fastlane test
  - stage: release
    deploy:
      provider: script
      script: fastlane beta
      on:
        tags: true
```

Let's review the code in the preceding snippet of the `.travis.yml` file:

- We use `jobs` to declare a series of build steps. The `release` stage will not run if the `tests` stage fails.
- On the `release` stage, we use the `script` deployment provider, which allows any kind of deployment to be run. Be sure to check the Travis documentation for all the providers it supports.
- With `on: tags: true`, the release stage will only be run when the build was triggered by a tag creation.

This concludes our section on fastlane.

You should now be able to kickstart any iOS project, and automatically upload new versions of your app with fastlane. While we just covered the basics, there is always more to learn about tools such as this one. Fastlane is driven by a strong community and grows in features every day. If you are interested, the project is open and you can always contribute on their GitHub repository: https://github.com/fastlane/fastlane.

Now that we are experts in setting up open source projects, let's have a look in the next section at a few tips and tricks for setting up and maintaining open source projects.

Becoming a maintainer, tips and tricks

Maintaining an open source project is fun, full of surprises, and sometimes hard. The following tips have been gathered from experience and discussions with other maintainers.

The README.md file

The README.md file is perhaps the most important file in your project. It describes what your project does.

It has an .md extension, so it's written in Markdown, the same language as your Swift documentation, so if you were not previously familiar with it, you should be by now.

Ideally, it should contain multiple sections:

- A title that should match the repository, folder, and package-manager names
- A short description, which is the hook, indicating what your project does, in a nutshell
- A table of contents, if your readme is very long
- Instructions for installation
- Instructions on how to use your project
- Instructions on how to contribute to the project
- The license for the code you are open sourcing

I didn't invent those on my own, but a standard readme specification is actively worked on here: https://github.com/RichardLitt/standard-readme/blob/master/spec.md.

The LICENSE.md file

Perhaps it should be added before README.md, but a licence file is always welcome, so your users know what to expect from your project.

If you do not include one, people usually assume any kind of usage of your project (the unlicenced licence), including just copy-pasting the code, is permitted. All licenses are not created equal, so always make sure you select one that is appropriate from the beginning. The Choose a License website (https://choosealicense.com/licenses/) can be useful when you need to determine the licence to be used.

The CODE_OF_CONDUCT.md file

A code of conduct is usually the next addition you want to make to your project. As you are opening yourself up to the public, you want to establish clear rules as to what to expect from contributors, and what contributors can expect (and not expect) from the maintainers. Now more than ever, good behavior in human interactions is expected, and rooting out bad actors should be a priority of the maintainers.

A popular code of conduct is the Contributor Covenant, adopted by many communities. Have a look at their website: https://www.contributor-covenant.org.

Issues, Pull Requests, and more

Now that you have a readme, a licence, and a code of conduct, you're open for business! It's time to give some thought to how to welcome the new users that have issues with your project, or potential contributors who open pull requests.

GitHub and GitLab have us covered with issue and pull-request templates (named description templates on GitLab). I recommend you take the time to add those to your repository. They can offer the following benefits:

- Help triage issues faster
- Help users troubleshoot their implementations first
- Help you gather more information as you ask for it (such as a version number)
- Enforce a proper description when opening pull requests

This is perhaps one of the most important parts to iterate on as your project grows.

No is temporary, yes is forever

This is an old saying, but in open source, it is very, very hard to remove a feature once it's merged, as you never know whether you're going to break a user's code.

We use this adage, and we are not afraid of saying **no**. Once you merge someone's code, it becomes part of the repository, and ultimately yours. As a maintainer, you retain ownership and stewardship of the project. You could not imagine how many users are actually happy with maintainers saying no, to ensure consistency with the vision of the project, or simply because you do not want to add a particular feature as untested.

Summary

In this final chapter, we covered one of the most important aspects of innovation in the software world: sharing your code with the world. While anyone can upload a few lines of Swift to GitHub, publishing a successful project is a particular art form. As of now, you should be able to use Jazzy to generate beautiful HTML documentation of your code. Using GitHub, Travis, or even GitLab to host and iterate on your project is now second nature. For your iOS apps, you are able to refactor complex shell scripts into simple actions with fastlane. Finally, your repository isn't naked with just code, but sports a useful README, a license, and you, as a fresh maintainer, are ready to deal with your first issues, merge and close your first pull requests, and pledge to respect and appreciate your users.

Reflecting on what we covered through this book, we started with the first part of our journey laying out the foundation of knowledge required to tackle design patterns properly. You now have a great understanding of the Swift language, and how the compiler helps you manage memory automatically. Foundation, the standard library provides a great base set of tools to work on any Swift project, so you are able to recognize when to use those tools and choose them appropriately. Lastly in this first arch, we covered how to mix Swift and Objective-C.

The second section was dedicated to the main design patterns you will encounter in Swift, based on the Gang of Four's patterns, and we have covered most of them. You also learned how to use Sourcery, a code generation tool for patterns that require more boilerplate. All the patterns we covered are ready to use and I hope you'll always use this work as a reference when refactoring existing code or extending your projects. We ventured in some swift specific patterns that you will encounter in many projects. We made a quick foray into architectural patterns and now, you should be able to write better MVC and switch when necessary to MVVM. Lastly, we covered dependency injection as well as futures and promises as those two concepts are used by many libraries and help write cleaner programs.

The last act was dedicated to additional skills and advanced techniques you will employ during your journey as a programmer. Covering using and creating packages, testing and open sourcing, this last section is designed as an extension to this book. You can most probably universally apply the concepts discussed to all programming languages as the practices described fall under the best practices. Applying the divide and conquer strategy, splitting your project into independent modules, creating unit and integration tests, and running them periodically on continuous integration services is always a sign of a healthy code base.

Other Books You May Enjoy

If you enjoyed this book, you may be interested in these other books by Packt:

Hands-On Full-Stack Development with Swift
Ankur Patel

ISBN: 9781788625241

- Get accustomed to server-side programming as well as the Vapor framework
- Learn how to build a RESTful API
- Make network requests from your app and handle error states when a network request fails
- Deploy your app to Heroku using the CLI command
- Write a test for the Vapor backend
- Create a tvOS version of your shopping list app and explore code-sharing with an iOS platform
- Add registration and authentication so that users can have their own shopping lists

Hands-On Server-Side Web Development with Swift
Angus Yeung

ISBN: 9781789341171

- Build simple web apps using Vapor 3.0 and Kitura 2.5
- Test, debug, build, and release server-side Swift applications
- Design routes and controllers for custom client requests
- Work with server-side template engines
- Deploy web apps to a host in the cloud
- Enhance web content with Bootstrap
- Manage user access using authentication framework
- Design for API gateway
- Develop an iPhone app to work with web services
- Deploy your app as a microservice in a cluster
- Deploy Swift web services with a RESTful API design

Leave a review - let other readers know what you think

Please share your thoughts on this book with others by leaving a review on the site that you bought it from. If you purchased the book from Amazon, please leave us an honest review on this book's Amazon page. This is vital so that other potential readers can see and use your unbiased opinion to make purchasing decisions, we can understand what our customers think about our products, and our authors can see your feedback on the title that they have worked with Packt to create. It will only take a few minutes of your time, but is valuable to other potential customers, our authors, and Packt. Thank you!

Index

W

Made in the USA
Las Vegas, NV
29 November 2020